We're Doomed. Now What?

Also by the Author

War Porn
Learning to Die in the Anthropocene

We're Doomed. Now What?

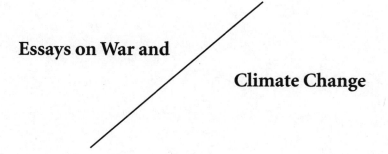

Essays on War and

Climate Change

ROY SCRANTON

Published by
Soho Press, Inc.
853 Broadway
New York, NY 10003

Library of Congress Cataloging-in-Publication Data

Names: Scranton, Roy, 1976– author.
We're doomed, now what?:
essays on war and climate change / Roy Scranton.

ISBN 978-1-61695-936-4
eISBN 978-1-61695-937-1

1. Civilization, Modern—21st century. 2. Climatic changes. 3. War.
4. Social change. I. Title
CB428 .S425 2018 909.82—dc23 2017055380

Interior design by Janine Agro

Printed in the United States of America

10 9 8 7 6 5 4 3 2 1

For Sara

Where do we find ourselves? In a series of which we do not know the extremes, and believe that it has none.

—Ralph Waldo Emerson, "Experience"

Contents

· ·

I. Climate & Change

II. War & Memory

III. Violence & Communion

IV. Last Thoughts

· ·

I.

CLIMATE
& CHANGE

We're Doomed. Now What?

The time we've been thrown into is one of alarming and bewildering change—the breakup of the post-1945 global order, a multispecies mass extinction, and the beginning of the end of civilization as we know it. Not one of us is innocent, not one of us is safe. The world groans under the weight of seven billion humans; every new birth adds another mouth hungry for food, another life greedy for energy.

We all see what's happening, we read it in the headlines every day, but seeing isn't believing, and believing isn't accepting. We respond according to our prejudices, acting out of instinct, reflex, and training. Right-wing denialists insist that climate change isn't happening, or that it's not caused by humans, or that the real problem is terrorism or refugees, while left-wing denialists insist that the problems are fixable, under our control, merely a matter of political will. Accelerationists argue that more technology is the answer. Incrementalists tell us to keep trusting the same institutions and leaders that have been failing us for decades. Activists say we have to fight, even if we're sure to lose.

Meanwhile, as the gap between the future we're entering and the future we once imagined grows ever wider, nihilism takes root in the shadow of our fear: if all is already lost, nothing matters anyway.

You can feel this nihilism in TV shows like *The Walking Dead* and *Game of Thrones*, and you can see it in the pull to nationalism, sectarianism, war, and racial hatred. We saw it in the election of Donald Trump. Nihilism defines our current moment, though in truth it's nothing new. The Western world has been grappling with radical nihilism since at least the seventeenth century, when scientific insights into human behavior began to undermine religious belief. Philosophers have struggled since then to fill the gap between fact and meaning: Kant tried to reconcile empiricist determinism with God and Reason; Bergson and Peirce worked to merge Darwinian evolution and human creativity; more recent thinkers glean the stripped furrows neuroscience has left to logic and language.

Scientific materialism, taken to its extreme, threatens us with meaninglessness; if consciousness is reducible to the brain and our actions are determined not by will but by causes, then our values and beliefs are merely rationalizations for the things we were going to do anyway. Most people find this view of human life repugnant, if not incomprehensible.

In her book of essays *The Givenness of Things*, Marilynne Robinson rejects the materialist view of consciousness, arguing for the existence of the human soul by insisting that the soul's metaphysical character makes it impervious to materialist arguments. The soul, writes Robinson, is an intuition that "cannot be dispelled by proving the soul's physicality, from which it is aloof by definition. And on these same grounds, its nonphysicality is no proof of its nonexistence."

The biologist E. O. Wilson spins the problem differently: "Does free will exist?" he asks in *The Meaning of Human Existence*. "Yes, if not in ultimate reality, then at least in the operational sense necessary for sanity and thereby for the perpetuation of the human species." Robinson offers an appeal to ignorance; Wilson, an appeal to consequences; both arguments are fallacious.

Yet as Wilson suggests, our dogged insistence on free agency makes a kind of evolutionary sense. Indeed, humanity's keenest evolutionary advantage has been its drive to create collective meaning. That drive is as ingenious as it is relentless, and it can find a way to make sense of despair, depression, catastrophe, genocide, war, disaster, plagues, and even the humiliations of science.

Our drive to make meaning is powerful enough even to turn nihilism against itself. As Friedrich Nietzsche, one of Western philosophy's most incisive diagnosticians of nihilism, wrote near the end of the nineteenth century: "Man will sooner will nothingness than not will." This dense aphorism builds on one of the thoughts at the core of Nietzsche's philosophy, today so widely accepted as to be almost unrecognizable, that human beings make their own meaning out of life.

In this view, there is no ultimate, transcendent moral truth. As Nietzsche put it in an early essay, "On Truth and Lies in a Nonmoral Sense," truth is no more than a "mobile army of metaphors, metonyms, and anthropomorphisms." If we can stomach the moral vertigo this idea might induce, we can also see how it's not necessarily nihilistic but, in the right light, a testament to human resilience.

The human ability to make meaning is so versatile, so powerful, that it can make almost any existence tolerable, even a life of unending suffering, so long as that life is woven into a bigger story that makes it meaningful. Humans have survived and thrived in some of the most inhospitable environments on Earth, from the deserts of Arabia to the ice fields of the Arctic, because of this ability to organize collective life around symbolic constellations of meaning: *anirniit*, capital, jihad. "If we have our own why in life," Nietzsche wrote, "we shall get along with almost any how."

When he wrote "Man will sooner will nothingness than not will," Nietzsche was exposing the destructive side of humanity's meaning-making drive. That drive is so powerful, Nietzsche's saying, that when forced to the precipice of nihilism, we would choose meaningful self-annihilation over meaningless bare life. This insight was horrifically borne out in the Götterdämmerung of Nazi Germany, just as it's being borne out today in every new suicide attack by jihadi terrorists—even as it's being borne out here at home in Trump's willfully destructive politics of rage. We risk it when we stumble toward another thoughtless war, asking young men and women to throw their lives away so we might continue believing America means something. As a character in Don DeLillo's novel *White Noise* remarks: "War is the form nostalgia takes when men are hard-pressed to say something good about their country."

Nietzsche wasn't himself a nihilist. He developed his idea of truth as a "mobile army of metaphors" into a more complex philosophy of perspectivism, which conceived of subjective truth as a variety of constructions arising out of particular perspectives on objective reality. The more perspectives we learn to see from, the more truth we have access to. This is different from relativism, with which it's often confused, which says that all truth is relative and there is no objective reality. Fundamentally, Nietzsche was an empiricist who believed that beyond all of our interpretations there was, at last, something we can call the world—even if we can never quite apprehend it objectively. "Even great spirits have only their five fingers breadth of experience," he wrote. "Just beyond it their thinking ceases and their endless empty space and stupidity begins."

Nietzsche's positive philosophical project, what he called his "gay science," was to create the conditions for the possibility of a human being who could comprehend the meaninglessness of our drive to make meaning, yet nonetheless affirm human existence: a human being who could learn *amor fati*, the love of one's fate.[1] This was his much-misunderstood idea of the "overman." Nietzsche labored mightily to create this new human ideal for philosophy because he needed it so badly himself. A gloomy, oversensitive pessimist and self-declared decadent who eventually went mad, he struggled all his life to convince himself that his life was worth living.

Today, as every hour brings new alarms of war and climate disaster, we might wish we could take Nietzsche's place. He had to cope only with the death of God, after all, while we must come to terms with the death of our whole world. Peril lurks on every side, from the delusions of hope to the fury of reaction, from the despondency of hopelessness to the promise of destruction.

We stand today on a precipice of annihilation that Nietzsche could not have even imagined. There is little reason to presume that we'll be able to slow down global warming before we pass a tipping point. We've already exceeded 1.5° Celsius above pre-industrial temperatures and there's more warming baked in.[2] The West Antarctic ice sheet is collapsing, Greenland is melting, permafrost across the world is liquefying, and methane has been detected leaking from sea floors and Siberian craters: it's probably already too late to stop these feedbacks, which means it's probably already too late to stop apocalyptic planetary warming. Meanwhile the world slides into hate-filled, bloody havoc, like the last act of a particularly ugly Shakespearean tragedy.

Accepting our situation could easily be confused with nihilism. In a nation founded on hope, built with "can do" Yankee grit, and bedazzled by its own technological wizardry, the very idea that something might be beyond our power or that humans have intrinsic limits verges on blasphemy. Right and left, millions of Americans believe that every problem has a solution; suggesting otherwise stirs a deep and hostile resistance. It's not so much that accepting the truth of our situation means thinking the wrong thought, but rather thinking the unthinkable.

Yet it's at just this moment of crisis that our human drive to make meaning reappears as our only salvation . . . if we're willing to reflect consciously on the ways we make life meaningful—on how we decide what is good, what our goals are, what's worth living or dying for, and what we do every day, day to day, and how we do it. Because if it's true that we make our lives meaningful ourselves and not through revealed wisdom handed down by God or the Market or History, then it's also true that we hold within ourselves the power to change our lives—wholly, utterly—by changing what our lives mean. Our drive to make meaning is more powerful than oil, the atom, and the market, and it's up to us to harness that power to secure the future of the human species.

We can't do it by clinging to the progressivist, profit-seeking, technology-can-fix-it ideology of fossil-fueled capitalism. We can't do it by trying to control the future. We need to learn to let our current civilization die, to accept our mortality, and to practice humility. We need to work together to transform a global order of meaning focused on accumulation into a new order of meaning that knows the value of limits, transience, and restraint.

Most important, we need to give up defending and protecting *our* truth, *our* perspective, *our* Western values, and understand that truth is found not in one perspective but in its multiplication, not in one point of view but in the aggregate, not in opposition but in the whole. We need to learn to see not just with Western eyes but with Islamic eyes and Inuit eyes, not just with human eyes but with golden-cheeked warbler eyes, coho salmon eyes, and polar bear eyes, and not even just with eyes but with the wild, barely articulate being of clouds and seas and rocks and trees and stars.

We were born on the eve of what may be the human world's greatest catastrophe. None of us chose this, not deliberately. None of us can choose to avoid it, either. Some of us may even live through it. What meaning we pass on to the future will depend on how well we remember those who have come before us, how wisely and how gently we're able to shed the ruinous way of life that's destroying us today, and how consciously we're able to affirm our role as creators of our fated future.

Accepting the fatality of our situation isn't nihilism, but rather the necessary first step in forging a new way of life. Between self-destruction and giving up, between willing nothingness and not willing, there is another choice: willing our fate. Conscious self-creation. We owe it to the generations whose futures we've burned and wasted to build a bridge, to *be* a bridge, to connect the diverse human traditions of meaning-making in our past to those survivors, the children of the Anthropocene, who will build a new world among our ruins. [2015/2017]

Arctic Ghosts

At the top of the world, a great wheel is spinning. Circling the Arctic Ocean, a current called the Beaufort Gyre drives pack ice clockwise around the pole. It pulls warm Pacific currents through the Bering Strait north and west above Siberia, pushes into the East Siberian Sea and the Transpolar Drift, then rolls away from Russia and whips south against Greenland and the archipelagic frontier forming the rocky distant rim of the Canadian Shield. As winter descends and the seas freeze, the gyre drives newly formed ice against the landfast floe edging those northmost coasts, thickening the ice in ridges and layers, and bit by bit forces drift ice into the straits that form the Northwest Passage. As winter thaws to summer, the pack ice breaks up into the Chukchi Sea, where warm Pacific waters join the gyre as it turns again in its grinding cycle.

The pack ice that the gyre drives around the top of the world breathes with the seasons, expanding in winter, contracting in summer, regular as a heartbeat. Over the past thirty years, though, the total amount has shrunk: minimum summer sea-ice area has decreased by more than half, as has estimated summer sea-ice thickness. Even more alarming, total summer sea-ice volume is less than a quarter of what it was a generation ago. Think of how an ice cube melts in three dimensions. Scientists at the Polar Science Center and the National Snow and Ice Data Center expect summer sea ice to disappear entirely as early as 2030. Some people are calling this dramatic decline the "Arctic death spiral." It will mean the end of the Arctic as we know it.

The Beaufort Gyre is just one wheel in a vast convolution of interconnected wheels that make up the global climate system: the El Niño Southern Oscillation, the Gulf Stream, the carbon cycle, and many, many more. As one wheel speeds up, slows down, changes, or disappears, it affects all the others, feeding back into the system. The Arctic death spiral will work like that: as white ice melts into dark water, it will diminish Earth's ability to reflect light and heat back into space, thus increasing overall warming. Methane and other carbon compounds frozen in Arctic permafrost will thaw and flow into the atmosphere, intensifying greenhouse-gas effects and increasing overall warming. Deep-ocean circulation, which depends on differences in temperature and salinity to move water around the world, will slow and shut down, radically changing regional climates, contributing to sea-level rise, and increasing overall warming.

To see the Arctic death spiral firsthand and to see the Arctic before it melted, I took a seventeen-day "adventure cruise" with the outdoor expedition company Adventure Canada: "Into the Northwest Passage 2015."

Cedar Swan, Adventure Canada CEO: "On my first trip, when I was fourteen, we were cruising in a little fjord just south of Kanger-lussuaq. We came right up to the foot of a glacier, and we were Zodiacking there and it was amazing and everything was wonderful. Then I went back to that exact same glacier in 2007, and there was nothing but rocks."

Tagak Curley, Inuk hunter, former Canadian legislator, co-founder of the territory of Nunavut, Adventure Canada resource staff: "I can confirm that the seasons have changed. We had colder weather when we were kids. The freezing and snow would normally come a lot earlier, even the first week in September. And now, mostly, almost about a month later we start seeing freezing on the lakes. In terms of the sea, it's dangerous in some parts to travel on the sea ice in October, even November. If that were forty, fifty years ago, the base would be solid and the floe edge would be a few miles away from the shore line."

———

Our journey began in the Alpine Room of the Sheraton Gateway Hotel Toronto. Enthusiastic Adventure Canada staff in migraine-blue shirts with polar-bear logos went over the basic outlines of our cruise. A total of 191 fellow "adventurers" listened politely, a crowd of mostly white, mostly silver-haired retired couples in various stages of physical decline, with a few singletons and only a smattering of younger blood— I counted a half-dozen under fifty, including myself. The plan was to sail north up the west coast of Greenland, go west into Canada through Lancaster Sound, then sail north around Victoria Island and down through the Prince of Wales Strait to Kugluktuk, although our final route would depend on the sea ice. Along the way, we'd clamber into black-hulled Zodiac boats for a series of landings and excursions. It was hammered home to us that this wasn't just a cruise but an "expedition," and that we had to be ready for anything.

From Toronto, we flew to Kangerlussuaq, Greenland, where we boarded the MS *Ocean Endeavour*, a 450-foot-long converted ferry built in Poland, ice class 1B, first registered as the *Konstantin Simonov* in Russia, now owned by the ship-management company FleetPro, based in Switzerland. The weather in Kangerlussuaq was auspicious, warm and clear, with temperatures in the forties and fifties Fahrenheit, where they would remain for the entire cruise. We steamed that night into a refulgent midnight sunset, magenta and coral clouds glowing over the craggy gneiss walls of the fjord, and in the morning woke at Sisimiut, a Greenland fishing town comprising many small, brightly colored square houses, like Legos scattered in the sun. The ship spent the day taking on supplies while we wandered around town. A shop sold gleaming silver sealskin gloves and wiry balls of musk-ox yarn. Sled dogs yipped and howled from their yards.

The next day we anchored at Ilulissat, 171 miles farther north, another town of bright square houses and home to a UNESCO World Heritage site, the Ilulissat Icefjord: a thirty-mile-long channel choked with giant icebergs calved from one of the world's most swiftly collapsing glaciers. The Jakobshavn Glacier has been melting back at a consistent rate of more than a hundred feet a day, dumping more than 38 billion tons of frozen water into the sea each year. In the days before we arrived, a nearly five-mile-square chunk fell off the face—what some observers think might have been the largest single calving ever seen from that glacier. The iceberg-choked fjord that the glacier emptied into seemed unreal, like a breathtaking modernist abstraction in white and blue and silver, 3-D, vivid, luminous, massive, and grave.

Jakobshavn is responsible for about 10 percent of all of the icebergs that Greenland produces. From Ilulissat, they follow the current north along the coast to Kap York, where they turn and wheel back south along Baffin Island, Labrador, and Newfoundland, slowly melting their way into the North Atlantic. Leaving Ilulissat, we sailed with them, stopping along the way for picturesque hikes at Karrat Fjord and Kullorsuaq Island. From Kap York we diverged from the current and sailed north out of Baffin Bay, to the most northerly point we would reach, just a smidge beyond seventy-eight degrees. A thin, shining line of pack ice, cutting across the gray water of Smith Sound and cloaked in a low fog, blocked us from going any farther. We didn't know it at the time, but this would be the only significant sea ice that we would see.

That day, August 26, we Zodiacked in down a long, spectacular fjord to land at Etah, a lush glacial valley rich with tundra, mosses, grass, and wildlife. We saw birds, musk oxen, and Arctic hares, but the most striking sign of life was in the innumerable bones littering the valley floor. A great cairn of them had been heaped up on the beach near a couple of Inuit hunting shacks, testifying to Etah's plenty: caribou antlers and musk-ox hooves, walrus skulls and seal spines.

A mile or so back from the cairn was the glacier face. Gently sloping to the moraine at its base, the glacier poured a stream of water out into a large pond. Its north edge had melted back in a curious way, creating a passage and, within, a small cave leading back under the ice. Standing inside the glacier, you could watch the vast Greenland ice sheet melting right before your eyes. You could feel it, slick, cold, and glistening under your hand. You could hear it drip, drop by drop, into pools among the rocks. Greenland is losing about three hundred billion tons of ice every year. Over time, that ice is going to raise sea levels by more than twenty feet. Drip by drip, drop by drop.

Bernadette Dean, Inuk hunter, seamstress, advocate of Inuit culture and language, member of the Nunavut Water Board, Adventure Canada resource staff : "I've lived in the North all my life. It's my home. The last few years we've had cold winters, but ten or twelve years ago we started noticing the freeze-up was later and later, and in lots of cases it was dangerous for hunters traveling on the sea ice. Another thing I've noticed is the change in the wind patterns. Easterly wind is more common now than it used to be. And the molting season of the seal seems to be a lot longer."

Dr. Mark Mallory, seabird biologist, Canada Research Chair in Coastal Wetland Ecosystems, Acadia University, Adventure Canada resource staff: "Moving north, climate change hits you like a tidal wave: all the scientists, that was their focus, all the talk amongst Inuit communities and community members was about how things had changed. In 1999, we were told that the typical temperatures we could expect in the summer might be 10 to 12 degrees Celsius. By the time we left Nunavut in 2012, it was very common to have at least one week in Iqaluit over 20 degrees, 24 or 25 degrees on some days."

Chris Dolder, Adventure Canada assistant expedition leader: "We were going out into Smith Sound and we're trying to traverse

eastward to get to Etah, and we found ourselves going alongside a
tabular berg. We steamed over two hours down one face of this berg,
well over twenty-two nautical miles. One face. This is the first time
that we'd encountered something that large. Why is that? Because
the ice shelves at the top of Ellesmere Island are breaking apart."

———

Ecotourism, adventure tourism, expedition tourism—call it what you
will, wilderness-oriented group tours remain an ethically dubious
proposition. Built on and often glorifying a tradition of brutal,
racialized colonial domination, adventure tourism restages the
white-supremacist conquest of "nature" and "natives" as a carefully controlled consumer encounter with "pristine wilderness" and
"indigenous cultures." And while it's nowhere near as violent as the
heritage it celebrates, it cannot help but change the places and people
it objectifies as "experiences," in ways both obvious and subtle.

Adventure Canada CEO Swan, along with nearly every staff
member I spoke with and several of my fellow passengers, expressed
an alert and sometimes pained awareness of the problem—in this
case, a history of environmental and cultural exploitation stretching
from the fur trade and whaling days to more recent Canadian efforts
to forcibly assimilate Inuit. Lecture programming on the *Endeavour*
focused heavily not only on environmental issues and climate
change, but also on Inuit culture and history. Two esteemed Inuit
leaders, Bernadette Dean and Tagak Curley, were on the cruise as
resource staff, in addition to a biologist, a zoologist, a botanist, an
archaeologist, a geologist, and a historian. Generally speaking, the
hope was that the experience would make passengers more conscious of the very history of despoliation it reprised, and that the
positive increase in social awareness thus achieved would outweigh
any negative impacts, not the least of which came from the *Ocean
Endeavour* burning ten to twenty tons of fuel every day.

"For us, as a company," Swan told me, "I feel that there's value in bringing people to a place that brings them so far out of their regular life that it gives them a little jolt. To say, 'Hey, it's not all pavement and Walmarts and provincial parks.' To have that wake-up call to remind us that we're a very small part of a much larger picture."

Swan introduced me to her resource staff, with whom I had many long conversations. I talked with biologist James Halfpenny about polar bears and sea ice, I talked with zoologist Ree Brennin Houston about environmental education, and I talked with Tagak Curley, one of the founders of Nunavut, about Inuit perspectives on climate change. Their voices resonated through our journey like a chorus. One of the most interesting people I spoke with was Ian Tamblyn, a sandpaper-voiced folk singer who'd been coming to the Arctic for decades. When I asked him about climate change, his merry eyes grew somber and their charming twinkle dimmed. "I'm not a scientist," he said. "I'm a musician. But I've seen these things. I've seen the Northwest Passage change in my lifetime. What it is, if it's not scientific evidence, is bearing witness. I've seen it happen."

James Halfpenny: "Once we lose the multiyear ice, that's a major tipping point. And I think we're probably going to see an ice-free North Pole in five, maybe fifteen years."

Ree Brennin Houston: "We need to look at what's coming at us with our eyes open. The Arctic will be ice-free. The Arctic ecosystem will change."

Ian Tamblyn: "I think about it all the time. To me, it's the slow disaster. It's so beautiful . . . so beautiful. And it's a disaster. It will eclipse everything."

———

Grise Fiord, Canada's northernmost community, is a small village of about 150 people, mostly Inuit, and two Royal Canadian Mounted

Police officers who rotate through every couple of years. Perched on a desolate, rocky stretch of Ellesmere Island, the village was founded in 1953 through a Canadian government resettlement scheme to assert national sovereignty in the far north. Inuit from Quebec Province were promised land, support, and good hunting, then shipped hundreds of miles above the Arctic Circle and more or less abandoned. They were isolated by sea ice, visited by a government ship once a year, and spurned by the local RCMP. Informed on arrival that hunting in the region was severely restricted because of recent wildlife protections, the resettled Inuit struggled to survive in near-starvation conditions, coping with neglect, malnutrition, depression, and suicide. In recent decades, after the founding of the Inuit-governed territory of Nunavut, the settlers and their descendants were offered the chance to return to the south. Many took it. The ones who remained proudly call Grise Fiord home.

Our cultural expedition there started with a visit from Grise Fiord's elders to the *Ocean Endeavour*. They sat awkwardly onstage in the Nautilus Lounge while Cedar's two-year-old daughter danced around them. There were some speeches, then a Q&A. Among the questions about native dress, seal hunts, how much food costs in the north, and the effect of technology on kids today, one passenger asked: "Is the weather changing in Grise Fiord?" This seemed apt: the Inuit name for the town, Aujuittuq, means "Place that never thaws," but the bay we'd anchored in was mostly clear, save for a few icebergs in the distance and a chunk of ice melting in the shallows.

John Houston, a bushy-browed, bearded filmmaker and culturalist on staff with Adventure Canada who had grown up in the north and lived among Inuit all his life, translated the question into Inuktitut. One of the female elders took the microphone and spoke, then John translated back: "Yes, she's really seen those changes. One of them is the loss of snow. Another is warmer air. The ice is melting much more quickly. The shorefast ice vanishes in the spring almost overnight. And there are many more changes, many changes. There are a lot of signs of climate change here."

Then Larry Audlaluk, one of the senior elders, stood up and took the mike from Houston. He spoke in English. "I want to dispel a notion about polar bears," he said. "I hear a lot about polar bears, a lot about what people down south think about polar bears. I want to tell you that polar bears are very healthy. There are very many polar bears, far too many of them. The ice hasn't affected our polar bears. The polar bear is just fine."

I was perplexed. Why was he talking about polar bears in response to a question about climate change? And weren't polar bears threatened?

In the Canadian Arctic, it turns out, polar bears are political. The fundamental conflict is between international environmental concerns and local economics. On one side, scientists and environmentalists argue that the polar bear is endangered by climate change, specifically by the loss of sea ice. The United States has declared the bear threatened and has lobbied to ban international trade in their pelts. On the other side, Inuit in Canada depend on bears as one of the few sources of cash in what is mainly a subsistence economy. As Houston explained to me: "There isn't that much cash income for senior hunters since Greenpeace and friends basically gutted the fur trade. The real cash income for a senior hunter would be to guide a nonresident sport polar-bear hunt, the purse for which can be $20,000 or more. In many cases it would be, by far, the majority of their annual cash income." In addition to the purse, a single pelt can sell for up to $10,000 Canadian.

Complicating the polar-bear question are two factors. First, while scientists have a strong case for describing what's going on with bear populations, they don't have very strong data to back that case up. Andrew Derocher, a biologist at the University of Alberta and the author of *Polar Bears: A Complete Guide to Their Biology and Behavior*, told me that the bears are a highly specialized apex predator dependent on sea-ice ecosystems for their main prey, ringed seals. Less ice means fewer bears. "We expect to lose about two-thirds of the polar-bear population by midcentury," he said. Yet he also told me that current estimates for the global polar-bear population, around 20,000 to 25,000, have a margin of error of plus or minus 40 percent (meaning the range could be anywhere from 12,000 to 35,000). Data on the bears is spotty, out-of-date, and hard to gather. Inuit call the polar bear Pihoqahiak, "the ever-wandering one," characterizing nomadic tendencies that, for biologists, make the bear difficult and expensive to study. The simple fact is that if we want to know what's going on with polar bears, we need more science.

The second factor complicating the polar-bear question is that Inuit and outfitters from Labrador to Cambridge Bay have reported seeing more bears today than in the past. Tagak Curley told me: "We know for a fact, from our forefathers, from the time we were little boys, that polar bears are increasing. I think you will see that anywhere. As my friend Mikitak Bruce said, 'Nanuit nungujjangit-tualuit.' Polar bears will never disappear." Even if Derocher is correct in predicting that polar bears will be affected by loss of habitat, local observers may still be right: polar-bear populations have probably grown in recent decades, after midcentury overhunting was curtailed in the 1970s. In addition, decreasing pack ice would likely send bears inland for food, where they'll run into more humans, thus giving the appearance of greater numbers.

Whether polar bears were endangered or adapting, the stark poverty of Grise Fiord made a much more compelling case for polar-bear economics than Larry Audlaluk had. The houses in town were bleak, the few residents we saw grim. A scowling grandma in a dirty jacket drove by on an ATV. Our tour guide, Rose, showed us the medical center, clean but sparse, and the co-op, a dusty, blighted general store restocked by ship each September. The prices were two to three times what you'd pay in Toronto or New York. Most people, Rose told us, relied on country food like seal, musk ox, and whale.

We were taken to see a statue of a stout Inuk woman glaring at the sea, the official memorial honoring the sacrifice Inuit had made to Canadian national sovereignty. We were brought into the town's cultural center and given samples of raw Arctic char and Beluga blubber, offered crude sealskin handicrafts and photographs of the memorial for purchase, and shown a performance of Inuit throat-singing and traditional dress. Two of my fellow passengers told me how much they admired Inuit for not being resentful and angry like some other indigenous peoples were.

One of our other tour guides showed us his bear pelt. It was his second kill, he said; he'd shot the bear himself, from about ten feet away. He was sixteen years old. The bear's thick white fur was rough to the touch.

It was the same bear that appeared on the Adventure Canada logo. The same bear that's become an icon for climate-change activists. The same bear that's used to sell Coca-Cola. Who had the right to decide what this bear's life meant? Who was entitled to say what it was worth?

John Houston: "When you talk about time, often our people—white people—have tried to present themselves in a patient, tolerant, long-suffering, forbearing sort of a way, and the expression that sums it up that I've been hearing ever since I was a kid was: 'Well, of course, it takes time.' It's a very tricky and complicated phrase, when the colonizers sigh to each other and say 'It takes time.' What do they mean? Well, it takes time to eradicate the native in the person, doesn't it? That would take time."

Ian Tamblyn: "I've argued for Inuit rights and claims. The injustices done to them and our First Nations have been horrendous. It's a really embarrassing part of Canada's history. But whether the future of those rights is a right or a romantic notion, I don't know. Sometimes I think the Inuit people see our presence in the Arctic as transitional. That one day we won't be here. I don't know if that will ever be the case."

Bernadette Dean: "People need to understand the true facts, and they need to change their attitude—whatever attitudes they may have about aboriginal peoples everywhere—and incorporate aboriginal values. When you come from a place like this, and you've lived here all your life and you know the seasons and you follow the plants and you follow what the land is doing, and then you get researchers who come up here for two or three months of the year and they're acknowledged experts . . . All those people, when it comes to October, November, December, January, February, March, April, May, June, they're not going to be up here. I'll be here. Tagak will be here."

———

Sir John Franklin's 1845 expedition to find the Northwest Passage was manned by adventurers who lived the motto of Enlightenment philosophy: *Sapere aude!* (Dare to know!) Like us, they had believed that with technology, ingenuity, and daring, they could master the unknown. Franklin's ships, the HMS *Terror* and *Erebus*, were outfitted with all the latest cutting-edge equipment, including steam engines, reinforced hulls, and three years' worth of canned foods. They were crewed by brave, resilient, and skilled sailors. They were commanded by veterans of the Napoleonic Wars with years of experience in the Arctic.

Somewhere in those frigid Northern waters, though, the ships caught fast in the ice. As the stout-hearted crew succumbed to starvation, hypothermia, and disease, they turned on each other, descending into madness and cannibalism. Franklin's expedition ended in disaster. Franklin's arrogance may have been partly to blame, as well as his cultivated ignorance of Inuit knowledge, but the real culprit—as Owen Beattie established conclusively in

1984—was the lead used to seal the canned food that Franklin had brought to ward off scurvy. Beattie and his team proved this by performing autopsies on three sailors Franklin had buried: Able Seaman John Hartnell, Royal Marine William Braine, and Petty Officer John Torrington. The men's bodies lay interred on Beechey Island, a small, bare rock rising up out of Parry Channel.

Today, as more and more cruise ships and private yachts ply the Northwest Passage, Beechey Island has become an important tourist stop. Indeed, when we arrived there on the morning of August 30, we found a 170-foot, custom-built Benetti yacht named *Latitude* in the harbor, with a covered runabout tethered beside. By the time our fifth Zodiac had unloaded for the day's expedition, rumors were flying that Leonardo DiCaprio was on board (he'd been spotted camping on Baffin Island in July and had been in Canada filming *The Revenant*). Our ship's videographer thought he'd spotted Michael Fassbender as well.

Later that morning, after most of us had already done our sightseeing and returned to the ship, a polar bear ambled up out of the water onto the beach. It was the fourth bear we'd seen. Those of us who'd already returned massed on the sundecks at the rear of the *Endeavour*, snapping photos, while Zodiacs swiftly ferried back everyone still on the island. Meanwhile, the *Latitude*'s runabout broke away and motored in toward shore, coming to rest about a hundred yards from the bear. The bear watched the runabout closely. We watched the bear. Then, after several minutes, the bear suddenly looked up, startled, and fled. Photographs and video showed a drone flying from the runabout and buzzing the bear. Assistant expedition leader Chris Dolder vowed to report the incident to Canadian authorities.

That night, compounding the excitement about Beechey, the bear, Leo, and the drone, we were led in a rousing rendition of Stan Rogers's Canadian anthem "Northwest Passage," treated to a special Franklin Expedition–themed dinner, and invited to dress up in costume for an explorer-themed dance party. The mood was high, charged with a peculiar mix of compulsory fun, emotional release, and cultural pride.

In the late 1840s, after the Franklin Expedition failed to return to England, the Royal Navy and Lady Jane Franklin funded numerous search-and-rescue attempts. The rescue expedition led by Dr. John Rae was the most successful in terms of actual information but was also the most controversial: Rae brought back reports from Inuit that the Franklin Expedition had degenerated into cannibalism. The news was a scandal, and Rae was attacked in the press by Charles Dickens. The controversy ended Rae's career.

One of my fellow passengers, a retired microbiologist from Los Angeles, was dismissive of Franklin's allure. "What's the big deal?" she asked. "He fucked up and he died. End of story."

"Maybe it was the sense of mystery," I offered. "The fact that they never found his ships."[1]

She was skeptical. And as I looked around the dance party at all the pale, pink-cheeked Canadians dressed like Vikings and British explorers, it occurred to me that she was right. It wasn't mystery. It wasn't even *Sapere aude*. What the Franklin Expedition glorified was the war of Man—white men—against Nature. Franklin was indeed a tragic figure, and the tragic flaw he embodied was a will to power that knew no bounds. He was doomed because "nature" proved, finally, unconquerable, but in honoring his memory, we were celebrating and carrying on the war he'd waged.

As the MS *Ocean Endeavour* burned another fifteen tons of carbon, sailing blithely through placid, warming seas, Franklin's war against Nature was being replayed by retirees dancing to Abba in Viking helmets, confirming Marx's well-known observation that history repeats itself the first time as tragedy, the second time as farce.

Ian Tamblyn: "We live in different times at different times. The arguments that Tagak and Bernadette are making are in a different time frame than the time frame we live in. What they're arguing is really good, but there's another wheel that's turning. The effect of European trampling is not over."

Heather McGregor, postdoctoral research fellow at the University of Ottawa, author of Inuit Education and Schools in the Eastern Arctic: "If climate change demands of every human on this earth that we put aside some of our national affiliations and look at this as something that we need to tackle transnationally, beyond the borders that have made sense to us up until now, I'm still not sure that we can do that without recognizing the history of relationships between indigenous and non-indigenous people. If there's going to be climate-change cooperation, it needs to be done within the context of the call for decolonization."

Stefan Kindberg, expedition leader, Adventure Canada: "It's all over the Arctic. It's not only this part. It's the Russian Arctic, it's the Scandinavian Arctic. It's the Arctic everywhere."

———

The "Idea of the North" has long been a whirl around a void, a dreamland, a question to be answered. As Margaret Atwood writes, "Popular lore . . . established early that the North was uncanny, awe-inspiring in an almost religious way, hostile to white men, but alluring; that it would lead you on and do you in; that it would drive you crazy, and, finally, would claim you for its own." This conception of the Arctic brings with it a sexual politics, a racial politics, and a geopolitics, all of them calling for assertions of white male mastery—from the search for the Northwest Passage to claims for Canadian sovereignty to the idiotic death chant "Drill, baby, drill!"

Yet for thousands of years before Franklin tried to pierce the Northwest Passage in 1845, humans eking out a tenuous existence there knew very well what the North was made of. It was giant bones and *qalupalik*, *angakkuit* who could turn from animals to men and back again, *anirniit* that were sometimes wind and sometimes women, sometimes waves and sometimes seals. Their world was neither Edenic nor sublime but fraught with constant danger from bone-cracking ice, ravenous bears, and innumerable unseen spirits.

"The greatest peril in life lies in the fact that human food consists entirely of souls," an Inuk named Ivaluardjuk told Danish anthropologist Knud Rasmussen a century ago. "All the creatures that we have to kill and eat, all those that we have to strike down and destroy to make clothes for ourselves, have souls, like we have, souls that do not perish with the body, and which must therefore be propitiated lest they should revenge themselves on us."

Those nomadic Arctic hunting cultures have been destroyed by colonialism, by modernity, by industrialization, as completely as were those of the great Iroquois nations and the Nambikwara of Brazil. We no longer live in the world of Ivaluardjuk, in which humans must battle and propitiate invisible spirits. But we no longer live in the world of Franklin, either, in which the white man is locked in an unending war with Nature. The Enlightenment hero's "Idea of the North," that conception of the Arctic as a sublime encounter with pristine wilderness, was being destroyed by the very ship I sailed on and the very passengers I traveled with.

We live today in a world in which humanity has been struck low, perhaps lower than ever before. Unwitting agents of our own demise, unable to control the immense technologies we so arrogantly believed were ours, incapable of exerting the rational collective will necessary to save our civilization from destruction, we find ourselves reduced to something less than human, lacking even the dumb instinct for survival we see in plants.

Geologists, scientists, and other thinkers have advanced the idea that the Earth has entered a new epoch, one characterized by the advent of the human species as a geological force. They're calling this epoch the Anthropocene. Some thinkers suppose this idea implies that we have advanced beyond nature, that the world is now completely human, but while they grasp the truth that we've left the Enlightenment's division between "Man" and "Nature" behind, they've grasped that truth by the wrong end. The Anthropocene implies not the supersession of nature by human civilization, but the opposite: the reduction of human civilization to the status of a fossil. On a geological time scale, we're just another rock.

As the *Endeavour* sailed south from Beechey Island, I sat with Ian Tamblyn over a glass of chardonnay, watching the sun drop into a black and iceless sea. "When Students on Ice started, their motto was 'Save the Pole, Save the Planet,'" he recollected. "In recent years, that logo's disappeared, in part because of the reality of the situation. It's heartbreaking for me, because these kids really want to save the planet. They're totally dedicated to it. But a few years ago, one of [Prime Minister Stephen] Harper's ministers came on the trip, and he told the students that global warming should be seen as an economic opportunity. I don't understand why they did that, but at the same time, that's a reality. It's a reality that our prime minister sees, and a reality that others see as well. What do we do? Do we try to save a planet that can't be saved, or do we adapt? I've got a generation of kids who are still living in a paradigm of saving the planet. Others see that we're beyond that and that it cannot be saved. And so a Machiavellian politician will say, 'Let's look for opportunity where we can. Let's look for the rare metals under the glaciers. Let's open the Northwest Passage.' Again, going back to my lifetime, I've seen that transition—of going from a pre-climate-change world, to a climate-change world, to a post-climate-change world. We're acting it out. But I've never actually been allowed to say these things. It's not part of the party line."

Ree Brennin Houston: "I do hear people say, 'Well, what's the point?' *What's the point*!? It'll make the Earth completely uninhabitable for life as we know it. Bacteria and whatever will survive, but I

care about life as we know it. We need to be fighting all we can to
decrease greenhouse gases."

James Halfpenny: "To be honest, the North is doomed. The Inuit
way of life is gone. They can't go out on the ice to hunt, it won't be
long before it's only annual ice, and I suspect there may be a time
when there's no ice. There just ain't a rosy picture there."

Tagak Curley: "Maybe it's like the elders say: '*Ajurtnarmat.*' Nothing
to be done."

———

The first cruise ship to transit the Northwest Passage, the MS *Lind-blad Explorer*, did so in 1984. In 2015, six other cruise ships made the
passage with the *Ocean Endeavour*, plus at least seven private yachts,
two cargo ships, and a tanker. A similar total in 2016 included the
MS *Crystal Serenity*, an 820-foot-long luxury liner that carried more
than a thousand passengers on a thirty-two-day cruise from Seward,
Alaska, to New York City.

As the *Ocean Endeavour* sailed west through Coronation Gulf
toward our final destination, Kugluktuk, I was overtaken by the
realization that what I'd come to see was already gone. The Arctic
was changing in response to global warming faster than anywhere
else on Earth, and by the time I'd gotten there, it had already been
through the hottest years and the most precipitous declines in
sea ice ever recorded. The five record lows for sea-ice extent had
all occurred in the past eight years. The lowest recorded seasonal
maximum occurred in February 2015, and the same year ranked
fourth-lowest in summer sea-ice extent, bottoming out at 1.7 million square miles on September 11, but that year's record low for
sea-ice maximum was shattered again in 2016, as the planet warmed
beyond anything human civilization had ever seen.

If it is true, as the Buddhists teach, that nothing is ever what it is for very long, then it is also true that nothing is ever wholly lost. Things morph from one form to another, as energy and matter coalesce and transition back and forth from waves to beings. Any truly empirical view of life must admit that the universe is flux, time change, and death nothing more than a shift between states. As the Earth's gyres and floes wheel and pass, diminish and crescendo, there is no final end, no doom, no death spiral, for as each wheel turns another and turns into another, every end is a new beginning.

Passengers board and disembark. Ships sail east and west. Planes fly in and out of Iqaluit, Sydney, Beijing, NYC. Traffic thickens and thins along the Brooklyn-Queens Expressway, the lights along Manhattan turn off, turn on, as the coal-fired grid ebbs and surges. The stock market rises and falls, days turn into weeks, weeks turn into years, money changes hands, and carbon flows from under the earth into the sky. Ice melts into the sea, drop by drop. Another UN convention meets. Another election cycle begins. Another hottest summer ever passes.

As we stood in our life jackets below decks the last day, waiting to Zodiac ashore for our flight to Edmonton, we were met by passengers coming aboard for the next cruise: "Out of the Northwest Passage 2015." Another crowd of silver-haired adventurers, our group's uncanny twins, smiling in confusion as we cheered them on. [2015/2017]

Anthropocene City

Imagine an oyster. Imagine waves of rain lashing concrete, a crawdad boil, a fallen highway, and a muddy bay. Imagine a complex system of gates and levees, the Johnson Space Center, a broken record spinning on a broken player. Imagine the baroque intricacy of the Valero Houston oil refinery, the Petrobras Pasadena oil refinery, the LyondellBasell oil refinery, the Shell Deer Park oil refinery, the ExxonMobil Baytown oil refinery, a bottle of Ravishing Red nail polish, a glacier falling into the sea. Imagine gray-black clouds piling over the horizon, a chaos spiral hundreds of miles wide. Imagine a hurricane.

———

Isaiah whirls through the sky, gathering strength from the Gulf of Mexico's warm waters. City, state, and federal officials do the sensible thing, evacuating beach towns and warning citizens and companies in Texas's petro-industrial enclaves from Bayou Vista to Morgan's Point to prepare for the worst.

The massive cyclone slows and intensifies as it nears the barrier islands off the coast, with wind speeds reaching over 150 mph. By sunset, several hours before landfall, the storm's counterclockwise arm is pushing water over the Galveston Seawall; by the time the eye finally crosses the beaches east of San Luis Pass, the historic city of Galveston has been flattened by twenty-foot waves.

As Isaiah crosses into Galveston Bay, it only grows in strength, adding water to water, and when it hits the ExxonMobil Baytown refinery, some fifty miles inland, the storm surge is over twenty-five feet high. It crashes through refineries, chemical storage facilities, wharves, and production plants all along the Houston Ship Channel, cleaving pipelines from their moorings, lifting and breaking storage tanks, and strewing toxic waste throughout east Houston.

The iridescent, gray-brown flood rises, carrying jet fuel, sour crude, and natural gas liquids into strip malls, schools, and offices. By the time Isaiah passes inland, leaving the ruined coast behind, more than two hundred petrochemical storage tanks have been wrecked, more than a hundred million gallons of gas, oil, and other chemicals have been spilled, total economic damages for the region are estimated at over a hundred billion dollars, and three thousand six hundred eighty-two people have been killed. By most measures, it is one of the worst disasters in US history: worse than the 1906 San Francisco Earthquake, worse than Hurricane Katrina, worse than the terrorist attacks of September 11.

The effects ripple across the globe. The Gulf Coast is home to roughly 30 percent of the United States' proven oil reserves; the Gulf Coast and Texas hold 35 percent of its natural gas reserves. The refineries and plants circling Galveston Bay are responsible for roughly 25 percent of the United States' petroleum refining, more than 44 percent of its ethylene production, 40 percent of its specialty chemical feedstock, and more than half of its jet fuel. Houston is the second busiest port in the United States in terms of pure tonnage and is one of the most important storage and shipping points in the country for natural gas liquids. Isaiah shuts all that down. Within days of the hurricane's landfall, the NYSE and NASDAQ plummet as the price of oil skyrockets. Fuel shortages ground flights throughout the country, airline ticket prices soar, the price of beef and pork shoots up, and gas prices at the pump leap to seven or eight dollars a gallon. The American economy slips into free fall.

Meanwhile, as the oil-poisoned water in east Houston flows back toward the sea, it leaves behind it the worst environmental catastrophe since the BP Deepwater Horizon spill. Rather than diffusing into open water, though, all the sludge is cradled within the protective arms of Galveston Bay.

The good news is that Isaiah hasn't happened. It's an imaginary calamity based on models and research. The bad news is that it's only a matter of time before it does. Any fifty-mile stretch of the Texas coast can expect a hurricane once every six years on average, according to the National Weather Service. Only a few American cities are more vulnerable to hurricanes than Houston and Galveston, and not one of those is as crucial to the economy.

The worse news is that future hurricanes will actually be more severe than Isaiah. The models Isaiah is based on, developed by Rice University's Severe Storm Prediction, Education and Evacuation from Disaster (SSPEED) Center, don't account for climate change. According to Jim Blackburn, SSPEED's co-director, other models have shown much more alarming surges. "The City of Houston and FEMA did a climate change future," he told me, "and the surge in that scenario was 34 feet. Hurricanes are going to get bigger. No question. They are fueled by the heat of the ocean, and the ocean's warming. Our models are nowhere close."

——

Imagine Cobalt Yellow Lake. Imagine Cy Twombly's "Say Goodbye, Catullus, to the Shores of Asia Minor." Imagine colony collapse. Imagine refugees drowning off the shores of Asia Minor. Imagine causality, a bicycle tire, a million lost golf balls, a Styrofoam cooler, a bucket of crab claws, polyurethane, polypropylene, three copitas of mezcal, polyester, polyacrylic acid, polybutylene terephthalate, barbecue sauce, polycarbonate, polyether ether ketone, polyethylene, a Waffle House, polyoxymethylene, polyphenyl ether, polystyrene, the Wizard of Oz, polysulfone, polytetrafluoroethylene, polyvinyl chloride, a pair of pink Crocs.

————

I made a reservation aboard the MV *Sam Houston* to take a boat tour of the Houston Ship Channel, the fifty-mile artery connecting Houston to the Gulf of Mexico, and the densest energy infrastructure nexus in North America. It seemed the perfect place to ask Timothy Morton about hyperobjects, dark ecology, and strange loops—some of the concepts he's been developing, as one of the leading thinkers of "speculative realism," in the effort to make philosophical sense of climate change.

The thinkers behind speculative realism, including Morton, Graham Harman, Quentin Meillassoux, and Jane Bennett, share a predilection for weird writers, woolly European metaphysics, and big ideas like the Anthropocene, but they'd likely resist being lumped all together. Graham Harman's "object-oriented ontology," for instance, argues that objects are autonomous in a way that keeps them from ever really connecting, perpetually withdrawing from each other in spite of apparent relations, while Jane Bennett's "vibrant matter" tells us that everything is equally alive and equally interwoven, humming together in a humongous, homogeneous web in which a lost glove, an F-117 stealth bomber, and an Iraqi child are all basically the same kind of stuff. Morton, for his part, is more concerned with a critique of "Nature," arguing that we need to get past our cherished "culture/nature" divide in order to see ourselves as always already bound up in a dark mesh of ontological feedback.

As different as these thinkers are, though, they share a few key ideas. First, they all argue against what Meillassoux calls correlationism, the idea that human access to reality is limited to mere correlation between things-in-themselves and our thoughts about them. Our access to reality, they each insist in their own way, is more mysterious and complicated than just finding the circle-shaped thought for the circle-shaped thing. Second, for all these thinkers, things in the world have their own vitality independent of their relations to humans. A spoon has its own reality, as does an ocelot, a painting by Redon, or a Panamax container ship. Objects don't *need* human subjects to be meaningful, they argue, not even objects made by humans. Third, these thinkers all believe ontology trumps epistemology. Instead of asking how we can know things, that is, they insist we should be asking what it means for things to exist in the first place. The signature move that ties all this together is the willingness to indulge in speculative metaphysics—pondering what reality, deep down, really *is*. Spurning both mainstream analytic philosophy and the critical Marxist-Hegelian tradition, these thinkers have decided that what the world needs from philosophy isn't analysis, interpretation, or even transformation, but imagination.

Whether or not any of this makes any sense will depend on whom you ask. While speculative realism has generated a lot of buzz in literature departments and art magazines, its coherence and influence remain much debated. Some argue that object-oriented ontology is just a new way to fetishize commodities, especially the ones we call art. Others argue that the ideas behind speculative realism are specious and ignorant of the philosophical tradition. Climate scientists and academic philosophers, meanwhile, have hardly seemed to notice that speculative realism exists.

One of the reasons speculative realism exerts such a draw on artistic and literary types, I suspect, is because its thinkers make interesting aesthetic choices. This is especially true of Morton, who has a gift for the phrase. His book titles, capsule formulations of the ideas they elaborate, rumble with portent. Consider *Hyperobjects: Philosophy and Ecology after the End of the World*, *Ecology without Nature: Rethinking Environmental Aesthetics*, or *Dark Ecology: For a Logic of Future Coexistence*. Indeed, on the page Morton is a dizzying, acrobatic thinker; to read him is to take a wild ride through

Romantic poetry, Western philosophy, literary theory, and climate change—imagine Slavoj Žižek on psilocybin.

In person, Morton is gentle, funny, and self-effacing, equal parts Oxbridge and cybergoth. We drove out to the ship channel in his white Mazda. As we rose and fell through the soaring grandeur of Houston's swooping highway exchanges, we talked about writing practice and work-life balance: Morton had two books coming out in 2016 and was writing two more, and when he's not busy writing, spending time with his kids, giving lectures, blogging, or collaborating with Björk, he teaches courses on literary theory and "Arts in the Anthropocene" at Rice University, where he holds the Rita Shea Guffey Chair in English.

Turning off the highway, we descended into the petro-industrial gray zone that sprawls from Houston to the sea. A Port of Houston security guard checked our IDs, and we drove past hundred-foot-long turbine blades, massive shafts, and what looked like pieces of giant disassembled robots. I asked Tim how he liked living in Houston.

"This is the dirty coast," he said. "Dirty in the sense that something's wrong. We're holding this horrible, necessary energy substance, and it's like working in an emergency room or a graveyard or a charnel ground. You're basically working with corpses, with fossils from millions of years ago, you're working with deadly toxic stuff all the time, stuff that has very intense emotion connected to it. If I was going to find a word that described Texan-ness, I'd use the word 'wild'—phenomenologically, emotionally, experientially wild."

We parked and boarded the MV *Sam Houston*. As the boat spun away from the pier and headed east, Tim and I went out on deck. Across the brown-black water enormous claws and magnets shifted scrap metal from one heap to another, throwing up clouds of metal dust, while the engine thrummed through my feet and the wind whipped across the mike of my voice recorder.

"The thing is," Tim said, "being aware of ecological facts is the very opposite of thinking about or looking at or talking about nature. *Nature* is always conceptualized as an entity that's different or distinct from me somehow. It's in my DNA, it's under my clothes, it's under the floorboards, it's in the wilderness. It's everywhere except for right here. But ecology means it's in your face. It *is* your face. It's part of you and you're part of it."

Several industrial recycling companies line the upper reaches of the Houston Ship Channel, including Derichebourg Recycling USA, Texas Port Recycling, and Cronimet USA, all recognized emitters of one of the most potent carcinogens known to science, hexavalent chromium. Behind the giant cranes and heaps of scrap lies the predominantly Hispanic neighborhood of Magnolia Park, whose residents have long complained of unexplained smoke and gas emissions, persistent pollution, and strange, multicolored explosions.

"The simplest way of describing that is *ecology without nature*," Tim continued. "That doesn't mean I don't believe in things like coral. I believe in coral much more than someone who thinks that coral is this 'natural' thing. Coral is a life form that's connected to other forms. Everything's connected. And how we think about stuff is connected to the stuff. How you think about stuff, how you perceive stuff, is entangled with what you're perceiving."

In among the recycling yards sat Brady's Landing, a steak-and-shrimp restaurant. Through its plate-glass windows, dozens of empty white tables shone like pearls in black velvet. I imagined diners eating crab-stuffed trout, watching the water rise up over the Ceres wharfs across the channel, rise up over the pilings at the edge of Brady's Island, rise up over the restaurant's foundations and up the windows, one foot, two feet, six feet, and the glass would crack, creak, and burst open, and the tide would rush in over fine leather shoes and French cuffs and napkin-covered laps and lift them, the diners, their tables, plates, pinot noir, and crab-stuffed trout, lift them and spin them in a rich and strange ballet.

"It's like when you realize you're actually a life form," Tim said. "I'm Tim but I'm also a human. That sounds obvious but it isn't. I'm Tim but I've also got these bits of fish and viral material inside me, that *are* me. That's not a nice, cozy experience; it's an uncanny, weird experience. But there's a kind of smile from that experience, because ecological reality is like that. Ecological phenomena are all about loops, feedback loops, and this very tragic loop we're on where we're destroying Earth as we know it."

Interstate Highway 610 loomed above, eighteen-wheelers and SUVs rolling through the sky. In the distance, gas flares flashed against the cloud cover. Pipes fed into pipes that wrapped back into pipes circling pipes, Escher machines in aluminum and steel.

"Ecological thinking is about never being able to be completely in the center of your world. It's about everything seeming out of place and unreal. That's the feel of dark ecology. But it isn't just about human awareness: it's about how *everything* has this uncanny, looped quality to it. It's actually part of how things are. So it's about being horrified and upset and traumatized and shocked by what we've been up to as human beings, and it's about realizing that this basic feeling of twistedness isn't going away."

A voice boomed out from the bowels of the boat as we broke from the highway's shadow: "First refinery to the right is Valero. This refinery began operations in 1942. It will handle 145,000 barrels of oil per day." Directly behind Valero lay Hartman Park, with its green lawns and baseball diamonds—the jewel of Manchester, one of the most polluted neighborhoods in the United States. Manchester is blocked in on the north by Valero, and on the east, south, and west by a chemical plant, a car-crushing yard, a water treatment plant, a train yard, Interstate 610, and a Goodyear synthetic rubber plant. In 2010, the EPA found toxic levels of seven different carcinogens in the neighborhood. The area is 88 percent Hispanic.

"At some point," Tim said, "instead of trying to delete the twisty darkness, you have to make friends with it. And when you make friends with it, it becomes strangely sweet."

––––––

Imagine Greenland. Imagine Kellogg Brown & Root. Imagine Uber, the Svalbard Seed Vault, a roadkill raccoon, six months in juvie, Green Revolution, amnesia. Imagine ZZ Top. Imagine White Oak Bayou flooding its banks. Imagine Mexican gardeners wielding Weed Eaters. Imagine boom and bust, the murmur of Diane Rehm, sizzurp, a sick coot, Juneteenth, coral bleaching, amnesia. Imagine losing Shanghai, New York, and Mumbai. Imagine "In the Mood." Imagine amnesia.

––––––

From Houston, the ship channel goes south through Galveston Bay, cutting a trench approximately 530 feet wide and 45 feet deep through the estuary bottom to where it passes into the Gulf of Mexico. As you follow the channel south along I-45, strip clubs and fast-food franchises give way to bayou resorts and refineries, until the highway finally leaps into the air, soaring over the water with the pelicans. It comes down again in downtown Galveston, once known as the Wall Street of the South: a mix of historic homes, dry-docked oil rigs, beach bars, and the University of Texas Medical Branch. The gulf spreads sullen and muddy to the south, its greasy skin broken by distant blisters of flaming steel.

Galveston Bay is a Texas paradox. One of the most productive estuaries in the United States, it offers up huge catches of shrimp, blue crab, oysters, croaker, flounder, and catfish and supports dozens of other kinds of fish, turtles, dolphins, salamanders, sharks, and snakes, as well as hundreds of species of birds. Yet the bay is heavily polluted, so full of PCBs, pesticides, dioxin, and petrochemicals that fishing is widely restricted. The bay is Houston's shield, protecting it from the worst of the Gulf Coast's weather by absorbing storm surges and soaking up rainfall, but hydrologists at Rice University are worried that it might also be Houston's doom: The wide, shallow basin could, under the right conditions, supercharge a storm surge right up the ship channel.

The fight to protect Houston and Galveston from storms has been going on for more than a century, ever since Galveston built a seventeen-foot seawall after the Great Storm of 1900, a Category 4 hurricane that killed an estimated ten to twelve thousand people. The fight has been mainly reactive, always planning for the last big storm, rarely for the next. The levees around Texas City, for instance, were built after Hurricane Carla submerged the chemical plants there in ten feet of water in 1961. Today, Hurricane Ike, which hit Texas in 2008, offers the object lesson.

Hurricane Ike was a lucky hit with unlucky timing. Forecasts had the hurricane landing at the southern end of Galveston Island, and if they'd been right, Ike would have looked a lot like Isaiah. Instead, in the early morning hours of September 13, 2008, Ike bent north and hit Galveston dead on, which shifted the most damaging winds east. The sparsely populated Bolivar Peninsula was flattened, but Houston came out okay.

Still, Ike killed nearly fifty people in Texas alone, left thousands homeless, and was the third costliest hurricane in American history. It would have been the ideal moment for Texas to ask Congress to fund a comprehensive coastal protection system. But that Monday, September 15, Lehman Brothers filed the largest bankruptcy in United States history, and the next day the Federal Reserve stepped in to save the failing insurance behemoth AIG with an $85 billion bailout. Nature's fury took a back seat to the crisis of capital.

Since then, two main research teams have led the way in preparing for the next big storm: Bill Merrell's "Ike Dike" team at Texas A&M Galveston (TAMUG), and the SSPEED Center at Rice University, led by Phil Bedient and Jim Blackburn. Despite shared goals, though, the relationship between the two teams hasn't always been easy. Bill Merrell's cantankerous personality and obsessive drive to protect Galveston have clashed with SSPEED's complex, interdisciplinary, Houston-centric approach.

Dr. Merrell's Ike Dike has the blessing of simplicity, which softens the sticker shock: It is estimated to cost between $6 billion and $13 billion. The plan is to build a fifty-five-mile-long "coastal spine" along the gulf. The plan's main disadvantage is that a strong enough hurricane could still flood the Houston Ship Channel, because of what Dr. Bedient calls the Lake Okeechobee effect.

"The Okeechobee hurricane came into Florida in 1928 and sloshed water to a twenty-foot surge," Dr. Bedient explained. "Killed two thousand people. But Lake Okeechobee is unconnected to the coast. It was just wind. Galveston Bay has the same dimensions and depth as Lake Okeechobee in Florida. So imagine we block off Galveston Bay with a coastal spine, and we have a Lake Okeechobee."

Dr. Bedient worked on the Murphy's Oil spill in St. Bernard Parish, Louisiana, where flooding from Hurricane Katrina ruptured a storage tank, releasing more than a million gallons of oil, and ruined approximately 1,800 homes. One of Dr. Bedient's biggest worries is what a storm might do to the estimated 4,500 similar tanks surrounding Houston, many of them along the Ship Channel. If even 2 percent of those tanks were to fail because of storm surge, the results would be catastrophic.

The SSPEED Center advocates a layered defense, including a midbay gate that could be closed during a storm to protect the channel. On its face, the plan seems unwieldy, but SSPEED's models show it could stop most of the surge from going up the ship channel, with or without the Ike Dike, at an estimated cost of only a few billion dollars.

On the government side, various entities are at work in the ponderous and opaque way of American bureaucracy. The US Army Corps of Engineers has its own research and development process and is working on a study of the Galveston-Houston area as part of its more comprehensive Gulf Coast research agenda, which could, eventually, lead to a recommendation for further studies, feasibility and cost-benefit analyses, environmental impact reports, and perhaps someday a project, which, were it funded by Congress, might even get built. One must be patient. It took the Army Corps of Engineers twenty-six years to build the Texas City Levee. When Katrina hit New Orleans and breached the levee system there, the Corps had been working on it since 1965, and it was still under construction.

Meanwhile, the Gulf Coast Community Protection and Recovery District is working to synthesize SSPEED and TAMUG's work into its own proposal. The GCCPRD was established by Texas governor Rick Perry in 2009, in the wake of Ike, but wasn't funded until 2013, when the Texas General Land Office stepped in with a federal grant from the Department of Housing and Urban Development. The GCCPRD board comprises county judges from Brazoria, Chambers, Galveston, Harris, Jefferson, and Orange counties, three additional members, and a president, currently former Harris County judge Robert Eckels, and has hired Dannenbaum Engineering, a local company with a strong track record in public infrastructure, to put the report together. The GCCPRD takes its lead from the GLO, headed today by Commissioner George P. Bush, and the specific language of the HUD grant restricts their work to analysis and general-level planning. Any more specific plans will have to come later, pending additional funding.

If there's one thing Houston can teach us about the Anthropocene, it's that all global warming is local. I went down myself to see representatives from all of these organizations—the USACE, SSPEED, TAMUG, the GLO, and the GCCPRD, plus the Texas Chemical Council and the Bay Area Houston Economic Partnership—testify before the State of Texas Joint Interim Committee on Coastal Barrier Systems (JICCBS), a special committee of the Texas state legislature, held at the TAMUG campus in Galveston.

Over five hours of presentations, talking points, and questions, a rough sense of the future began to take shape. As I sat in the back row listening to politicians ask about how various projects might affect insurance rates, how long different projects might take to build, and how the pitch could be put to the US Congress asking for the billions of dollars needed, I imagined a single white feather, numinous in the golden light of the Power Point, drift across the conference room, float over the heads of the senators, administrators, and scientists, and rise, rise, rise on an ever expanding wave of confidence.

What obstacles might have remained between this roomful of committed public servants and the building of one of the largest coastal infrastructure projects in the world seemed for a moment insubstantial. The fact that environmental impact studies taking years to complete had yet to be started, that any of the land in question would have to be bought or seized under eminent domain, that all the planning at this stage was merely notional and actual designs would have to be bid on, contracted out, and approved, that there was no governmental agency in place to take responsibility for a coastal barrier system and maintain it, much less build it, and that somebody still had to come up with the money, somewhere, perhaps somehow convincing divided Republicans and embattled Democrats in the US Congress to send a bunch of Texas pols and their cronies a check for $13 billion— these were all mere details, nothing to worry about. I felt sure the political will manifest in that conference room would find a way.

And I had total confidence that those same feelings of goodwill, pragmatism, and accomplishment would be found, more or less, at the next Joint Interim Committee on Coastal Barrier Systems meeting, and the next academic conference on "Avoiding Disaster," and the next policy symposium on energy transition, and the next global conference on sea-level rise, and the next plenary on carbon trading, and the next colloquium on the Anthropocene, and the next Conference of Parties to the United Nations

Framework Convention on Climate Change, and the next, and the next, and the next, and the next, and the next, and journalists would report on it, and philosophers would ponder it, and activists would tweet about it, and concerned people like you would read about it. The problem is, it's not enough.

According to Jim Blackburn, "Even a locally funded project would probably be three years in the permitting and another six to eight years in construction." Most local politicians, however, seemed to prefer the Ike Dike, necessarily a Federal project. "I have heard more than one person say our plan is to wait until the next hurricane comes," Blackburn said, "and then depend on guilt money from Washington to fix the problem."

Bill Merrell told me much the same thing: "We see local politicians in general content with doing nothing. The do-nothing option is pretty gruesome. It gets you a storm, sooner or later, that's going to kill thousands of people and cause at least $100 billion in damage. The cost of doing nothing is horrendous. But trying to get politicians from doing nothing to doing something is really hard. I think I've started to appreciate that more. I didn't realize it would be as hard as it was."

Two weeks after the JICCBS meeting, Houston was inundated with more than a foot of rain in less than twenty-four hours, almost two feet in some neighborhoods. Flooding damaged more than 200 homes and killed eight people. By the end of the month, it was the wettest April the city had ever recorded. More rain and more floods hit Texas in May and June, then a week of precipitation in August dumped more than seven trillion gallons of water on Louisiana, with some areas accumulating more than twenty inches of rain. Flooding killed thirteen people and damaged 146,000 homes.

Imagine Earth. Imagine "Pretty Hurts." Imagine Lakewood Church, wind-lashed magnolias, a bottle of Topo Chico, the Astrodome. Imagine surface and depth, weather drones, the Geto Boys, thermodynamic disequilibrium, a body in a hole. Imagine the economy slowing, snowy egrets nesting in a live oak, becoming one with the Ocean of Soul, a Colt Expanse carbine. Imagine purple drank and a bowl of queso. Imagine *Terms of Endearment*. Imagine stocks and flows, a pearl, a rhizome. Imagine the end of the world as we know it.

———

The *Sam Houston*'s ninety-minute tour of the Houston Ship Channel only goes a few miles out before turning around at the LyondellBasel refinery, one of the largest heavy-sulfur-crude refineries in the United States, processing around 268,000 barrels a day. The loudspeaker voice offered us complimentary soft drinks. I asked Tim Morton whether dark ecology had a politics.

"Obviously," he said, "it's not just that unequal distribution is connected to ecological stuff. It *is* ecological. It's not like we need to condescend to include fighting racism and these other issues under the banner of ecological thinking. It's the other way around. These problems were *already* ecological because the class system is a Mesopotamian construct and we're basically living in Mesopotamia 9.0. We're looking at these oil refineries and it's basically an upgrade of an upgrade of an upgrade of an agricultural logistics that began around 10,000 BC and is directly responsible, right now, for a huge amount of carbon emissions but also absolutely necessitated industry and therefore global warming and mass extinction."

We passed the CEMEX Houston Cement Company East Plant, the Gulf Coast Waste Disposal Authority's Washburn Tunnel Wastewater Treatment Facility, the Kinder Morgan Terminal, and Calpine's Channel Energy Center, a natural gas steam plant.

"This is where I have to say something English, which is 'Give us a chance, mate.' Because we can't do everything all at once, and we come to the conversation with the limitations and the skill sets that we have, and we're getting round to stuff. But maybe the first thing to do is to notice: We. Are. In. A. Shit. Situation. Maybe the first thing to do is go, okay, we're causing a mass extinction the likes of which hasn't been seen since the end-Permian extinction that wiped out 95 percent of life on Earth. Dark ecology has a politics, but it's a very different kind of politics because it means that the idea that humans get to decide what reality is needs to be dismantled. It's an ontological war."

Off our starboard, Public Grain Elevator #2 poured wheat into the hold of a Chinese freighter, a hundred yards from a giant mound of yellow Mexican gypsum. The Valero refinery rose again to port, flare stacks burning against the sky, just beyond where Sims Bayou broke off from the channel and meandered in toward South Park and Sunnyside, poverty-stricken African American neighborhoods largely abandoned by Houston's government. One area of Sunnyside was recently rated the second most dangerous neighborhood in America. Seventy-six percent of the children there live in poverty. Residents have a 1 in 11 chance of becoming a victim of violent crime.

"Take hyperobjects," Tim said, staring fixedly at the Valero refinery. "Hyperobjects are things that are so huge and so long-lasting that you can't point to them directly, you can only point to symptoms or parts of them. You can only point to little slivers of how they appear in your world. Imagine all the oil on Earth, forever, and the consequences of extracting and burning it for the next 100,000 years. That would be a hyperobject. We're going through this ship channel and these huge gigantic entities are all symptoms of this even larger, much more disturbing thing that we can't point to directly. You're in it and you *are* it, and you can't say where it starts and where it stops. Nevertheless, it's this thing here, it's on Earth, we know where it is."

We passed Brady's Landing and Derichebourg Recycling and Brays Bayou. The boat motored back much faster than it had gone out, and I had to strain to catch Tim's voice against the noise of the wind and water.

"My whole body's full of oil products," he said. "I'm wearing them and I'm driving them and I'm talking about them and I'm ignoring them and I'm pouring them into my gas tank, all these things I'm doing with them, precisely *that* is why I can't grasp them. It's not an abstraction. It's actually so real that I can't point to it. The human species is like that: instead of being this thing underneath appearance that you can point to, it's this incredibly distributed thing that you *can't* point to. The one thing that we need to be thinking right now, which is that *as a human being* I'm responsible for global warming, is actually quite tricky to fully conceptualize."

The *Sam Houston* throttled down and bumped against the wharf, the crew laid out the gangplank, and we disembarked. Tim and I got back in his white Mazda and he punched the destination into his phone.

"Make a U-turn," the fembot voice commanded. We drove out past the guard shack and over some railroad tracks, then out onto the highway.

"Anybody who's got any intelligence or sensitivity working with this stuff very quickly gets into dilemma space," Tim said, changing lanes. "I think it's a matter of nuance, how you work with that. I admire any mode of thought that goes as quickly as possible to this dilemma space, but we've only just begun to notice the 'we' doing these horrible things, and it's okay to be completely confused and upset. We're in shock, and that's on a good day. Most days it's just grief work because we're in a state of total denial. I am too. I can only allow myself to feel really upset about what's going on for maybe one second a day, otherwise I'd be in a heap on the floor all the time crying."

We took Alt-90 to I-10, passing a Chevron and a Shell and a Subway and Tires R Us and Mucho Mexico, then rose into the flow of traffic cruising the interstate west.

"We're constantly trying to get on top of whatever we're worrying about, but if you look at it from an Earth magnitude, that's magical thinking. We've given ourselves an impossible-to-solve problem. The way in which we think about the problem, the way in which we give it to ourselves, is part of the problem. How do you talk to people in a deep state of grief when you're also in that deep state of grief?"

The lanes split and we wove from I-10 to 59 and then, just past Fiesta Mart's enormous neon parrot, slid down the ramp to Fannin Street.

"I think there's an exit route, actually," Tim said, "but it's paradoxical. It involves going down underneath: it's not about transcending in any sense, it's about what I call subscending. There's always so much more about weather than just being a symptom of global warming. It *is* a symptom of global warming, but it's also a bath, these little birds over here, it's this wonderful wetness on the back of my neck, it's this irritating thing that's clogging up my drain."

We passed Fannin Flowers and then turned onto Bissonnet Street, rolling by the Museum of Fine Arts, with its special exhibit on Art Deco cars, and the Contemporary Art Museum, which was featuring an exhibition about the colonization of Mars. We turned in past Mel Chin's *Manilla Palm*, a giant fiberglass and burlap tree erupting out of a broken steel pyramid, then turned again, tracking back toward my apartment, past expensive new condos and down the dead end where I lived. Bamboo rose against the fence at the end of the road. Tim parked by the curb and shut off the Mazda.

"It boils down to knowing that global warming is a catastrophe rather than a disaster. Disasters are things that you rubberneck as they're happening to other people because you're reading about it in the Book of Revelation. It isn't now. A catastrophe, on the other hand, is something that you're inside of and it's got this weird, loopy, twisty structure to it. Disaster's like: everything's being destroyed and I can see perfectly how everything's being destroyed. Catastrophe's more like: OMG, I am the destruction. I'm part of it and I'm in it and I'm on it. It's an aesthetic experience, I'm inside it, I'm involved, I'm implicated."

A cardinal flew across the street, a streak of red against the green.

"I think that's how we get to smile, eventually, by fully inhabiting catastrophe space, in the same way that eventually a nightmare can become so horrible that you start laughing. That's how you find the exit route. I feel like maybe part of my job is giving people that."

————

Imagine black. Imagine black, black, black, blue-black, red-black, purple-black, gray-black, black on black. Imagine methane. Imagine education. Imagine wetlands. Imagine a brown-skinned woman in white circling the Rothko Chapel chanting "Zong. Zong. Zong." Imagine a regional, comprehensive approach to storm-surge risk management, lemonade, the Slab Parade, increased capacity, complexity, attribution studies, progress, a wine-and-cheese reception, TACC's Stampede Supercomputer, an integrative place-based research program, Venice's Piazza San Marco, sea-level rise, Destiny's Child. Imagine a red line. Imagine two degrees. Imagine flare stacks. Imagine death.

————

Maybe it was the eleventh straight month of record-breaking warming. Maybe it was when the Earth's temperature hit 1.5 degrees Celsius over pre-industrial levels. Maybe it was new reports that Antarctica and the Arctic were melting faster than anyone expected. Maybe it was when Greenland started melting two months early, and then so quickly that scientists didn't believe their data. Maybe it was watching our world start to come apart, and knowing that nothing would be done until it was too late.

We've known that climate change was a threat since at least 1988, and the United States has done almost nothing to stop it. Today it might be too late. The feedback mechanisms that scientists have warned us about are happening. Our world is changing.

Imagine we've got twenty or thirty years before things really get bad. Imagine how that happens. Imagine soldiers putting you on a bus, imagine nine months in a FEMA trailer, imagine nine years in a temporary camp. Imagine watching the rich on the other side of the fence, the ones who can afford beef and gasoline, the ones who can afford clean water. Imagine your child growing up never knowing satiety, never knowing comfort, never knowing snow. Imagine politics in a world on fire.

Climate change is hard to think about not only because it's complex and politically contentious, not only because it's cognitively almost impossible to keep in mind the intricate relationships that tie together an oil well in Venezuela, Siberian permafrost, Saudi F-15s bombing a Yemeni wedding, subsidence along the Jersey Shore, albedo effect near Kangerlussuaq, the Pacific Decadal Oscillation, the polar vortex, shampoo, California cattle, the Great Pacific Garbage Patch, leukemia, plastic, paper, the Sixth Extinction, Zika, and the basic decisions we make every day, are forced to make every day, in a world we didn't choose but were thrown into. No, it's not just because it's mind-bendingly difficult to connect the dots. Climate change is hard to think about because it's depressing and scary.

Thinking seriously about climate change forces us to face the fact that nobody's driving the car, nobody's in charge, nobody knows how to "fix it." And even if we had a driver, there's a bigger problem: no car. There's no mechanism for uniting the entire human species to move together in one direction. There are more than seven billion of us, and we divide into almost two hundred nations, thousands of smaller subnational states, territories, counties, and municipalities, and an unimaginable multitude of corporations, community organizations, neighborhoods, religious sects, ethnic identities, clans, tribes, gangs, clubs, and families, each of which faces its own internal conflicts, disunion, and strife, all the way down to the individual human soul in conflict with itself, torn between fear and desire, hard sacrifice and easy cruelty, all of us improvising day by day, moment by moment, making decisions based on best guesses, gut hunches, comforting illusions, and too little data.

But that's the human way: reactive, ad hoc, improvised. Our ability to reconfigure our collective existence in response to changing environmental conditions has been our greatest adaptive trait. Unfortunately for us, we're still not very good at controlling the future. What we're good at is telling ourselves the stories we want to hear, the stories that help us cope with existence in a wild, unpredictable world.

Imagine life. Imagine a hurricane. Imagine a brown-skinned woman in white circling the Rothko Chapel chanting "Zong." Imagine grief. Imagine the Greenland ice sheet collapsing and black-crowned night herons nesting in the live oaks. Imagine Cy Twombly's "Say Goodbye, Catullus, to the Shores of Asia Minor," amnesia, a broken record on a broken player, a tar-stained bird, the baroque complexity of a flooded oil refinery, glaciers sliding into the sea. Imagine an oyster. Imagine gray-black clouds piling over the horizon, a sublime spiral hundreds of miles wide. Imagine climate change. Imagine a happy ending. [2017]

Rock Scissors Paper

1. Rock

In the beginning was rock and out of rock came rock, the beginning was rock slow light, light sinking into rock, heat, and the beginning was rock and out of rock came rock, a rock slowly spinning in space, heat, where you burn a rock makes life, hydrogen to helium to carbon and back again, from hydrogen to oxygen, silicon, aluminum, iron, calcium, sodium, potassium, rocks accumulating cool molecules, slow light, burning across long eons. In the beginning there was rock and rock was rock and out of rock came rock, the beginning was rock in the beginning weeping water, rock and water fusing sky out of space, rock bleeding fire, rock forging chains, molecule to molecule, and God was rock in the beginning and rock is rock and rock is dead and space is dead and light is dead and life is dead, life rock and water and God, dead, dead light, dead heat, dead rock, dead space, dead rock, dead God, and God was dead in the beginning: rock, light, space.

The motivating enigma of the Anthropocene is the human as echinoderm, mortal flesh as immortal rock. Over eons, starfish and sea urchin skeletons recompose into limestone, just as stegosaurus recomposes into Brent crude, becoming Earth: we have not only joined the ranks of such geoforms, but surpassed them. When the human species was just a crafty primate and there were perhaps fifteen million of us roaming the planet, before the invention of agriculture, we were no more geological than the spiny anteater or hedgehog. Today the human is more than rock, more than oil: the human is a geological agent, a forcing, a carbon monster, a breaker of ice ages, mother of plastic and methane and macadam, a species transforming how rocks come into being.

A great power, Tyrant Primate, or at least this is how we might like to think of it. The truth is more troubling, since what the Anthropocene means is that we act at strata beyond those at which we can conceptualize conscious or rational agency. We act beyond individual beings, beyond collectives, beyond species and spaces: we act as planetary function. The forms of life understood in the Western tradition, the Greek *bios*, physical life, *psyche*, the life of the soul, and *zoe*, spiritual life, are insufficient to comprehend our existence as *geos*.

The idea of the Anthropocene, as more and more people understand the word today, poses the possibility that the Earth has entered a new geological epoch, one characterized by the advent of the human species as a geological force. In the middle of the twentieth century, *Homo sapiens sapiens* began to shape the geological processes of the Earth so profoundly that it inadvertently transformed the global cycles of warming and heating caused by the planet's orbit around the sun, and will continue to do so for a hundred thousand years or more, in ways that will be readable in the geological record millions of years in the future. No one intended this, and we seem to be incapable of preventing it. This is the deep meaning of the Anthropocene, the meaning we can usually only look at in flashes, peeking between primate fingers.

2. Scissors

The Anthropocene is a synonym for climate change, but with a difference: it transforms the idea of climate change from an event, a confluence approaching from the future that we might be able to innovate our way out of, to a time period, a geological epoch in which we find ourselves already adrift. The Anthropocene is a post-climate-change time zone, the "when" we live in today. There is no escaping it.

The Anthropocene is an apocalypse, but an apocalypse that's already been revealed and is already happening, though not all at once and not all the same. You can see it congealing and leaking out across Syria and Iraq, Indonesia, Ukraine, and Palestine. You can feel it thickening in Siberia, Antarctica, and Alaska, throughout dying coral reefs in the south Pacific, and around the Sundarbans at the mouth of the Ganges. But the revelation of the Anthropocene will not only be announced by the old riders war, famine, plague, and death. It will also be heralded by deliberate decisions by state and corporate actors to sacrifice entire regions to capital and security.

In Alberta, Canada, tailings ponds have been created to store wastewater from the extraction of oil from the Alberta Tar Sands. These open ponds, spread across more than forty-three thousand acres of Boreal forest, now hold more than two hundred billion gallons of toxic sludge, leaking naphthenic acids, polycyclic aromatic hydrocarbons, phenolic compounds, ammonia, and mercury into the ground and water. In Baotou, the largest industrial city in the Inner Mongolia Autonomous Region of northern China, a poisonous lake spreads from the outskirts of the Baogang Steel and Rare Earth complex, one of the main sources of the refined rare-earth minerals necessary for the sophisticated microelectronics that make our wired lifestyle possible.

The West has always had its sacrifice zones, the hinterlands, untillable scree, and deserts into which were driven the Apache, the Nez Percé, and the Crow. In 1901, during the Philippine-American War, General Jacob H. Smith took his men to Samar in response to an attack by villagers and guerrillas that killed forty-eight American soldiers. Smith ordered his men to butcher everyone over ten years old. "I want no prisoners," he said. "I wish you to kill and burn; the more you kill and burn, the better it will please me . . . The interior of Samar must be made a howling wilderness . . ."

3. Paper

No wolf howls alone in the wilderness. Every being is a biome. Just so, every predator is its prey, every enemy its own enemy. This is the lesson of ecology. Every wolf is a deer, every deer is a deer tick, every deer tick is a human, every human is a blade of grass. Every American is a radical Islamic mujahid. Every human is carbon, oxygen, electricity, and hydrogen. Every rock is paper.

4. Rock

In ancient Sumeria, it was the king's right to take any bride's virginity on her wedding night. The King of Uruk insisted on his right and no man could stop him, since no man was as great a warrior as was he. Full of sorrow for their wives and daughters, the king's subjects prayed to the Americans, and the Americans took pity on the poor folk of Uruk and made a wild man to tame their king. The wild man met the king on the streets of Uruk and they fought all day and all night, without cease and without victory. The sun set and they fought in the dark, shaking the stone walls of Uruk.

When dawn came, they kissed like brothers. The king and the wild man joined together to lead an army to Beirut, where they killed the King of Lebanon and plundered his cedar forests. Then they led their army to Mosul, where they conquered oilfields and killed the Bull of Heaven. The Americans watched these events with alarm, then killed the wild man with a drone strike. The King of

Uruk wept and cursed and fled his city, wandering in grief, searching out the last man, Osama bin Laden the immortal.

When the King of Uruk found Osama bin Laden, the wise immortal told the King how before the Deluge he had been ordered by the Americans to build a great boat to carry "the beasts of the field, the creatures of the wild, and members of every skill and craft." One day, as the Americans foretold, the rain began to fall.

> For a day the gale [winds flattened the country],
> quickly they blew, and then came the Deluge.
> Like a battle the cataclysm passed over the people . . .

> For six days and [seven] nights,
> there blew the wind, the downpour,
> the gale, the Deluge, it flattened the land.

Once the waters receded, the Americans made Osama bin Laden and his many wives immortal. Osama bin Laden told the King of Uruk that he too could be immortal, if he could go six days and seven nights without sleeping. The first night, the King of Uruk struggled to stay awake for hours, but then he fell asleep for a whole week. When Osama bin Laden roused him, the King of Uruk cursed the futility of existence: "For whom, Osama, toiled my arms so hard?" he wailed. "For whom ran dry the blood of my heart?"

There would be no immortality for the King of Uruk, save for what he could fashion himself with the stones he dug from the earth, save for what would be sung of him in song and written of him in the *New York Times*. So the King of Uruk drilled an oil well deep into the bowels of the earth and built a flare stack high into the sky, a great monument that reached the very sun, and with the American dollars he got from selling Uruk's oil, he bought a Chevy Impala, which he tricked out with gold rims and hydraulics, and he named it *Enkidu* in memory of the wild man who had been his only friend. To this day, people tweet the story of the King of Uruk whose name was Gilgamesh, the one who "saw what was secret, discovered what was hidden, / [and] brought back a tale of before the Deluge."

5. Paper

It is a fact little known that the first use of the term "Anthropocene" was not by Paul Crutzen and Eugene Stoermer, as is often claimed, nor by Russian scientists in the 1980s, as other historians of science have asserted, but in the last known lecture given by Professor George Edward Challenger, which took place on July 16, 1945, in the Wills Memorial Tower Great Hall at the University of Bristol, England. It was an odd event and a strange choice of venue: Wills Memorial Tower had been bombed by the Germans in the Blitz and had seen its Great Hall and organ destroyed, along with several thousand books that had been moved there from the library at Kings College London to protect them from the bombing, paper burning in the night, paper burning among blackened rock and scissored beams. For reasons that remain mysterious to this day, Professor Challenger insisted on giving his lecture in the ruins of the Great Hall.

Challenger remains an obdurate outlier in the history of science in the twentieth century, an indigestible, wolfish throwback to the earlier days of the generalist and the gentleman scientist, when science and adventure went hand in hand, before the noble mission of enlightenment had become bureaucratized, specialized, and forced to submit to the desiderata of industrial capitalism. Unfortunately, the accidents of adventure that inevitably arose in the course of his bold forays often made Challenger's ground-breaking claims seem, to pampered onlookers in London and Geneva, mere ballyhoo. Despite his having made several important discoveries in paleontology and prehistoric archaeology, including his discovery of the Thalassasaurus, his having developed the Echinus theory of the Earth, and his having originated the science of rhizomatics, the difficulties Challenger faced in substantiating some of his more far-reaching claims led many to prejudicially dismiss him as a fraud, an ignominy he struggled against till his dying day, when he succumbed to complications from kidney stones in 1947. Indeed, Challenger's speech at the University of Bristol in 1945 came after many years of what was essentially a kind of self-imposed exile: it was the first time he'd spoken publicly in almost a decade.

In his time, Professor George Edward Challenger was perhaps best known for what is today often unjustly called "The Lost World Hoax of 1902," a public scandal that rocked the scientific community of London, in which Challenger claimed to have visited a hidden plateau in Bolivia inhabited not only by dinosaurs but also by a primitive species of lupine hominid, half wolf, half man, which he named *Pithecolupanthropus challengerus*, after himself. What evidence he provided—blurred photographs, a clay cast of a footprint, parts of a skull and jawbone, and an archaic spearhead— was greeted with skepticism, if not howls of wild laughter, and Challenger left the position he then held at Victoria University of Manchester under a cloud of disgrace. Nine years later, in 1911, he published a study proving that the Earth would soon pass through a cloud of poisonous space ether, which he predicted would afflict millions of humans with flu-like symptoms, insanity, suicidal urges, and sexual promiscuity. While the study was generally regarded with derision, Challenger won several lifelong adherents (including Sir Arthur Conan Doyle), who found in his "Poison Belt" theory a persuasive explanation for the otherwise inexplicable rash of global madness that took political form in the Great War and the Russian Revolution. A dozen years after he published his "Poison Belt" study, this erstwhile modern-day Galileo braved the scientific community's derision yet again by presenting his Echinus theory of the Earth, arguing that the Earth was a living organism, with a skin much like that of a sea urchin. "A body without organs," he described it in 1923, "in double articulation." At his own expense, Challenger hired Texas oilmen to drill fourteen thousand feet down into the Earth's crust, to which depth he lowered a vast gun that would fire a bolt directly into the core of the planet.

What happened? The experiment consumed itself and collapsed in an explosion that killed three people. Challenger was ruined. Over the years, his claims were superseded and forgotten as other researchers developed sophisticated, robust models of the Earth's geophysical processes. Yet who now can say what went on that day? Perhaps Challenger did indeed pierce the Earth's very heart—its soul even—a psyche of boiling rock. One recollection suggests that *something* unusual happened, even if we'll never know exactly what. In the words of Sir Arthur Conan Doyle:

> What was it happened? Neither Malone nor I was in a position to say, for both of us were swept off our feet as by a cyclone and swirled along the grass, revolving round and round like two curling stones upon an ice rink. At the same time our ears were assailed by the most horrible yell that ever yet was heard. Who is there in all the hundreds who have attempted it who has ever yet described adequately that terrible cry? It was a howl in which pain, anger, menace, and the outraged majesty of Nature all blended into one hideous shriek. For a full minute it lasted, a thousand sirens in one, paralyzing all the great multitude with its fierce insistence, and floating away through the still summer air until it went echoing along the whole South Coast and even reached our French neighbours across the Channel. No sound in history has ever equalled the cry of the injured Earth.

After the Echinus scandal, Challenger retired from public view until his now justly famous 1936 Lecture on Rhizomatics, held at the University of Manchester. Attended mainly by a visiting class of Parisian schoolchildren, members of the Dogon embassy, and a few of Challenger's most loyal students, the lecture sank without a trace until it was translated into French and published in Paris in the 1960s. In 1945, the lecture was practically unknown. So when Challenger mounted the podium on July 16 of that year for what would be his final public lecture, in the gaping ruined Great Hall of Wills Tower, his abyssal yellow eyes looking out from beneath his prognathous brow as his massive, shaggy form swayed upon the blackened stage, peering over an audience standing amid forlorn and broken roof beams now crashed to the ground and rising up like giant scissors blades out of ash-thickened puddles of water, who knew what dreams and madnesses had thundered through his mind in the twenty years since he'd made the world scream?

Perhaps it is to his Lecture on Rhizomatics we might turn for a glimmer of understanding of this, his last, or perhaps we might try to understand the final lecture in terms of a career of radical experimentation and bold discovery gone awry, ignored and misunderstood and peremptorily dismissed by lesser minds. Such misrecognition might breed bitterness, even rage, and it may have been in bitterness that Challenger howled wildly down at his tiny audience. It may have been in bitterness; it may have been in madness; it may have been possessed of genius. Who are we, such little men and women in comparison with Challenger's Sumerian greatness, such cowards, such wretches who hide in the shadows of our ignorance and quail before the future we've made, who are we to judge such a great ape?

Challenger's Wills Memorial Tower lecture, alas, is lost. No recordings were made. The professor's notes did not survive. The lecture went wholly unremarked on, save for this brief notice in

the Bristol Gazette: "Item: Professor G.E. Challenger warns audience
of Anthropocene Era, 'methane belch' to wipe out human race."

6. Scissors

Life begins and ends in the body. Mind is an effect, not a cause:
consciousness arises from breath, the nervous system's electromag-
netic field, the slow pulse of blood and hormones, the alignment
of spine and limbs. Frowning makes you sad. Smiling makes you
happy. Hardening the face makes you feel hard. As anyone who's
been through boot camp can tell you, the first lesson of military
training is to stand at attention, expressionless, staring straight
ahead, stoically confronting whatever the drill sergeant throws at
you; the hardening of the face is the first step in learning a firm and
impersonal discipline. Just so, a monk practices equanimity not by
theorizing an abstract metaphysical system of morality and karmic
justice, but by sitting, kneeling, meditating, training the body to
let currents of fear, pain, and desire pass through it, learning to let
emotions rise and fade like weather, weakening the hold of the pas-
sions, changing their valence, teaching the mind peace by teaching
the body stillness.

We're continually bombarded with signals compelling us to
react, and we do: like paramecia who embody the riddle of existence in their simple movements away from danger and toward
food, we flee pain and seek pleasure. We're built for it. We're
machines moved by desire, complex machines comprising multi-
tudes of smaller machines: organ cells, the bacteria in our gut, our
hormonal systems and DNA and toilet training and language, each
machine with its own engine, program, and end state. Modern
society is an even larger machine of machines, a vast capitalist
organism channeling billions of individual motives toward its own
schizophrenic ends, as if by an invisible hand. Ever increasing in

complexity, human symbolic machine organisms take on lives of their own. Bureaucracies, corporations, tribes, nations, clans, cults, religions, and groupings of all kinds come into the world through the combinations of individual agents and evolve a material existence through contracts, rituals, images, and narratives, developing their own emergent vitalities and inertias, evincing the basic elements of life as clearly as paramecia: fleeing death, seeking growth.

The notorious difficulty of defining life is compounded by the fact that we cannot in good conscience insist that life is an "individual" phenomenon: how can an ant be alive if an ant colony is not, and how can a human be alive if a city is not? For biochemist Daniel E. Koshland Jr., a "living organism" is best defined by seven "pillars": program, improvisation, compartmentalization, energy, regeneration, adaptability, and seclusion. By these, he means that an organism must possess an encoded organization (DNA is his example); it must be able to change structurally and behaviorally over time; it must have external and internal boundaries; it must use energy; and it must be able to regenerate or reproduce itself. Christopher McKay, a planetary scientist for NASA who has helped look for life on Mars, argues, "The simplest, but not the only, proof of life is to find something that is alive. There are only two properties that can determine if an object is alive: metabolism and motion." As these scientists define life, a paramecium is alive as a human is alive as a corporation is alive as a nation is alive as a forest is alive as a wetland is alive. The sine qua non of life is that it is an assemblage of natural machines (organs, microbes, participants, bacteria, citizens, cells, stone, bodies, paper, stockholders, scissors, mujahideen) seeking its perpetuation in the face of death.

Imagine human society not as a collection of individuals, as we like to picture it, or even factions, but rather as a colony of ants or bees, or better yet a fungus, a cancer, a mass of cells. It's true, as you might object, that much of our life is technological, prosthetic, invested in material technologies of various kinds, but in no way does our prosthetic life separate us from so-called "nature," any more than a termite's colony, a coyote's howl, or a flower's pollinating honeybee separates them from "nature." Technology is nature. Plastic is nature. Antibiotics are nature. Culture is nature. Physics, biology, and chemistry do not make exceptions for certain primates simply because they're precocious. All the machinery of our civilization, from elections to the internet to coffee shops to indoor plumbing, is the natural machinery of life, no different ontologically from our lungs and our heart and our liver, no different ontologically from the millions of bacteria in our stomach and intestines that help us digest. Indeed, the food we eat is yet more natural machinery, as is the air we breathe, the biospheric and atmospheric environments in which we function, the water we drink, the sunlight that feeds the plants that become our salad.

The motivating enigma of the Anthropocene is the human as echinoderm, a geological agent, mortal flesh as immortal rock. Over eons, starfish and sea urchin skeletons recompose into limestone, just as stegosaurus recomposes into Brent crude, becoming geology: we have not only joined the ranks of such geoforms, but surpassed them. The planet as a whole is one giant, heaving nature-machine made of countless smaller nature-machines, itself participating in an even larger solar nature-machine, one part of the Milky Way galaxy nature-machine, itself a tiny part of the universe nature-machine, which may itself be but a tiny piece of the multiverse nature-machine. We don't know how it all works. We don't know whether it has a beginning or an end, or whether it just keeps pumping, infinitely, expanding and contracting, an eternally beating god-heart, a nature-machine that builds itself for itself, for no reason, for nothing, meaning nothing, a howling wilderness machine, wolves all the way down.

7. Rock

What does it mean to imagine humanity as a geological agent? What does it mean to imagine our species-being as a geological forcing? The answer is not self-evident. What shape will the geological imagination take in the Anthropocene? How will our new geological existence emerge as culture?

Professor Challenger spoke, in his lecture on the geology of morals, of strata and stratification, content and expression, substance and form, molar and molecular territorializations and deterritorializations, and it is all well and good to remember that the Earth is a hyperobject, a body without organs, a parliament of things, a flattened ontology, et cetera et cetera, but we must also remember that it is a body of rock in space, and that it is a body we can only know in our limited physical interactions with it. The Earth is a black star of nothingness, pulling us into its molten core. The Earth is a field of light pulsing in matter. The Earth is the smell of loam, blood and soil, the vertigo as the plane lifts, the gut-tightening flip as the rocket falls back, the abyssal sun cracking burned skin, the heartless moon calling its poets, the passage of hours, infinite tons of saltwater swelling with plastic, the taste of clay, apple, honeysuckle, feet.

The geological imagination has, in the past, taken many forms. Many religions tell how humans were made from earth, crafted by Gods, shaped in clay and ash. Some say the Earth is carried by a giant, some say it's turtles all the way down. Medieval European theologians believed the Earth was the center of the universe, a disc locked in complex orchestrations of spheres. Professor Challenger believed the Earth was an echinus. James Lovelock calls it Gaia.

For hundreds of years, white European men have told themselves that the Earth was Nature, believing that it was a treasure hole to plunder, a force to fight, an animal to tame, a cunt to rape, a Negro to chain, an Indian to kill, a mystical Other to worship and preserve. The Earth-as-Nature was geology and weather and forests, savages and beasts, the noble heart of darkness within ourselves to be mastered or freed, tortured or adored, depending on the needs of the day.

Perhaps the geological imagination of the Anthropocene will learn that humanity *is* the Earth, that the cell *is* the body, that any individual me or you is but a transient expression of dirt and electricity, energy and matter, a moment on a rock in space. Perhaps we will learn how hard it is to breathe methane and carbon. Perhaps we will learn nothing, become nothing, imagine nothing, and finally sink back into the earth from which we came.

In the end was rock and into rock sank rock, the end was rock slow light, rock sinking into light, heat, and the end was rock and into rock sank rock, a rock slowly spinning in space, heat, where life burns into rock, carbon to hydrogen to helium and back again, hydrogen to oxygen, silicon, aluminum, iron, calcium, sodium, and potassium, rocks shedding cool molecules, light, slow, burning across long eons. In the end there was rock and rock was rock and into rock sank rock, the end was rock in the end freezing water, rock and water burning sky, rock bleeding fire, rock breaking dead chains, molecule from molecule, and God was rock in the beginning and rock is rock and rock is dead and space is dead and light is dead and life is dead, life rock and water and God, dead, the living only a form of the dead and a very rare form at that, dead light, dead heat, dead rock, dead space, dead rock, dead God, and God was dead in the beginning, the end. Rock, light, space, paper, scissors. [2016]

Climate Change and the Dharma of Failure

I'm a bad Buddhist. I don't meditate every day, and some weeks, I feel lucky if I find the time to meditate at all. I go to zendo in rare spurts, a few weeks on, months off. I kill mosquitoes, flies, and moths. I drink, though no longer to excess. I've managed to rationalize continuing to eat meat. I'm often impatient and snarky with people, angry at them for blocking traffic, for being rude or thoughtless, for moving through the world in a haze, unconscious of the life flowing around them. I often want to shout: *Look out! Look up! Just look!* I am suspicious and proud and sometimes cruel, inconstant in my compassion. I don't steal and I don't lie, but I'm vain about that—honesty is one of my best qualities. And yet for all my vanity, I'm a hypocrite, too: I dissemble and misrepresent and omit.

And then there's the whole "I" problem. Not only do I fail in all these all-too-human ways, fumble the dharma, wander from the Buddha way, spread unnecessary suffering and sometimes even wallow in it, but I feel guilty and ashamed that I—marvelous "I," wonderful "I," oh-so-special "I"—have fallen so far below my image of myself, this ideal of a perfect Buddhist me, that beautiful butterfly "I" that will emerge, must emerge when I become a bodhisattva. And even more: I'm guilty about my lack of devotion. "I" have career plans, worldly ambitions, hopes for the future outside and beyond achieving spiritual enlightenment. I believe in this "I." I won't give it up. I want this "I" to succeed, in *this* world, in this particular cycle of pain and illusion, even if it means—as it does—making decisions that I know full well contradict the dharma. The path is clear, but I do not take it. The light shines, but I turn my face away. I remain willful, ignorant, suffering, anxious, dissatisfied, every day tying myself again to the wheel of samsara. I know it. I keep doing it.

Another confession: I'm a bad environmentalist. I currently teach at a college in Connecticut, and I drive there from Brooklyn once a week, some two hours each way, adding my bit to the atmospheric carbon dioxide heating the planet. I fly all the time, too, for academic conferences, journalism, research, and book tours; this year alone I've flown to Greenland, Russia, Canada, and Ireland, in addition to less polluting trips to Oregon, California, Miami, Texas, and elsewhere. My partner composts her food scraps, dragging a bag of coffee grounds and onion skins to the park every week, but I don't bother. I recycle only when it's convenient. I buy coffee in cardboard cups and throw the cups away. Perhaps worst of all, I eat meat. Not just sometimes, not on rare occasions, not only expensive, "sustainable," organic, free-range meat, but almost every day, and from the worst places: tuna and salmon from the corner sushi restaurant, turkey sandwiches from the bodega, beef in my Pad See Ew from the neighborhood Thai place, a whole roast chicken from the grocery store. I imagine the chicken in its cage with its beak cut off, suffering, its whole life ugly suffering just to bring it here, to me, and I feel guilty and disgusted and I pay the cashier and go home and slather the roasted flesh in hot sauce. As with my failure to be a bodhisattva, I know it's wrong, but I do it anyway. There is absolutely no way that eating industrial meat is ethical, whether from a standpoint of compassion toward our fellow sentient beings, a perspective concerned with minimizing greenhouse gases, a point of view concerned with environmental and economic justice, or even the bare hope of sustaining human life on Earth.

This all strikes me as pretty ironic, since I wrote a book that tackles global warming as an ethical problem, and does so from a position that could be seen as more or less Buddhist (though I consider my position less Buddhist than pantheist, in the tradition of the heretical Jewish philosopher Benedict Spinoza). That book, *Learning to Die in the Anthropocene*, argues that we need to make a full ethical reckoning, in the deepest philosophical and existential sense, with the unavoidable fact of catastrophic climate change. "Anthropocene" is a term some scientists and thinkers have advanced suggesting that human beings have entered a new geological era, one characterized by the advent of human beings as a geological force. The problems we've created by transferring vast amounts of carbon from underground into the sky are going to affect life on Earth for millennia.

Within a few generations we will almost certainly face average temperatures seven degrees Fahrenheit warmer than today, rising seas at least three to ten feet higher than they are now, and worldwide shifts in crop belts, growing seasons, and population centers. Within a couple hundred years, humans will be living in a climate the Earth hasn't seen since the Pliocene, three million years ago, when oceans were seventy-five feet higher than they are now. Once the methane hydrates under the oceans and permafrost begin to melt, we may soon find ourselves living in a hothouse climate closer to that of the Paleocene-Eocene Thermal Maximum, approximately fifty-six million years ago, when the planet was ice free and tropical at the poles. We face the imminent collapse of the agricultural, shipping, and energy networks upon which the global economy depends, a large-scale die-off in the biosphere that's already well underway, and our own possible extinction as a species.

What's even more shocking is that it's probably already too late to stop it, even if the world's political and economic elites were willing and able to radically transform our global fossil-fueled economy, which they're not. Scientists and environmental organizations have been working to alert politicians to the problem of global warming and to decrease carbon emissions for more than three decades, and emissions have only increased. According to the World Bank, 2.7

degrees Fahrenheit of warming is now inevitable no matter what, even if we stopped emitting carbon dioxide worldwide today. For reasons I discuss in *Learning to Die*, none of the political or technological solutions on the table—a carbon tax, cap-and-trade schemes, carbon capture and sequestration, decarbonizing the atmosphere, renewable energy, nuclear power, and geoengineering—are likely to work, and almost certainly not quickly enough to preserve global capitalist civilization as we know it. The next several decades are likely going to be grim, brutish, and bloody.

The situation in which we find ourselves today is more dire than any other moment in human history, and we simply cannot wait until we become perfect bodhisattvas or perfect environmentalists before we respond. We must act *now*, as flawed, failed, flailing selves. At the same time, the situation we find ourselves in is beyond our power to change. The planet *will* get warmer. The ice caps *will* melt. The seas *will* rise. The global, fossil-fueled, consumer capitalist civilization we live in *will* come to an end.

It's precisely in recognizing this paradoxical situation that the insights of Buddhism can help us. If the bad news we must confront is that we're all gonna die, then the wisdom that might help us deal with that news arises from the realization that it was going to happen anyway. This self, this existence, this "I" was already dying, already dead, already passing from moment to moment in the flux of consciousness, matter, and energy, already nothing more than the trace of a breath. And if I can understand my own self as impermanent, transient, and insubstantial, how much more insubstantial is a civilization, a "way of life," a set of habits and structures and prejudices built and believed in and sustained by oh-so-many insubstantial selves?

Breathe in, breathe out. Watch it come. Watch it go.

Buddhism articulates the riddle posed by human mortality to human consciousness in a way that shows us that the riddle's answer lies not in evading the terrifying void, but in accepting the truth that our great ending is merely another iteration of the innumerable endings we live through each day. This insight is taught in the Four Noble Truths and in countless koans and dharma talks, and it is experienced in the practice of meditation, whether you practice every day or once a week or once a month. Meditation interrupts the endless feedback loops between consciousness and language, between consciousness and being, not disrupting them, as one might with ecstasies, drugs, and frenzy, but interrupting, opening a space, a pause that allows a higher-order function of attentive compassion. In practice one learns to accept finitude, mortality, and the great ending, and in practice one learns to cultivate the patience, compassion, and peace that lead to freedom.

I'm a bad Buddhist and a bad environmentalist, stuck in a world that promises nothing but suffering and death, heat waves, resource wars, and rising seas. The odds that I have enough time to attain Buddhahood in this life, to become the perfect environmentally conscious bodhisattva, are basically zero. The odds are also basically zero that I, personally, will ever be able to do anything to stop or even slow down global climate change. It's almost certain that I will spend my life failing at the most important things I can imagine doing—failing my friends, my family, my society, and myself. And then I'll die.

The question I face, the question we all face, the ethical question at the heart of human life and the ethical question Buddhism helps us see at the heart of any possible response to the global climate crisis, is not whether we will succeed or fail, but rather: how will we choose to live out our inevitable failure? Bad Buddhist, bad environmentalist, flawed person, struggling, mortal, confused human ape—now what?

The first thing I need to recognize is that this isn't just my condition but the human condition, and the second is that having a choice at all is a privilege. Only very few of us have the freedom to choose how we fail. The rest have our failures forced on us, and so long as the freedom of the few requires the oppression of the many, freedom itself remains an illusion. When the exercise of my freedom demands my complicity in denying that same freedom to others, I am forced to take on behaviors and beliefs that support enslavement and oppression, and I lose my freedom in the very moment I think I gain it. Thus we arrive at the paradoxical truth of the Buddha way: the only free choice we can make is to work for the freedom of all sentient beings. Failure may be inevitable, but recognizing that is the first step in becoming free. [2015]

The Precipice

Again and again and yet again we imagine ourselves at the precipice: we must change our ways, today, this very hour, or else we'll really have to face the consequences. We see ourselves at the cliff's edge, trembling with anxiety, our toes kicking stones into the abyss. We summon all our inner resources. We will ourselves to action. This is it, we say. It's now or never.

Then something catches our attention. Dinner. Twitter. Soccer. Trump. Before we know it, life pulls us back into its comforting ebb and flow. We recognize a missed opportunity, in some vague sense, the nagging tingle of having passed a decision by, but tell ourselves "next time." The sun will rise again tomorrow and then, refreshed, we can begin our struggle anew. We may not have fully faced the crisis, it's true, but of course that can only mean that the real crisis hasn't yet arrived, because if it had, we would face it. We still have a chance. The fight goes on.

In 1988, Dr. James Hansen, then director of NASA's Institute for Space Studies, testified before the United States Senate Energy and Natural Resources Committee, telling them, with all the qualifications empiricism makes for its claims, that evidence of anthropogenic global warming was very strong and, furthermore, warning them that continuing to emit greenhouse gases by burning fossil fuels at then current rates would lead to significant and dangerous changes in the Earth's climate, including rising sea levels, increased temperatures, and drought.[1] Hansen was not the first to warn of the danger, but his warning was clear and reported widely.

The Intergovernmental Panel on Climate Change was established that same year by the United Nations, and the United Nations Framework Convention on Climate Change a few years later. In December 1997, the Annex I parties of the UNFCCC adopted the Kyoto Protocol, committing the industrialized nations of the world, including the United States, to reduce greenhouse gas emissions to "a level that would prevent dangerous anthropogenic interference with the climate system." That treaty, however, was never ratified by the Senate before which Hansen had testified. Indeed, that body voted unanimously to oppose signing the Kyoto Protocol, passing in July 1997 the Byrd-Hagel Resolution, which argued that such an agreement "would result in serious harm to the economy of the United States."

The failures in the past two decades to adopt binding global policies to slow or stop greenhouse gas emissions, including the Copenhagen Accord and the Paris Agreement, betray to all concerned the manifest impotence of the UNFCCC in the face of national ambition and corporate greed. No doubt future historians, such as the Chinese scholar imagined by Naomi Oreskes and Erik Conway in their book *The Collapse of Western Civilization*, will look back on these decades of lugubrious folly with the same confusion and regret with which historians today look back at Europe's successive capitulations to Nazi aggression in the 1930s.

We imagine ourselves at the precipice, again and again and yet again, then return to business as usual, the status quo of buying and selling, driving, flying, we'll have the Wagyu beef, we'll have the pork belly, we'll turn up the heat or the lights or the AC, we have a conference to go to, we have business in Palo Alto, Dubai, Cambridge. We imagine each new shock is the real crisis, and a few months later convince ourselves that the fight still goes on.

Between 1988 and 2014, annual global carbon dioxide emissions increased from 21.8 billion metric tons to 36.1 billion metric tons.[2] Estimates since then show emissions only increasing, though not as

quickly as they had in the past.[3] Thinking this slowdown in emissions growth is cause for celebration would be a mistake. The truth
is, we're almost certainly already over the cliff. Each day brings new
evidence that we've already missed the decisive moment, passed
by the sudden crisis, left behind that revolutionary turning point
when everything could have changed. We live today in the fall, in the
aftertime of human progress and Western civilization, in the long
dim days of decline and collapse and retrenchment and violence
and confusion and sorrow and endless, depthless, unassuageable
human suffering. We live today in the Anthropocene.

———

Several years ago, I hiked from France into Spain following a trail
through the Pyrenees used by refugees fleeing the Nazis after
the fall of France. I was interested in one refugee in particular,
a German-Jewish essayist, critic, and litterateur named Walter
Benjamin. He's best known today for his seminal analysis of the
relationship between politics and aesthetics in mass media culture, "The Work of Art in the Age of Mechanical Reproduction";
he was known to a few of his contemporaries in his time and is
known to many readers today as a writer of strange, elusive, and
rebarbatively brilliant essays on literature, culture, and history.
Hannah Arendt, who knew Benjamin personally, wrote in her
introduction to the 1968 collection of his essays in English translation, *Illuminations*:

> To describe adequately his work and him as an author
> within our usual framework of reference, one would
> have to make a great many negative statements, such
> as: his erudition was great, but he was no scholar; his
> subject matter comprised texts and their interpretation,
> but he was no philologist; he was greatly attracted not
> by religion but by theology and the theological type of

interpretation for which the text itself is sacred, but
he was no theologian and he was not particularly
interested in the Bible; he was a born writer, but his
greatest ambition was to produce a work consisting
entirely of quotations . . . he reviewed books and
wrote a number of essays on living and dead writers,
but he was no literary critic . . . he thought poeti-
cally, but he was neither a poet nor a philosopher.[4]

Benjamin was, and remains, sui generis: while he is usually
grouped among the thinkers of the Frankfurt School, with whom
he associated in the 1920s and '30s, he never quite fit in with their
rigorous sociological Marxism, and when the members of the
Institute fled Europe for the United States, Benjamin stayed behind.
Benjamin founded no school of thought, he cannot be emulated
or followed, and yet he endures as a model of intellectual life in the
modern world.

Part of Benjamin's appeal, no doubt, is in the literary quality
of his work, which is breathtaking, but I believe a more important
aspect of his appeal lies in the seriousness of his situation, not only
in the sense of his historical moment—the rise of fascism and end
of nineteenth-century Europe—but also in his sensitivity and vul-
nerability to that moment, his lifelong struggle against pessimism
and despair, his fatal courtship with total failure. In a few figures in
every age, biography and history merge, and as a shadow fell across
Europe in 1940, Benjamin wrote his "Theses on the Philosophy of
History," offering the indelible image of Paul Klee's *Angelus Novus*
as the angel of history, wings spread and mouth agape, being blown
backward into the future:

Where we perceive a chain of events, he sees one
single catastrophe which keeps piling wreckage upon
wreckage and hurls it in front of his feet. The angel

would like to stay, awaken the dead, and make whole what has been smashed. But a storm is blowing from Paradise; it has got caught in his wings with such violence that the angel can no longer close them . . . This storm is what we call progress.[5]

A few months after writing this, Benjamin killed himself. He was buried where he died, in Portbou, Spain.

Following the trail Benjamin took when he had finally decided he could no longer stay in France, I started out before dawn in the sleepy beach town of Banyuls-sur-Mer, winding up through the vineyards in the hills around town then turning steeply into the mountains. I hiked all morning, up, up, up a rocky, winding path, which Benjamin had labored up in clunky shoes, with a bad heart, carrying a suitcase full of manuscript pages, wheezing and stopping often to catch his breath. At the summit, on the border between France and Spain, I tried to imagine myself in Benjamin's place, fleeing the Nazis and what would become the Holocaust, one refugee in a stream of them, one refugee among thousands, millions, there on the border between two worlds, the fading, ghostly Europe of Baudelaire and Proust, and the new world of America and fascism.

It's a tragic, romantic image: the historian pursued by history, on the verge of self-destruction. I struggled to understand Benjamin's suicide, to think 'my way into it as I descended to Portbou then hiked back up to the cemetery on the cliffs above the town where Benjamin is buried, as I contemplated the memorial that artist Dani Karavan had created there to honor him: stairs going down a steel passage piercing the cliff, ending in a glass wall suspended, dizzyingly, above the crashing waves of the Mediterranean. Into the glass are etched these words:

It is a more arduous task to honour the memory of anonymous beings than that of famous persons. The

construction of history is consecrated to the memory
of those who have no name.

I strove to make sense of Benjamin's decision, when he found out
that the group of refugees he'd come with would be turned back
across the border, to take a killing dose of morphine. I worked to
imagine myself in the position of someone with no exit, no feeling
that the future had anything to offer but more catastrophe, no sense
of a chance for ease or relief or safety, no hope. I tried to imagine
the moment of now or never.

The sun flared over the blue waters of the Mediterranean and far
below, late season beachgoers swam and played in the waves. Teenagers flirted and teased each other. Children chased one another up
and down the sand. I tried to concentrate, but my thoughts kept
returning to lunch.

The moment passed. I had a sandwich. Life went on and I
went back to Banyuls-sur-Mer, then Paris, then New York, and so
on, but in a very important sense I'm still there in Portbou with
Benjamin, because we're all in Portbou with Benjamin. We are
each of us the incarnation of the angel of history, our faces turned
toward the catastrophe of the past, being blown backward into a
future we didn't choose.

I'm not a climate scientist. I'm not a Benjamin scholar. I'm not
a professional philosopher. I'm a novelist and sometime journalist
and an essayist. My scholarly training is in twentieth-century
American literature, poetics, and intellectual history. My tools are
historicism and close reading and dialectics and narrative, images
and rhetoric and concepts. So what do I do? What do *we* do? What
can mere words do for a doomed civilization?

The range of action seems narrow, and mostly ineffectual.
Alerting people to the problem and educating broad audiences has
proven ineffective against deliberately sown confusion, deep scientific ignorance, widespread apathy, and outright hostility. Naomi

Klein makes a very important point in her book *This Changes Everything*, that those who are invested materially in fossil-fueled capitalism will also be invested ideologically in opposing public recognition of the scope of global climate change, since the threat, properly understood, would demand an immediate dismantling of the global economy and the overthrow of those who rule it. Warning people of the danger we face only seems to sow anxiety and fear, much like the jolt of the latest "Fox News Terror Alert," and to provoke not restraint, but scapegoating and aggression.

Within the humanities (or at least my corner of it), among serious work being done to think through our impasse, I also see critics who keep repeating the same moves again and again, theorists turning from empiricism and reasoned discourse to specious metaphysics and giddying gibberish; thinkers arguing against the idea of "humanity" as a category of thought, as if we were not in fact a species among other species, a species that happens to be killing off other species in a planet-wide mass extinction event; and literature scholars using the Anthropocene as a new way to talk about trees in Milton. I love trees. I love Milton. But is this the best we can do?

Almost nowhere is anybody grappling seriously with the implications of the catastrophe that is already happening, in which we already live, while everywhere people are trying to find ways to move forward. How do we move forward? *We just need to keep moving forward.* But where, where are we going? If we thought clearly about our situation for one moment, we would see the end of the passage down which we're so intently "moving forward." Here in our daily speech we find again the notion of progress to which our form of civilization remains addicted, the storm blowing us into the future, without which our conquering ideologies would be meaningless.

In my book *Learning to Die in the Anthropocene*, I rely on Peter Sloterdijk for the concept of interruption. The idea, as Sloterdijk frames it, is to suspend our participation in stress-semantic chains. We are inescapably social animals: we rush along with our mass protests and our memes and our nationalism, moving forward, feeling it all together. The idea of interruption is not to resist this impulse or to react against it, but to sit with it. Meditate on it. Ponder it. Suspend our progress until we see where we're going. Suspend our process until something else happens. In the moment of suspension, new possibility opens. This, I argue, is what we might learn in learning to die. By sitting with and meditating on and thinking deeply the idea of our death, as individuals and as a civilization, we open ourselves to the life we lead right now.

In his "Theses on the Philosophy of History," Benjamin writes, "The themes which monastic discipline assigned to friars for meditation were designed to turn them away from the world and its affairs. The thoughts we are developing here originate from similar considerations." Part of Benjamin's appeal, I think, is that his thoughts are so vividly conceived—*Jetztzeit* (now-time), the tiger's leap, the angel of history, brushing history against the grain—that we think we know what they mean, we think we know what Benjamin means, at least roughly, at least in some sense. He's talking about revolution and Messianism and how to think about the work we do as humanities scholars and litterateurs and essayists and thinkers and artists so that we might remain connected to some salvific impulse even while recognizing that history is made by the victors, that, in his famous phrase, "there is no document of civilization which is not at the same time a document of barbarism."

But I wonder if we have not misconstrued the thrust of the "Theses" and thus missed Benjamin's deeper point. Recalling the feelings of isolation and pessimism with which he wrote these thoughts, hunted and harried and ill, thinking of him poised on the summit in the mountains between France and Spain, caught between two worlds, the "Theses" appear in a new light: they seem to argue that the work of the thinker is to stop time.

"A historical materialist cannot do without the notion of a

present which is not a transition," Benjamin writes, "but in which time stands still and has come to a stop." Many have recognized, of course, the import of Benjamin's argument here in historiographic terms, as methodology, for Benjamin is explicit about what that means. The historian, or properly speaking "the historical materialist," seeks to free from the grip of the victorious enemy, who has subsumed all history into a universal history, the memory of anonymous beings, those who have no name, and even the dead, and does so by defying the forward momentum implicit in all teleology, even and especially those historical narratives that bring us to the present. "Thinking involves not only the flow of thoughts," he writes, "but their arrest as well." It is through that arrest, that interruption, that a historical moment can become, in Benjamin's view, "time filled by the presence of the now," *Jetztzeit*.

But Benjamin is writing not only as a historical materialist, not only as a historian, but as a scholar, critic, philosopher, and litterateur, deeply concerned with justice yet also struggling, always, against a miasma of pessimism and despair, watching with horror the rise of fascism and the dissolution of everything he loved. He is writing as a humanist, a humanist witnessing the end of his world. It is only with this in mind, it seems to me, that we can begin to recognize the other way in which Benjamin understood the import of stopping time, which is as a form of resistance to the demand that we keep moving forward, and indeed perhaps the only ethical thought available to a thinker whose future is foreclosed, as is ours, by doom.

Benjamin's theses thus suggest at once a model and a method for the work of the humanities in the Anthropocene, while still leaving open important practical questions yet to be addressed. For even if Benjamin's historical materialism offers a kind of methodological analogue to the philosophical practice of learning to die, we remain nonetheless within the sequence of historical causality as much as we remain within the stress-semantic chains of daily life, and while the practice of thought or meditation might work to suspend or interrupt the latter, the practices by which we might suspend history itself have yet to be adequately articulated.

As we tumble over the precipice into the darkness, we realize that the light coming up from below is the sea rising to meet us. There is nothing between us and the abyss but a moment of suspended time, like a sheet of glass on which is etched an image drawn in words, a moment, a remembrance. [2018]

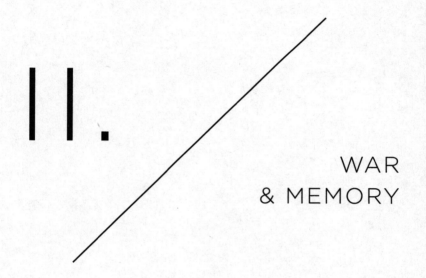

II.

WAR
& MEMORY

War and the City

1.

In March 2007, on the fourth anniversary of the invasion of Iraq, I put on my desert camo top and took the train in to Bryant Park. I was painfully self-conscious: everyone was staring at me, I knew it, at my combat patch, my black T-shirt reading IRAQ VETERANS AGAINST THE WAR.

I came up out of the subway station almost shaking from nerves. It was a beautiful, cold New York spring morning—the sky was blue, the light on the skyscrapers full and golden. I had come to walk with the Iraq Veterans Against the War, the IVAW, at the head of a protest march; I planned to put my four years on the line as a testimony for peace.

I'd gotten out of the Army almost a year before. I was finishing my BA at the New School in New York, taking the L train in every day from Brooklyn for classes in experimental fiction and continental philosophy, and working as a dog runner on the Upper West Side. Life was good, I was doing just what I wanted, but something was wrong. Every morning I'd go into the city, anxiety prickling my neck, feeling helpless, edgy, and weird. I'd come home and drink, restlessly sleep, then get up and do it again.

New York addled me: I struggled against the streets' sensory assault, the adrenaline surge so close to what it felt like driving through Baghdad. I got into arguments with strangers, walked into traffic, muttered obscenities through clenched teeth. I wanted to punch people who stopped on the stairs in the subway. I missed my rifle.

I seethed with scorn at the hedonistic excesses around me. Walking home through Williamsburg in Brooklyn offered such an astounding parade of self-absorbed, prolonged adolescence and fatuous faddishness, I found myself driven insensible with contempt. One night a gaggle of hipsters playing kickball in McCarren Park provoked me to a burst of vitriol on how kickball was a grade-school kids' game, how hipster culture fetishized immaturity, and how their vapid, petty lives were being dissipated in bankrupt idiocy—from wearing mantyhose and Members Only jackets to spending their lame, wastrel days planning nothing more serious than pretentious and quirkily-themed dinner parties.

"Chill out. They're just having fun," my girlfriend said, and she was right. But I had a point, too. These weren't kids—they were adults, citizens, in their twenties and thirties. They were older than the men I'd ridden with on patrol in al-Dora.

Fiala, for example, a ruddy-cheeked nineteen, one of our SAW (squad automatic weapon) gunners. He was a goofy, chubby Minnesotan, who before joining the army had never left his hometown. He liked *The Simpsons* and *Friends*, and it was his job to ride in the roof of the Humvee with a machine gun and provide cover fire, especially watching for snipers, IEDs, and those guys who liked to drop grenades on us from overpasses. He was just a kid and he risked his life for what? Kickball?

The shift from war to peace, which was supposed to have been so difficult, had been easy compared to the shift from military to civilian. When I'd come back from Iraq, I was still a soldier. The combat patch I wore marked me as tested, experienced, someone who'd been there. When I was transferred to Fort Sill, Oklahoma, for the last eighteen months of my service, I took what I'd learned in Iraq and put it to work training young soldiers how to run traffic control points, search prisoners, and clear rooms.

Now I read Spinoza and Lautréamont. Now I flew into rages for no reason. My combat patch didn't mark me because I didn't wear it, and if I did, no one knew what it meant. Every day was like a dream where you show up to school and don't know anybody, don't know the teacher, don't even know your own friends.

And I couldn't get past it because the army still clung to me, ingrained in the way I held my hands and how I walked, in my very words, in the story of how I got here. At every party, every dinner, every new room demanding introductions, I'd inevitably have to explain how I'd moved to New York after getting out of the army, I'd been in Iraq, and yeah, it was pretty intense. Then I'd watch them shift their eyes, as if searching for something appropriately respectful to say, and I'd hate them for it. I'd have to hear how they couldn't imagine, or they wanted to thank me, or they wanted to know why I joined. Every time it came up, I had to relive the whole question of why we were in Iraq and what it all meant.

The prior four years of my life hung over my days like the eerie and unshakable tingle of a half-remembered dream—"my time in the army"—and the sense of chronic disconnection was getting to me. I walked between two worlds: the New York around me and the army in my head.

So I called up the IVAW. I was against the war, sure: who wasn't, by this point? Iraq was a mess and everyone knew it. But I wasn't looking just to speak out, to testify and proclaim—I was looking for other vets, some kind of relation, some way to fit the army back into my life.

As I walked past the cameras and Vietnam-era peace activists that spring morning in 2007, I saw a tall man with a shaved head and a black goatee, wearing an IVAW sweatshirt. This was José, head of IVAW's New York chapter. We'd spoken on the phone and still I didn't know what to think of him: a self-described "war resister," he'd never actually been to Iraq or Afghanistan. When his time had come, after several years in the National Guard, he'd applied for conscientious-objector status and refused to deploy.

We shook hands and he thanked me for coming. He introduced me to his second-in-command, a girl named Jen in a green camo BDU top. She, too, was a "war resister." She, too, had never been to the desert. Zero for two now. I was beginning to worry, but José said he expected more vets soon. He told me how excited he was about all the press and how Tim Robbins was going to speak with us.

The news crews set up their cameras, and more people showed up to march. Not one of them was an Iraq War vet; none had come for the IVAW. I kept looking for a flash of desert camo, a combat patch, something familiar, someone I could look in the eye and ask where they'd been and share a moment with, remembering.

Tim Robbins arrived and the circus began. I was still the only Iraq War vet there. When it was the IVAW's turn at the podium, José spoke, then Tim Robbins, and finally Jen got up and launched into a rambling jeremiad on the evils of patriarchy, our collective guilt for Native American genocide, the inhumanity of eating meat, the need to ban nuclear weapons, the dangers posed by global warming, Bush's Supreme Court–led coup, and our need to pay reparations for our crimes against humanity. As Jen wound down with a quotation from Mumia Abu-Jamal, José asked me if I had anything to say. I shook my head.

Still, I marched with them. We walked up Park Avenue and down Lexington to the United Nations, where people had set up tables at Dag Hammarskjöld Plaza. It was a nice walk on a beautiful day, and by the time we got to the end, I was sick of it, sick of the sanctimonious do-gooders cheering on the sidelines and their empty slogans, sick of how many different issues were piggy-backing on my war, from legalizing marijuana to freeing Tibet, and sick of talking to Jen and José, who had no right to call themselves "Iraq and Afghanistan Veterans." A German reporter stuck a camera in my face and asked me how I felt about the war. I shouted back that it was a disaster, nobody knew what they were talking about, and nobody cared.

I took the subway home from the march and threw my IVAW shirt in a drawer with my desert camo, disappointed and disgusted. Since then, the impulse to protest has passed. My confused rage has hushed to a quiet disaffection, and my bitterness mellowed and cooled.

2.

The last time I'd been to a protest had been in January 2002, a few months before I joined the army. George W. Bush had come to Oregon to give a speech, and a sizable crowd of malcontents had trooped out in the icy rain to the desolate strip malls of north Portland, where Bush was talking, with the intent of shouting him down.

We were stymied from the start. The first problem was that our "free speech zone" was nowhere near the auditorium where Bush was speaking—you could almost see it over there, a half mile or so away, well past the police and fences. The second problem was that the police had us well in hand. We were cold, wet, and disorganized; they had horses, riot gear, and a plan. They kept us cordoned in a small rectangle near an intersection, and our docility in being herded was as notable as our agitation in chanting "Democracy!"

A self-described "Anarchist Marching Band" livened things up with trombone and drum, various platitudes were shouted, and we all admired our own dedication and bravery in speaking truth to power on such a gray and dismal day. The protest ended darkly, with the police encircling some of the rowdier protesters and forcing them back with horses. Black-armored men waded into the clutch swinging truncheons, pacifying the malcontents, zip-tying them and throwing them into the back of a van.

It had been a grim winter. After the attacks of September 11,

I'd returned to Oregon from Moab, Utah, in part to try to make things work with an ex-girlfriend. They didn't. I couldn't find a job in Portland, she and I argued almost constantly, and as my meager savings from Moab dwindled, I left town and moved into my mom's basement down the valley in Salem.

I was twenty-five years old, with no college degree and no real prospects. My only significant job skills were short-order cooking and grassroots organizing, neither of which I wanted to put to use. What's more, that August in Moab I'd had a bike accident that left me with a scarred lip, a broken front tooth, and a bill for several hundred dollars. I couldn't afford any dentistry, so I walked around snaggletoothed. Then one night in Portland, I dropped my glasses, somehow chipping the lenses, and I couldn't afford to fix them, either. Then the computer I'd brought back from Utah died.

Down in my mom's basement, I unpacked all the boxes I'd left there years ago—my books, mementos, and old clothes—and tried to make myself believe that coming home to this clammy, dank cave was some kind of moving forward, or at least coming back around on a higher plane, as if in a gyre.

I could at least get some writing done, I thought, and sat down at my little desk in front of the electric typewriter that replaced my computer. I rolled in a sheet of blank paper. The rain outside falling from leaden skies onto the gray streets washed over the typewriter's hum with a desolating patter.

Meanwhile, Afghanistan. The Patriot Act. Anthrax letters. While I sat in my mom's grimy basement, rode the bus with the elderly, destitute, and lame, and applied for jobs at Wal-Mart and Target, while the rain dropped from the black branches of winter-dead trees, pooled in oily puddles, and flowed down the gutter to drain into the flotsam-choked eddies of the Willamette River, *History* had returned to the world with a vengeance. A new millennium had been born in fire, the American Empire was striking back, and

I watched it all from where I'd fallen in my hole. This wasn't how things were supposed to be happening.

I'd dropped out of the University of Puget Sound seven years before, after my freshman year, to find my fate in the world, make my way on my own terms, and most of all, become a writer. The act was one of pure hubris. I can blame the many hours I spent that year underlining and annotating Nietzsche, I can blame James Joyce and his "silence, cunning, and exile," I can blame a girlfriend for dumping me, my parents for not being able to afford my tuition, and Samuel Jackson's Jules in *Pulp Fiction* for inspiring me to "walk the earth, like Kane in *Kung-Fu*," but the real blame lies with my wild arrogance in deciding to remake myself in words.

I spurned the safe path through college and decided I'd do things the hard way: I would spend the next year working and writing, reading and studying on my own, with my own syllabus, teaching myself style and technique. Then the following summer, I planned to hitchhike across the country to New Orleans, where I'd get a job and live the writing life.

I had a great dream that once I got out into the world, I'd find myself a circle of like-minded souls who'd refused to take the offered paths and insisted on going their own way, a brilliant literary-artistic collocation such as was found in Paris in the 1920s and '30s. I knew they were out there somewhere. All I had to do was find them, and once I did, I'd not only find the tribe to which I belonged, but I'd also find my fate, my connection to the greater world, my place in history. I'd join not just with other people but somehow with the Zeitgeist, and through it all I'd transform myself from the fat, nerdy, timid, white-trash loser I was into something stronger, more beautiful, and more profound.

Dropping out to become a writer was also in some sense political. It was a rejection not just of who I was and where I came from, but also of who I felt I was supposed to be and the choices I saw offered. A life spent earning a wage to waste on useless consumer goods and empty diversions seemed sterile and bleak. Becoming a writer was a choice for self-determination in the most radical sense, and literature seemed deeply connected to the ideals of freedom and democracy I'd imbibed wholesale growing up in the last decades of the Cold War. As I read Orwell, Whitman, Twain, Havel, Mailer, and Solzhenitsyn, the connection between writing and freedom seemed ever stronger and ever more true.

At first, things went more or less according to plan: I moved in with a friend in Salem, got a job, and started typing. The following spring, I said goodbye to the girl I'd been seeing, packed up the novel I'd written, and walked down Highway 99 with my thumb out. By the time I got to New Orleans, though, late in August, I was so lonely, stressed out, heartbroken, and busted, I only lasted a couple weeks. I had my mom wire money for a bus ticket home and, with my tail between my legs, slunk back to Oregon.

Several other misadventures followed over the next few years, including a torrid affair with a German woman ten years my senior who flew me to stay with her in Hamburg; two summers spent on the pow-wow circuit with a traveling hot-dog stand; a variety of low-down, no-account jobs; a failed attempt to go back to school at Southern Oregon University; a year spent working as a grassroots canvasser and activist with the Fund for Public Interest Research; a car trip through Mexico; the WTO protests in Seattle; a Rainbow Gathering; supporting a tree-sit; and a brief stint as a phone psychic. Through it all I kept writing, often badly, logging hundreds of thousands of words and hundreds of hours of revision.

Eventually I landed in Moab, where I got another job cooking breakfast and settled in for the long haul. I thought I'd stay and write, become a desert hermit, and leave the world to its troubles. After the compromises of grassroots fund raising and the disappointments of the WTO protest, I was done with eco-warriors, tree huggers, and anarchists; I wanted nothing at all to do anymore with the politics of our fallen world.

Then one morning I woke to find that several men had flown planes into the World Trade Center towers. I didn't see it; I didn't have a TV. My ex-girlfriend had called me and told me to turn on the radio.

Within a few months, I was in my mom's basement, listening to the rain fall. After everything, I was right back where I'd started but even worse off, and just as far from the Left Bank as I'd ever been. Moreover, I could see, if I kept on like this, there was a good chance I'd wind up slipping into drunken, self-loathing decrepitude, eventually writing bleak, dark-hearted stories about Great American Failures, if I managed to keep writing at all. This wasn't how things were supposed to be happening.

3.

People always want to know why I joined the army. They meet me now and see my bookish demeanor, my sensitive green eyes behind wire-rimmed glasses, and can't seem to fathom why a thoughtful, seemingly intelligent young man might want to put himself in harm's way in the service of American power when we're engaged in dirty, uncertain, and morally dubious wars.

The obvious answers are easy: adventure, excitement, travel, challenge. It was also a way to pull myself out of poverty. In 2002 I was back at my mom's house after years of trying to get away, an unemployed, desperate, snaggletoothed college dropout, stuck in a dead end. I'd had enough washing dishes, mopping floors, and scraping by, and the army offered money for college, full medical and dental, a regular check, and combat pay.

I also joined because I wanted to see. I wanted to see, first, if the American empire, out where it was happening, was as bad as all the Chomskyites said. I assumed it would be, but after several years of disappointment with the left followed by the frightening shock of 9/11, I was unwilling to take anti-imperialist polemic at face value. Furthermore, I was swayed if not convinced by liberal hawks like Christopher Hitchens and George Packer, who argued that in the "war on terror" there was something real at stake in terms of international peace, the spread of democracy, and the idea of a better world. Islamic fundamentalism seemed a real danger, and I thought maybe our open society, for all its deep flaws, was worth defending by force of arms. I wanted to see for myself what it felt like out there doing what Orwell called "the dirty work of empire."

I also wanted to see war. I wanted the material. All my life, from GI Joe to *Apocalypse Now* to Sartre, I'd been told that war was an experience beyond all others. It might destroy you, it might cripple you, but in it you'd confront yourself and the world in all its bedrock authenticity—there was no way around the physicality, seriousness, and death at the heart of war. It was inescapably true, in all its horrors, profoundly meaningful, in all its risks, and ultimately redeeming, in its test of character. I wanted to know what it felt like to get shot at; I wanted to know what it felt like to kill.

I wanted disillusionment and wisdom. I wanted the equanimity and poise of Conrad's Marlow sitting on a ship deck in the London dusk, telling the story of his boat trip up the Congo. I wanted to write with the confidence and authority of Hemingway, to be able to say how "Abstract words such as glory, honor, courage, or hallow were obscene beside the concrete names of villages."

I wanted the concrete names of villages. I wanted the shuddering opening to unknown vistas of the soul, truth in sudden flashes, something transformative and maybe crippling that would give me, like Edmund Wilson's Philoctetes, power in my very wound. I wanted to cut through the buzzing anomie of our feckless consumer society and see through to the realm of the real, even if it meant suffering from it the rest of my life. I wanted to cross over from innocence to experience, like all those heroes of literature, and come back with a novel.

Finally, I went to be a man. My dad was a sailor, and both grandpas, too, one uncle, a Navy helicopter pilot, and another did time in the National Guard. I'd been fascinated by all things military since I was seven or eight, and had collected patches, manuals, gear, and paraphernalia like I was stocking a tiny militia.

One night when I was ten or eleven, I ran away from home. I waited till midnight, then put on full camo fatigues and a web belt, packed my canteen, poncho, Swiss Army knife, and lensatic compass, smeared my cheeks with Army-issue olive-drab face paint, and rode my bike out to my grandma's house in the country, where I planned to live in the woods like Rambo or Patrick Swayze in *Red Dawn*.

I was so frightened by the time I got there, I woke up my grandparents and slept on their couch. I was turned over in the morning to my father, the one whose fury I'd been fleeing.

I was a sensitive kid. I loved to read, loved my mom, and cried at the slightest provocation. My dad made sure I knew this was unacceptable. His parenting style was taken straight out of boot camp, and he seemed to think that if shame failed to motivate me, fear would work in its place. The more he'd yell, the more I'd cry, the more I'd infuriate him, the more he'd threaten, the more I'd whimper and break. "You wanna cry," he'd shout down at me, "I'll give you something to cry about."

My dad was a large, red-bearded, red-faced bald man with thick, hairy arms and a bulging gut. He was a bully and, like most bullies, a coward and a liar—rough, uneducated, manipulative. For most of my childhood, he worked a succession of low-wage jobs, at a gas station, a porn shop, and a cannery, among others, but he eventually got certified as a marine electrician, which is what he'd done in the navy. He had a good job for a few years at the shipyard in Portland before he got laid off. He was not only massive and quick to anger, but also charming, mercurial, and funny. Even as I feared him I looked up to him, to his sheer physical bulk, his legendary years sailing the mythic Orient, his seething power and fickle affection.

My mom insisted, with a fervor all the more dubious for its force and repetition, that I had been wanted and planned, yet simple calculations put my conception some months before her senior year of high school; my dad at the time had been twenty-five. I wondered whose plan I could possibly have been.

It doesn't take much to make a child feel unwanted. I was well aware, and early, that my arrival had cut short the glory days of youth my father enjoyed and my mother never really had. My father's resentment at having to provide for a child he no doubt saw as a mistake was exacerbated by the death of his namesake, my younger brother Baby Dan, who died within a year of his birth, and my own failure to live up to Dad's militant standards of masculine behavior. I often felt he'd prefer I simply didn't exist.

He prided himself on never hitting me. He didn't have to. He bullied me with words, taught me to fight with them, taught me how they rend and destroy. One day when I was sixteen, he threatened me, like he always did when I pushed too far, but this time I dared him to follow through. I got in his face and shouted, "Hit me, then, if you're gonna talk about it so much." His fist spasmed and his eye twitched, then something happened: he seemed to shrink, diminishing in the half-light, like a gently collapsing red balloon. I turned my back on him that day, and for a long time after on what I thought it meant to be a man.

I read French poetry, I did theater, I went in drag for Halloween, I fooled around with other guys, I grew my hair long and channeled my anger into poetry, activism, and protests. For a while I thought I was an atheist anarchist nihilist revolutionary, then a secret, starry-eyed Emersonian ascetic, then a rabble-rousing martyr for redwoods and butterflies. Anything but that kind of blue-collar man my father was or the kind I thought society said I should be—violence-cheering, sports-watching, self-satisfied, anti-intellectual, domineering.

I paired a sensitive, feminine side with a deep insecurity about my masculinity, an unstable self opening into a gut-wrenching fear pounded in by my dad that I was never good or strong or tough enough, and no matter what I did or how I struggled to find my own way, I still always felt like I was treading water over a bottomless sea, a feeling of emptiness of meaning and will I was sure would end only with my self-destruction. By 2002, after years of struggling to remake myself somehow like James Joyce or Nietzsche, I had nothing to show but hands empty with failure. In my mom's basement, I faced a choice.

"Every man thinks meanly of himself for not having been a soldier," Dr. Johnson said, and when I decided to join the army in that grim February after 9/11, that's what I told my friends, the one who'd been a PETA activist and the one who'd marched with me against the President. They thought I was being flip, but my seemingly offhand remark held a truth deeper than I could have then admitted.

4.

I stumbled out of the cattle car and onto the drill pad, wobbling and sweating under two duffel bags and a backpack, while drill sergeants' smokeybear hats circled like killer UFOs, shadowing bulging eyes and red faces screaming, "You better move, private!"

When I'd rolled across the tracks to basic training, panting in the stuffy stink of fifty other recruits tense with fear and excitement, I felt an odd dissociation different from anything I'd felt before. In one way, I couldn't believe it was me—the hippie, the weirdo, the poet, the anarchist—here to learn the craft of making war. In another, deeper way, it was like I was coming home.

I did basic and advanced individual training at Fort Sill, Oklahoma, where I learned to operate the targeting computer that would be the focus of my military occupational specialty. I was a 13P, which is a combat arms MOS, but one of the nerdier ones. It would be my job to sit in a tracked vehicle behind the lines and send down targeting data to the giant multiple-launch-rocket-systems launchers, which would then fire long-range rockets armed with air-dispersed antipersonnel bomblets deep into enemy territory.

I'd gotten station-of-choice in my contract, so after AIT I headed for Germany, where I was assigned to the First Armored Division ("Old Ironsides"). Soon after arriving, I was made the battery commander's driver and unit armorer. I found myself suddenly responsible for half a million dollars of weapons and electronics I had no idea how to take care of. I knew how to maintain an M16 and vaguely remembered taking apart a SAW once in basic, but I was completely boggled by the Mk 19 automatic grenade launcher, the M2 .50 caliber machine gun, and all our night-vision goggles, coding machines, and GPS devices. As if the weapons weren't confusing enough, I also had to keep track of what got issued to whom and puzzle out the arcane Army bureaucracy involved in trying to get anything fixed. The previous armorer had given me two days of training before he split back to the States; my first-line supervisor, the unit supply sergeant who should have been my mentor, spoke a kind of English incomprehensible to non-Spanish speakers and spent most of his time cruising internet dating sites.

Over that fall and winter, I was so busy, overwhelmed by new responsibilities, frantically trying to learn the ropes, and taking two college classes on top of it all, that I hardly had any energy left to worry about the impending war with Iraq. When we were told for sure we'd be going, though, the formerly distracted curiosity with which we'd faced the future turned in an instant to an ominously solemn sense of fate.

We deployed to Kuwait in May 2003, then drove from there to Baghdad. Since the fighting war was over and our MLRS rockets all but useless, we were tasked to "needs of the Army." We worked a variety of missions: picking up old Iraqi mortar and artillery rounds, running IED patrols, and assisting cordon-and-search operations, among others. I was transferred from the arms room, which, since we all carried our weapons with us anyway, was merely storage, and spent my tour driving a Humvee.

To be honest, those brutal, maddening days in Baghdad in the summer of 2003, when I thought every morning I was going to die, were some of the sweetest and purest of my life. Each moment gleamed with transcendent splendor. I knew it was pure danger, just adrenaline and focus, and that over time my body and mind would lose the ability to cope with the stress. I knew that, as with any drug, I would develop a certain tolerance. Yet none of that changed the fact that I drove through the city with sparkly eyes, alive to the trees' shadows cutting the street, the aching, tender curve of a baker's Arabic neon sign, the lugubrious sweep of the gray-green Tigris, the manic systemic flow of traffic like waves, the ebb and pulse of foreign bodies.

Nor was I merely passive to the glory—I was action, movement, life itself. I could feel the shudder in the wheel at 50 mph through bumper-to-bumper rush, just my fingers on the column and my foot tapping lightly gas-to-brake as I swung two tons of steel around a truck piled twenty feet high with bricks, brushing between it and a van full of Iraqis, all of them gaping, maybe an inch on either side. Sweet like sex, the gut-grinning crunch of ramming a civilian car, angels singing as I sped through jammed intersections without stopping, God's own righteousness when I picked up my rifle to take a man in my sights.

Everything miserable and beautiful at once.

On the road, in the mix of it, I was pure motion. I did not wonder who I was or what I had to do or think about tomorrow. My fate was held in hidden hands and my horizon limited to the rising and setting sun. I saw we had to die and it was foolish to deny it. I saw our lives were merely preparation for the emptiness to come. I saw how all was vanity, how nothing mattered except forthrightness of purpose and motion. I saw how ridiculous we animals were to think ourselves so civilized, to think our words and thoughts mattered, when really we were nothing more than complicated meat, counting-beasts puzzling ourselves with specious enigmas. I saw we were nothing but guts and eyeballs, and the closer we lived in our skin, the more beautiful we became. I saw that the true glory of existence was in being free from existence itself, free from attachment, free from loss. I saw that only in the purity of fearless, thoughtless action were we truly alive.

The feeling passed. As the year wore on, I saw futures extending beyond the brilliance of those strange and dangerous days. I began to want to live again, finish school, write more, get married, maybe have kids. I wanted something more than the blur of the moment and the pseudo-truths of adrenaline and terror. I grew attached again to existence.

After the chaotic summer and fall of 2003, Baghdad seemed to calm. In early 2004, we ran patrols in the al-Dora neighborhood on the south side and I thought perhaps the door had opened to peace and stability. There were fewer bombings, ambushes, and attacks; the streets seemed quieter, the people less fearful and surly. My unit prepared to redeploy to Germany, and I looked back over my time in Iraq with a sense of relief and achievement. In simply making it through, in riding out the fear I felt every time we'd crossed the wire, in taking on a kind of hardness, and in learning to push myself past my limits, I'd proven whatever it was I'd needed to prove.

I have a picture of myself standing by my Humvee on an overpass in Baghdad, taken one afternoon when we'd set up an ad hoc traffic control point. I've got my M-16 and grenade launcher hanging across my body armor, and I'm standing looking into the distance like some dauntless conqueror, some Cortés, Ozymandias, or Alexander. My helmet's slightly too small for my head, and my fatigue pants are too big and baggy, giving me a clownish, dumpy, sort of pinhead look. I make a ridiculous soldier.

Yet I did my job. I moved when I was called upon. I stood fast when I was needed to stand fast. I felt I'd accomplished what I'd come for—my dad, after all, had gotten no closer to Vietnam than two nights spent on a destroyer tender in Da Nang harbor.

Unfortunately, we weren't done. Just before we were to leave, in the spring of 2004, Iraq erupted again into violence. Sunni fighters took Fallujah, captured four mercenaries, killed them, set their bodies on fire, and hung them from a bridge, while closer to home Muqtada al-Sadr's Mahdi Army took to the streets of Baghdad with RPGs and rifles. I was on the truck to go to the airport to fly back to Germany when we were told to download our gear. We had new orders, extending us in-country indefinitely.

The last few months in Baghdad, we mostly drove convoy security between the Baghdad airport and Karbala. I was bitter and angry; I felt I'd done my part, and I wanted to go home before I got killed. I was sick of Iraq, the army, my rifle, my boots, and the tension in every mission somewhere between boredom and terror.

After some weeks, I finally made it back to Germany, passed the sergeant's promotion board, and was transferred to Fort Sill. Through pure luck, I dodged another deployment and spent the rest of my time in the army training privates, going to sergeants' school, taking college courses, studying for the GRE, and applying to universities. I also began a novel about my war, typing away in the dark hours before first formation.

In April 2006, I threw my desert boots in a dumpster and took a flight to Berlin, leaving the war behind—or so I thought. The truth was, I'd just begun learning how to carry it with me.

5.

It's been a long four years, writing, thinking, reading, trying to understand the connection between thought and deed, who I was and who I became and why we use certain words for things. I've struggled with the ideas of innocence and experience, trauma and revelation, fiction and truth. I'm still not sure how to remember my war. I'm unsure about a lot of things.

My gravest doubt, to echo the soldier and philosopher J. Glenn Gray, is whether I've learned anything from my war at all. In the end, my adrenaline-drenched days driving through Baghdad, my moments of terror and hell-bent fury, and my chilling scrapes with death were just more mere human existence, a dazzled bath of glandular chemicals, nothing sublime.

I got my war stories, but I didn't find any authentic bedrock I could stand on and say, "This is real." I found no soldier's faith, no concrete names of villages. How we understand and account for violence, death, and destruction seems just as contingent and convention-ridden as any other aspect of human culture, and the notion that there's another "really real reality" somehow reachable beyond the physical, mental, and cultural constructs shaping our being in the world seems wholly naive. We find in war what we want to, what we expect, what we've been trained to see.

What's troubling, though, is that I've continued to want to believe, however tenuously, that I've had some sort of revelatory and existential encounter with "truth." I must have learned something profound, some steely-hearted Hobbesian revelation about the "way things really are," some peek into the heart of darkness, or at least something important about myself—right? Maybe, I tell myself, I just haven't figured it out yet. And how do I explain my disappointment in having to wonder whether or not I've had a revelation?

Equally troubling, I've found the moral authority imputed to me as a veteran gratifying and am reluctant to give it up, even though it depends on this very idea of an encounter with truth I don't wholly believe in. I like how it sets me apart, how people assume I know something they don't, how my war has made me special. Over time, I've gotten used to dropping Iraq into conversation like bait, and while this is certainly an improvement over the nervous, angry silence I lived in before, if I'd seen then the way I use it now, I would have been appalled at my easy cynicism.

Just a few years ago, I wanted to shout in people's faces. Now I walk down Sixth Avenue carrying my dirty little war like a card I hand over for credit. It doesn't buy anything on its own, but it does change the calculus: the Post Office gives veterans ten free points on their civil service exam; being a vet, having been to Iraq, gives me similar points in all kinds of ways, from publishing articles to sleeping with women. It might have even helped me get into graduate school.

And what's wrong with that? It's what I went for. I'd joined the army so I could write with authority not just about war but about history, love, life, meaning, and truth. George Orwell, Sam Fuller, Norman Mailer—these are the men I followed, men who went to battle in some sense already wanting to be writers. The tradition goes back to Hemingway at least—Hemingway the self-aggrandizing con artist who spent all of six weeks at the front, as a nurse, before getting himself blown up. He didn't even carry a rifle. I was in Iraq for thirteen months and had a grenade launcher—why shouldn't I own that moral authority? Or at least, if I think it's a question, step up and put it on the line.

So here it is on the line.

I had an easy deployment. I didn't kill anybody. I never even fired my weapon in combat. I mostly drove around Baghdad. I saw nasty things and met some nasty people. I got shot at. I twisted my ankle. Some of my fellow soldiers didn't come back in one piece, and some didn't come back at all. I remember the UN building's wreckage after it got car-bombed, Humvees burning on Route Irish, the sound of incoming mortar rounds, blood, smoke, and fear.

I remember hating the Iraqis. Hadjis, we called them, and it took me a few years to train myself out of using the word. I remember learning to despise weakness, incompetence, and stupidity—not least because they could get me killed—and learning to enjoy feeling pain and inflicting it on others, not least because it could help me stay alive. I remember the posturing and machismo of military culture and how I was so frightened of being deemed not manly enough, not brave enough, not tough enough, that I hid my love for poetry, my checkered hippie past, and much else besides.

Coming back from Iraq on leave through Dallas–Fort Worth, I remember being disturbed by all the people thanking me for my service. I remember dusty bodies in Baghdad streets. I remember standing with pride when I got pinned sergeant. I remember the day I got out and left Fort Sill, feeling so light, free, and full of hope, yet stricken with an unexpected and deeply unwelcome sense of loss. I remember the faces of friends I'll never see again.

Mostly I was lucky. I got everything I wanted: I got my college money; I got my teeth fixed; I saw the dirty work of empire up close, did it with my own two hands and learned its moral cost; I felt the ultimate exhilaration Winston Churchill spoke of, that of being shot at and missed; I saw the chaos of war and wrote a novel about it.

I proved to myself I was man enough, whatever that means. The last time I saw my dad was at my sister's wedding in October 2006. He tried to talk to me and I cut him down. As if seeing him for the first time, I understood in a flash what kind of man he would have been in the service: a braggart, competent but lazy, noisy, untrust-worthy, a moral coward. The roles we'd played in my childhood were now reversed: instead of me not meeting his standard of what a man was, now he failed to meet mine.

Since then, I've continued to struggle with what things mean, what a man is or what truth is, but with a difference. My struggle now is no longer merely in my soul but in the world. Rather than treading water in a metaphysical sea, my feet are planted on the simple, quotidian earth. With this body comes mortality, an end and eventual rot, but also the concreteness of human being, our animal life and breathing thoughts. [2010]

Memories of My Green Machine

War has its own logic.
—**J. Glenn Gray,** *The Warriors*

Memory: "The insights of one hour are blotted out by the events of the next, and few of us can hold on to our real selves long enough to discover the momentous truths about ourselves and this whirling earth to which we cling. This is especially true of men at war."[1]

My Green Machine 1: Unarmored but armed, woodland camo with olive drab liner, Charlie 6, a standard-issue M998 HMMWV. I drove it through traffic-choked, smoky Baghdad streets at the head of the convoy, waiting for the blacktop to explode in shrapnel and fire, watching overpasses for ambushes and rooftops for snipers, watching hadjis for sudden swerves. I gripped the wheel and tapped the gas, weaving unstopping through crowded intersections, feeling tires grip the road and weight shift from right to left. Every morning I opened the hood and lovingly ran hands along belts, rubbed oil between fingers, traced lineaments and undercarriage with tender eyes.

Posthumanism: Something has happened to "Man." Whether understood as "the subject," as "the human," as "Modern Man," or "Western White Male Hegemonic Identity Discourses," the problem of "Man" has been brought to a new pitch by various thinkers, more recent than Nietzsche, Darwin, and Marx, and the political question of our anthro-ontology has been raised to the status of imminent dilemma. We are, we're told, postmodern cyborgs engaged in apocalyptic biopolitics: "For millennia," writes Foucault, "man remained what he was for Aristotle: a living animal with an additional capacity for political existence; modern man is an animal whose politics places his existence as a living being in question."[2] Auschwitz, according to Agamben, has confronted us with the "metaphysical task *par excellence*," the "'politicization' of bare life."[3] We are decentered, fragmented, fluid, part thing and part animal, primitive and modern at once: "Beyond the edge of the so-called human, beyond it but by no means on a single opposing side, rather than 'The Animal' or 'Animal Life'"—and we should add here "The Object," "The Parliament of Things," "Commodity Life," and even "Technological Man"—"there is already a heterogeneous multiplicity of the living . . . a multiplicity of organizations of relations between living and dead, relations of organization or lack of organization among realms that are more and more difficult to dissociate by means of the figures of the organic and inorganic, of life and/or death."[4] We are, we are told, *posthuman.*

All this seems more or less taken for granted, as if in the realm of ideas the forces arrayed against anthrocarniphallogocentrism themselves formed a theoretical hegemony unwilling to confront the conditions of its possibility. Critics have come out to give the critics a good critique. Neil Badmington argues that posthumanism is not quite ready for prime time: "Posthumanism . . . needs theory, needs theorizing, needs above all to reconsider the untimely celebration of the absolute end of 'Man.'"[5] Daniel T. O'Hara asserts that posthumanist theorists have misread their Foucault, ditching his nihilistic Nietzschean-Heideggerian baggage in order to put him to work toward "liberal or social democratic" progressivism in the service of "all kinds of self-revising subjectivities," and argues that many of posthumanism's "prophetic discourses" are in fact not posthuman at all, but very much within a deeply humanistic Romanticism.[6] And Derrida, true to form, questions whether we have even begun to question the questions behind our question:

"It is thus not a matter of opposing another discourse on the same 'things' to the enormous multiplicity of traditional discourses on man, animal, plant, or stone, but of ceaselessly analyzing the whole conceptual machinery, and its interestedness, which has allowed us to speak of the 'subject' up to now."[7]

Yet something *has* happened. I would hazard, in fact, that it happened some time ago. On the "crisis of representation," Bernd Hüppauf writes: "The experience of the dissolution of subjectivity and its traditional patterns of orientation and values, the transformation of modes of perception, and the destruction of vast areas of landscape and experience of time and space have become constitutive elements of modern consciousness . . . It seemed impossible to restore the human face after it had been mutilated in the outburst of destruction after 1914."[8] Rather than maybe washing away on some beach in the future, then, perhaps the human has already passed—blown to pieces almost a century ago in a dismal and muddy gray trench.[9]

My Green Machine 2: Clearly technology has something to do with this. We didn't transform ex nihilo, nor were we shaped from within by some transcendental Idea. What marks modernity (and any prefix positing subsequent epochs) is the change in how we interact with our world: namely, our *technology*. Yet we must remember that "Technology is . . . no mere means. Technology is a way of revealing. If we give heed to this, then another whole realm for the essence of technology will open itself up for us. It is the realm of revealing, i.e., of truth."[10] What is the truth of technology? For Marx, it shows us the objectified social relations between humans, the way that we produce ourselves.[11] For Heidegger, it is an enframing that separates man from his essence.[12] For me, in this investigation and intervention, technology is the *war machine*—both the quasi-subjects who wield it and the quasi-objects who compose it. For the posthuman soldier, "*Technology is our uniform*."[13]

War: Beyond the gate, the roads were already thick with traffic and smog. The chaos out there, the crazy fucking hadji writing, lawless traffic, hidden danger and buzz and stray bullets and death all pressed like a hot wind, and as I stood smoking, waiting for the mission to start, I was suddenly filled with a deep sense of strength and power, of fortitude and righteous fury. I was overtaken by a sudden joy at being a soldier, feeling the charge in my fingertips and neck, so unbelievably just and good to have my rifle in my hands, ten pounds of killer steel, resplendent in the promise of three-round burst. Those fuckers out there, the victims, the insurgents and snipers and fedayeen, the hadjis in their man-dresses and turbans and rags—it might be their land and their city but I was a walking death star. We had full-auto SAWs and two .50 cals, whose rounds could blow chunks out of concrete. We had grenades and rifles and more ammo than we knew what to do with. We had knives and ceramic armored plates and steely, murderous hearts. We had handheld satellite-linked computers and ciphered radios and behind us the whole heaving Empire. We were storm troopers, force made flesh, gods in metal. I ran my palm over the blued metal receiver of my rifle, wanting death to flow from my eyes like magic. *This is what I was born to do,* I thought, *the apotheosis of life itself, the glory and the power.*

Route Map: Our mission is to explore phenomenologically and theoretically the fraught and complex question of the cyborg animal man, the *posthuman*, through what seems to be the most intense enactment of this all-too-contemporary crisis: modern industrial war. Donna Haraway called modern war "a cyborg orgy," and Alphonso Lingis recently argued that in our "postindustrial social economy," the soldier has become "the sole genuine hero, an individual integrally subordinated to order and utility, but at the same time superhuman in the savage and exuberant release of excess energies against a demonic enemy."[14] Both of these contemporary thinkers echo the thoughts of an earlier writer best known for his memoir of World War I: Ernst Jünger. Russell Berman writes in his preface to Jünger's *On Pain* that "Jünger's speculation on the intrusive expansion of technology into the realm of the body clearly anticipates the extensive recent discussion of the blurring between humans and machines."[15] Furthermore, Wolf Kittler suggests "that what Jünger calls 'organic construction' comes uncannily close to the man-machine symbiosis which is the basic assumption of cybernetics, the science that studies *Control and Communication in the Animal and the Machine* . . ."[16] As Jünger himself noted in 1934, "The growing objectification of the individual and its formations seen today is not new."[17]

New or not, our story happens in the present, even if the first "posthumans" were born almost a century past. Our hero is the cyborg soldier. Our setting is Baghdad, Iraq. Our subject is the experience of men at war.

WARNO: First, war is normal. As the anthropologist Paul Richards notes in his study of contemporary war, we must take as our starting point "an assumption that may at first seem paradoxical—that to understand war we must first deny it special status. War, like peace, is organized by social agents."[18] In her brief but important book on photography and war, *Regarding the Pain of Others*, Susan Sontag critiques our contemporary "conviction that war is an aberration . . . That peace is the norm." She asserts rather that throughout history, "War has been the norm and peace the exception."[19] According to the bioarchaeologist Phillip Walker, "As far as we know, there are no forms of social organization, modes of production, or environmental settings that remain free from interpersonal violence for long."[20] We must begin by taking war as something as essential to humans as any other social activity found in our long historical and prehistorical record. The first clear evidence of mass human violence is almost ten thousand years old; the first evidence of the end of war has yet to be seen.[21]

It is also important to resist interpretations of the experience of war that rely too heavily on narratives of trauma and recovery. Much contemporary discussion of war seems to focus on its traumatic aspects, but in many ways this serves only to pathologize and obscure the subject. As Allen Feldman has pointed out, "trauma" itself is a political, historical, and aesthetic concept that often serves to "archaize violence, commodify the past, isolate the 'traumatized' from peer communities, and promote short-term cathartic-empathic identification," and it also risks inducing the "repression of memory" and "compulsive repetition."[22] Relying too heavily on a hermeneutics of trauma not only marginalizes a central human experience and runs the risks Feldman points out, but also betrays the evidence of history. Yuval Noah Harari has worked to historicize the "disillusionment narrative" so central to our understanding of war since 1914 by comparing it with earlier memoirs: "As the case of Renaissance military memoirists clearly indicates, there can be warriors and warrior castes that are intimately familiar with war and all its horrors, yet see it as an acceptable and even a desirable vocation. It all depends on people's worldview—not on war's 'true face.'"[23] Glenn Gray puts the problem succinctly: "There are soldiers in the Anglo-Saxon world and perhaps many more in Teutonic and Slavic lands . . . for whom death is a fulfillment. Unless we try to understand the motivation for this kind of soldier, we can make no claim to grasping the full nature of *Homo furens*."[24]

Normalizing war doesn't solve all our problems, however, because for most Westerners, war is something they've never seen or heard or felt except through a screen. As Sontag puts it:

> "We"—this "we" is everyone who has never experienced anything like what they went through—don't understand. We don't get it. We truly can't imagine what it was like. We can't imagine how dreadful, how terrifying war is; and how normal it becomes. Can't

understand, can't imagine. That's what every soldier, and every journalist and aid worker and independent observer who has put time under fire . . . stubbornly feels. And they are right.[25]

Journalists, anthropologists, and participant-observers like myself must face what Ivana Maček identifies as "one of the major methodological problems of the anthropology of war, namely, how to communicate experiences of war, or how to express the existential threat and pain . . ."[26] We must work toward understanding war in all its complexity, and we must meet this complexity with all our resources. "This demands a constant sociocultural-emotional engagement from everyone in contact with a war," writes Maček. "The process calls upon all our creativity to find new ways of understanding each other, new ways of communicating the most important aspects of our experiences."[27]

War has its own logic, a logos we must be willing to hear, a logos characterized by, among other things, fragmentation and transformation.

Shark Attack: A trailerful of nervous boys sweating under the weight of bags of gear, we flinch in the glare of the opened door and under the howls of sergeants wobble into light—"Doubletime, private!"—two minutes to heave to the drill pad while the sergeants circle and close like sharks—"Too slow! You're dead, private. You're dead now!"—the rims of their smokeybears plunge into your face like the razored halos of red devils, their voices hard and loud, and when you flinch, move, stumble, mutter, blink—Wham!—there's a fucker screaming in your eyeball like you just raped his mom, and thus our first lesson: MOVEMENT UNDER FIRE. In just a handful of the longest hours of my life, mostly spent in pain, we began the sixty-three-day transformation from dirtbags into soldiers. From a gaggle of individuals each doing his own thing, from a motley blend of black, white, brown, Northern, Southern, Eastern, Western, city, and country, we'd learn to think, move, and speak as a unit—and by the time we would finally cross the stage in our graduation ceremony, we would have learned to believe deeply in our mechanization. Humming in our sense of accomplishment, each of us tin soldiers would know we'd done something bold and honorable to be stamped and molded so fiercely, to be made into tools of the big green machine.[28]

Homo furens: There are many transformations in war. One comes before, transforming a man into a soldier; another comes after, turning a killer back into a citizen. One, on the field of battle, changes a soldier into a fighter: "The soldier who has yielded himself to the fortunes of war . . . is no longer what he was. He becomes in some sense a fighter, whether he wills it or not . . . He must surrender in a measure to the will of others and to superior force. In a real sense he becomes a fighting man, a *Homo furens*."[29] Another change, into what Jonathan Shay calls the berserk state, turns men into irrational beasts and invincible gods, strewing red-eyed carnage.[30] As Jünger describes it, "The fighter, who sees a bloody mist in front of his eyes as he attacks, doesn't want prisoners; he wants to kill."[31] Transformation is the key to unlocking the enigma of war. Hiding in occupied France in 1940, Simone Weil wrote this in her brilliant study of our oldest war story:

> Herein lies the last secret of war, a secret revealed by the *Iliad* in its similes, which liken the warriors either to fire, flood, wind, wild beasts, or God knows what blind cause of disaster, or else to frightened animals, trees, water, sand, to anything in nature that is set in motion by the violence of external forces . . . The art of war is simply the art of producing such transformations, and its equipment, its processes, even the casualties it

inflicts on the enemy, are only means directed toward
this end—its true object is the warrior's soul.[32]

Dogs of War: At first, Basic Training is like living in a kennel. It's like
living in a kennel and knowing it, being conscious of descending
to the level of brute animal being—higher brain functions like
imagination, thought, empathy, and analysis all shut down. The
most you can handle is taking a thirty-inch step, putting one foot in
front of the other, moving your feet the way you're supposed to, and
you're fucking that up too and they're on you and guess what, you're
doing pushups again. You cannot succeed. You cannot escape. You
cannot be free from the noise and hate and constant surveillance.
Punished as a group for individual infractions, you learn to watch
the others and bully them just like the drill sergeants do—at first
to keep your ass from having to push, then later just because you
can, because after getting shit on all day, it feels good to fuck with
somebody smaller than you. A rough and ready hierarchy forms:
the toughest, meanest, and quickest at the top, the weak, compassionate, and slow bullied by all.

Animal Man: "It is a general principle . . . ," wrote Freud in his celebrated debate with Einstein on the question of war, "that conflicts
of interest between men are settled by the use of violence. This is
true of the whole animal kingdom, from which men have no business to exclude themselves."[33] What would it mean to consider man
an animal, and to ask if the roots of war lie in our animal being?[34]
The primatologist and anthropologist Richard Wrangham has
considered this question by looking at the way chimpanzees, unprovoked, form raiding parties to attack and kill outnumbered male
chimpanzees in other troops. He presents a convincing adaptive
explanation for why chimpanzees engage in lethal group raids, his
"imbalance-of-power hypothesis," which explains that unprovoked,
calculated aggression has been selected for as a trait conducive to

both individual and group reproductive success.[35] Wrangham uses the imbalance-of-power hypothesis to back up the "chimpanzee violence hypothesis," which "proposes that human warfare is built on pre-human tendencies."[36]

"A combination of three points . . ." Wrangham writes, "suggests that selection has favored unprovoked intergroup violence in human males: the prevalence of human war raiding, the similarities of chimpanzee and human lethal raiding, and the ability of the imbalance-of-power hypothesis to explain the mammalian distribution of lethal violence."[37] His conclusion implies that violence, both individual and organized, is as much a biological part of human life as are sex and eating, that aggression and the drive for dominance are neither vestigial atavisms nor social maladaptations but rather species traits, and that we have little reason to hope that our long history of war and murder might someday come to end.[38]

In fact, what seems to have occurred is not an abatement of violence but its intensification and increase through industrialization, from the meat-grinding cannons, Maxims, and wire of World War I to the apocalyptic annihilation held in reserve in ballistic-missile subs currently prowling lightless depths under Arctic ice. The technological revolution of mass industrialization changed warfare as radically as it has the rest of the world, and it was in the trenches of World War I that this change was seen in its most intense, dramatic, and horrific form. "Under the conditions of technological warfare," writes Hüppauf, "the destructive elements of modernity were condensed to the extreme and forcefully imprinted on the modern mind."[39]

Steel Helmet: "He was the first German soldier I saw in a steel helmet, and he straightaway struck me as the denizen of a new and far harsher world . . . The impassive features under the rim of the steel helmet and the monotonous voice accompanied by the noise of the battle made a ghostly impression on us. A few days had put their stamp on the runner, who was to escort us into the realm of flame, setting him inexpressibly apart from us . . . Nothing was left in this voice but equanimity, apathy; fire had burned everything else out of it. It's men like that you need for fighting."[40]

Warrior Ethos: What kind of man is needed for fighting? An animal become a machine. How do we create such a thing? Through training, institutionalization, the bureaucratization and mechanization of warfare, the objectification of man and his indoctrination through pain: "One immediately notices by every kind of rigorous training how the imposition of firm and impersonal rules and regulations is reflected in the hardening of the face."[41] This is a physical, mental, and even narrative process. It is also a moral process: "The vast and distant military and civilian structure that provides a modern soldier with his orders, arms, ammunition, food, water, information, training, and fire support is ultimately a moral structure, a *fiduciary*, a trustee holding the life and safety of that soldier."[42] It is, finally, a process that the soldier must learn to accept, internalize, and even come to love. "In highly mechanized armies," writes Gray, "many a soldier gains a certain fulfillment in serving the machine with which he is entrusted."[43] The soldier learns, in training and in battle, to objectify the world, himself, and others. He learns to repeat after the drill sergeants: "Pain is weakness leaving the body." He learns "to serve a different deity," a deity concerned "with death and not life, destruction and not construction."[44] He learns to love war, to take pleasure in it, to "delight in destruction," and to master pain.[45] He learns the love of discipline and violence.

Master of Discipline: His name was Drill Sergeant Krugman. He was a sniper in the light infantry in Alaska, and we hated him with fierce, fierce ardor. He was the ultimate authoritarian, and I still think back fondly sometimes to our first day there, his big black boots shining in my face as he walked up and down the line, the burn in my arms and chest and hips, the puddle of sweat on the floor under my chin. "Down," he said, and we lowered ourselves to the level of his rippled boot soles. "Up," he said, and we pushed up past the toe gleaming like a Vulcan mirror, past the ankle where the boot narrowed and up the leather along the leg where it widened, the laces taut and strong, the hide smooth, to the top of the boot where the snugly bloused trousers slid into the leather like a hand inside a glove. "Three-five, Drill Sergeant," we gasped, weak and broken. We did not deserve his love. "Down," he said, and down we went. He smoked us all day long.

The Art of Pain: "Tell me your relation to pain," writes Jünger, "and I will tell you who you are!"[46] Indeed, not only are we "who we are" in our relation to pain, but in our history and knowledge of it; we are who we are in our scars. "The constitution of memory through coercion and the spectacle of pain is the constitution of the political subject . . ." writes Feldman. "For Nietzsche, as later for Foucault, the body marked by discipline and punition serves as an exemplary site for the coming together of political forces and constitutes a formation of domination, a place where power is ordered and a topos where that ordering attains a certain visibility . . ."[47]

If, as Elaine Scarry asserts, "War is relentless for taking for its own interior content the interior content of the wounded and open human body," then learning the art of war is learning the art of pain.[48] According to Jünger,

> The heroic and cultic world presents an entirely different relation to pain than does the world of sensitivity. While in the latter . . . it is a matter of marginalizing pain and sheltering life from it, in the former the point is to integrate pain and organize life in such a way that one is always armed against it . . . Indeed, discipline means nothing other than this, whether it is of the

priestly-ascetic kind directed toward abnegation or of the warlike-heroic kind directed toward hardening oneself like steel. In both cases, it is a matter of maintaining complete control over life, so that at any hour of the day it can serve a higher calling. The central question concerning the rank of values can be answered by determining to what extent the body can be treated as an object.[49]

The soldier is formed not only in the mastery of pain, but also in the training to cause it. As Scarry points out, "In battle . . . the soldier's primary goal . . . is the injuring of enemy soldiers . . ."[50] The soldier must learn how to use force, which, according to Weil, is "that *x* which turns anybody who is subjected to it into a *thing*. Exercised to the limit, it turns man into a thing in the most literal sense: it makes a corpse out of him."[51] The way a soldier exercises force and makes corpses is not with his bare hands, but through tools, weapons, the objects that constitute the technology of war. Violence, as Hannah Arendt points out, "is distinguished by its instrumental character."[52] The soldier identifies himself with his technology, his rifle, his body armor, his tank or Humvee, because it is his *uniform*, while at the same time the material world around him comes to life because now *it* has the power to kill *him*, whether through an IED buried under a pile of street trash, "hostile territory," the unseen fire of a sniper, or the potential failure of his own equipment.[53] Meanwhile, he comes to see the enemy as a target, a corpse, something less than human.

Fucking Hadjis: We held them all at gunpoint, making them sit with their hands on their heads. "Don't fucking look at me," we shouted. "Eyes on the ground!" Our work crew had turned into our prisoners, because one of them had tried to steal some 9mm rounds from the ammo depot where they worked. "Fucking hadjis," someone muttered, as we waited for orders from higher. Eventually the lieutenant picked five: the thief, his brother, the leader of the work crew, one guy who'd had nothing to do with it but had been angry and disobedient, and another guy who might've known the thief somehow. We zip-stripped their thumbs and put sandbags on their heads and threw them in the back of a truck. We took them back to Battalion, where they were interrogated, then we took them to the MP station. The lieutenant had me help him fill out the paperwork: name, address, next of kin, offense. He had their names scribbled on a notepad, nearly everything else was left blank. The MPs started processing them, shoving each one up against the fence and twisting his arms behind him: "Spread your fucking legs! Don't fucking look at me! You fucking looking at me?"

By the time the Abu Ghraib photos came out, most of us hated the Iraqis so much, we didn't really care. Command came down with platitudes about unacceptable behavior, but the rest of us knew the score. They were the enemy, all of them, the whole fucking country, maybe even the kids. "You know what?" one of our sergeants told us. "Fuck 'em."

The Face of the Enemy: "Since humans relate to each other through social cues, rendering the enemy without (and outwith) society is an essential aspect of setting up a target to be hit," writes Paul Richards.[54] Dehumanizing the enemy is such a common feature of war, in fact, that we can almost take it for granted.[55] The enemy is not always defined as subhuman, especially not among professional soldiers who feel they are fighting other professional soldiers, but all too often the image of the enemy's subhuman status is a central feature of modern war.[56] This may have something to do with race, as suggested by Gray, and no doubt the worst acts of dehumanization—both physically and symbolically—occur in colonial or imperial wars. Yet this might also have to do with mass mobilization and the need for propaganda. Shay frames the problem thus:

To our modern mind the enemy is detestable—by definition. "Well, he's the enemy, ain't he?" said one veteran. "You couldn't kill them if you thought he was just like you." This apparently self-evident truth—that men cannot kill an enemy understood to be honorable and like oneself—is something this veteran learned as part of his culture . . . Vietnam-era military training reflexively imparted the image of a demonized adversary . . .[57]

As Shay points out quite clearly in his discussion of trauma, dehumanizing the enemy has a real effect on the soldier, making his own objectification darker, meaner, and potentially more destructive. As Gray describes his own experience, "It is not the suffering and dying that sickens [the warrior] so much as it is the brutalization of the emotions and the corruption of the heart which prolonged fighting brings."[58]

My Weapon: I watched the man come into my sights, right where I had him set up. Another time, I jammed the rifle stock into my shoulder and aimed at the driver behind the windshield. Another time, all I had to do was chamber a round, pulling back the charging handle with a click and riding it forward, and I got my message across. My big black gun was power incarnate: M16A2 5.56mm rifle with 40mm M203 grenade launcher, well-oiled and fastidiously clean. I took her with me everywhere. I cradled her in my arms and nightly rubbed her down and reached to touch her in my sleep. 11.79 pounds with a thirty-round; I was naked without her. I went home on leave in the middle of my tour, and the whole two weeks I kept coming to with a shock because when I reached for her, she wasn't there. With my rifle I was a soldier: I could kill, I wielded force, I held power. The Iraqis we moved among were something less, something less potent, something I could push around. Without my rifle I was nothing, a target, merely passive. My rifle gave me my world.

The Worldhood of the Rifle: "Possessions are for the combat soldier his only assurance of protection against a threatening world," writes Gray. "He cares for them, often with more attention than he pays to his own body."[59] A soldier's things, from Achilles's shield to the gear in Tim O'Brien's *The Things They Carried*, are more than mere tools, more even than just fetishes.[60] They are world-forming, in a Heideggerian sense, and world-destroying, as in Scarry's analysis.[61] The rifle reveals a world.[62]

In *Being and Time*, Heidegger puts forward a description of the way we encounter "entities in the world" such that they are world-disclosing. "Taken strictly," he writes, "there 'is' no such thing as *an* equipment. To the Being of any equipment there always belongs a totality of equipment, in which it can be this equipment that it is."[63] He explores this phenomenology from the specific utility of any piece of equipment to the environment toward which and in which said equipment exists.

> In roads, streets, bridges, buildings, our concern discovers Nature as having some definite direction. A covered railway platform takes account of bad weather; an installation for public lighting takes account of darkness, or rather of specific changes in the presence or absence of daylight—the "position of the sun." In a clock, account is taken of some definite constellation in the world-system . . . When we make use of clock-equipment, which is proximally and inconspicuously ready-to-hand, the environing Nature is ready-to-hand along with it.[64]

Mutatis mutandis, a rifle comes along with a world of conflict and an enemy to be destroyed.

Normally, according to Heidegger, "Things" are phenomenologically ready-to-hand in their daily instrumentality, but they become
world-disclosing (or present-to-hand) in their "conspicuousness,
obtrusiveness, and obstinacy," that is, as obstacles, failures, and
absences.[65] When we encounter the obstacle, failure, or absence of an
object, we encounter as if newly seen the "toward-this" toward which
the object is directed, "and along with it everything connected with
the work—the whole 'workshop'—as that wherein concern always
dwells."[66] This newly-revealed context announces itself as the world.

But in war there is something else: the presence of death and
the death-dealing, death-defying, and "civilization-destroying"
utility of arms and armor opens the possibility of a greater awareness of the "world" as it is disclosed through the world-destroying
character of the equipment involved.[67] The soldier's rifle, that is, is
ready-to-hand and present-at-hand at once; the soldier moves in an
enchanted world of magical objects, where any common "Thing"
has the power to kill, and where the human is always reducible and
being reduced to the status of a mere "Thing," an "object," a target,
a tool, or a corpse. "So, too, the ordinary soldier . . . dwells every day
in the midst of determinate wounds and indeterminate meaning."[68]
In this liminal world of life and death, where every subject is an
object and every object a death-dealing subject, a refined and vivid
fetishism is more than an atavistic reflex of the narrative animal.
The dangerous, heterogeneous relationships between things and
Being, between object, animal, and man, the "multiplicity of organizations among realms," form the essence of the cyborg soldier's
experience of war. As Gray wrote in 1959, "Those thinkers who
believe that a new type of man is bound to emerge as a product of
our technological development might well study in detail over the
last century the varying relation of men to their weapons of war."[69]

Storm of Steel: "The incredible massing of forces in the hour of destiny, to fight for a distant future, and the violence it so surprisingly,

stunningly unleashed, had taken me for the first time into the depths of something that was more than mere personal experience. That was what distinguished it from what I had been through before; it was an initiation that had not only opened the red-hot chambers of dread but had also led me through them."[70]

Thinking War: The "posthuman" transformation is apocalyptic, emancipatory, dehumanizing, profound. The effect of modern industrial warfare on the soldiers in World War I has been noted, but its effect on thought is widespread, complex, and yet to be made fully clear. Through the deadly heterogeneity of war, our narratives of selfhood are fragmented and reformed in strange, precarious, and threatening ways. One possibility is the creative metamorphosis of individuals within ever-renewing social-cybernetic networks of increasing richness and potential; another possibility is the increasing alienation, atomization, and commodification of the destabilized subject; yet a third possibility, embraced by Heidegger and Jünger, is totalitarianism. There may be others, more or less nihilistic.

Jünger's embrace of the world of the cyborg soldier raises important questions about the future of that world. According to Hüppauf, "Jünger's claim in 1963 that many of his observations are no longer surprising or provocative, but have become part of everyday experience, seems justified."[71] One of the most disturbing potential aspects of the posthuman, when taken in its full destructive and creative potential, is that as it manifests itself in death and war making (and the Schumpeterian "creative destruction" of global capital), it constricts the range of human possibility to a narrower and narrower horizon. Paraphrasing Jünger, Kittler writes: "The gestalt of the worker [read: warrior] stalls, brings to a standstill in the sense of challenging, provoking, defying, and hunting down any being in the world—including that eminent being-there, 'Da-sein,' which man is."[72] This happens not only in the biopolitics of concentration camps and nuclear missiles, but in the very experience of war itself. The horizon of being contracts and intensifies: time shrinks from days to hours to minutes, space transforms into an ominous world of fetishes and threats, and other people divide into allies and enemies. Thought gives way to matter: in the phenomenological ethos of war, "Thinking tends to become not only painful but more and more unnecessary."[73] When posthumanism goes to war, the war is total. Simone Weil writes:

> Once the experience of war makes visible the possibility of death that lies locked up in each moment, our thoughts cannot travel from one day to the next without meeting death's face. The mind is then strung up to a pitch it can stand for only a short time; but each new dawn reintroduces the same necessity; and days piled on days make years. On each one of these days the soul suffers violence. Regularly, every morning, the soul castrates itself of aspiration, for thought cannot journey through time without meeting death on the way. Thus war effaces all conceptions of purpose or goal, including even its own "war aims." It effaces the very notion of war's being brought to an end. To be outside a situation so violent as this is to find it inconceivable; to be inside it is to be unable to conceive its end.[74]

After-Action Report: The line of the horizon rose and bulged in weird and jagged shapes, framed by drifts and columns of smoke. A great turquoise egg, split as if by a giant, loomed in the distance among the buildings, towers, stacks, minarets, and palaces. Crossed by highways thick with cars, bunched in dense collections of hovels and alleys, scarred by megalomania, occupation, shock and awe, the city met us every day with the same cratered face, verging between a sneer and a smile.

Until I got used to the idea of my own death, until I got used to the randomness of things, I saw wires in every trash bag. Watching my speed, watching the traffic around us, watching for the next exit, watching our escorts, I also watched the trash along the streets, the everywhere garbage and corpses of goats and chunks of concrete and abandoned tires, the filth that could kill me.

The city's skin: trash and sand and smoke, hiding instant death. Up close, far away. War is no place for imagination. Coming up over the river, the apocalyptic panorama fading into the desert, swinging off the exit back into the mess, crammed junctions, bodies pressed wall-to-wall, narrowed sky and muezzin windows. The sun, the shade, blurs of brown and passing colors, little boys in lavender pants and huddled packs of wives in black burkas.

I already feel like a cliché. My memory feels false: checkpoints, translators, freestyle, friendly fire. But there was nothing false about it then, the flood of light and the fear of death. The truth is, I never got used to it.

The city pulsed around us, a big heart beating traffic and smoke. We were only little things, action figures in the field of play, army guys moved around, scattered by fire, piled up, and boxed away. [2010]

Back to Baghdad

1.

Ali was going to kill me.

I lurched to my feet, groping for my glasses, as a vision flared across the dark: Around six the next evening, I go up the Mansour Mall's four flights of escalators to the food court, passing on my way glitzy Western-style clothing shops and overpriced Chinese tech stores. The food court is packed, as Meethaq had told me it would be, and I scan the crowds of young Iraqis and Baghdadi families for his face. Meethaq's going to introduce me to his friend Ali, who worked as a terp for the Americans during the war.

The skin on my neck prickles—I want to leave but I go on, pulled in, anxious but incapable of doing anything different. I pass through segregated clusters of twenty-somethings, the men together in leather-fringed blue jeans, with manicured stubble and faux-hawks, the women on their own, keeping nominal hijab in elaborate colored scarves and high-heeled shoes. People are talking all around me, but their conversations are drowned out by a rising ringing and beating in my ears.

Somewhere between Burger Queen and Pizzarro's I stop and turn. There he is. I don't know his face, but he knows mine from the cell-phone picture Meethaq took, and I see the recognition in his eyes as he steps toward me, smiling, one hand reaching for mine, the other reaching in his jacket for the trigger to his explosive belt.

"Allahu akbar," he says, and turns the world to fire.

As I sat in my Baghdad hotel room in the dark, hours yet from dawn, all the pieces slid into place. First, the location. Mansour Mall had good security, but I was sure that if somebody wanted to sneak in a PBIED (personally borne improvised explosive device), they'd be able to. There had to be at least one service entrance, and there was no way they were checking every box of merchandise that came into the mall. More important, the Mansour Mall was Baghdad's biggest and most modern shopping center. Opened a year before, in 2013, it was a beacon of global commerce. All sorts of consumer goods gleamed under the relentless lighting, from Xboxes to Timberland shoes to Versace purses. The top floor housed Baghdad's most modern movie theater, showing *Transcendence* and *Captain America: Winter Soldier*. Young men and women gathered, browsed, and even mingled, out from under the watchful eye of parents and religious authorities.

For the extremists in the Islamic State of Iraq and Syria (ISIS), the al Qaeda–spawned movement that had been sending suicide bombers into Baghdad and had, in January, conquered Fallujah and most of Ramadi, Mansour Mall would be a symbol of both Western influence and Iraqi prime minister Nouri al-Maliki's national leadership. It would therefore be a perfect target for an attack three days before Iraq's upcoming national elections, the first since the Americans had left in 2011. Even a small PBIED in the crowded food court could kill dozens. And all the better for ISIS if one of them was an American journalist and a former US soldier.

Second, there was Meethaq. I wanted to believe his passionate hope for Iraq's future, his heartfelt patriotism, and his hospitality, but something—perhaps these very qualities—didn't compute. Meethaq studied at the Iraqi Foreign Service Institute, training to be a diplomat. He'd met me the day before in a charcoal gray suit and a conservative striped tie, and we'd had an awkward but friendly conversation over Diet Pepsis in the food court. He was thirty-one, had studied at the Osaka School for International Public Policy in

2008 and 2009, and before entering the Foreign Service Institute had worked three years at the Japanese Embassy. You wouldn't think, observing his calm, professional demeanor, that he'd spent most of his adulthood negotiating life under a foreign occupation, that his college years had been interrupted by an invasion, or that the two years after graduating college, during the sectarian civil war, had been so painful and difficult that he refused to talk about them.

Meethaq seemed representative of the educated Sunni upper middle class that had before 2003 formed Iraq's political and cultural elite. I expected him to be pessimistic, resentful, and grim, given that he was an intelligent young man who, as a Sunni, would have seen privilege turn into prejudice, and who lived in a failing state under increasingly autocratic rule, with dim prospects ahead and two decades of bad blood behind. Instead, Meethaq expressed earnest ambitions for his country: a fervent faith in Iraq's potential as a developing economy and a viable democracy. Although his hair was prematurely gray and his face serious beyond his years, when he talked about the future, his eyes shone.

"We're a new generation," he told me. "We can make the change. Iraq has suffered for thirty years, and that has closed people off from one another. As a new generation, we can make the reforms our country needs. We want to say to the world that Iraq is a new country. It has a new government. Iraq is a free country. Iraq is peaceful . . . The media has created this false perception of Iraq and of Arab countries. We're not extremists. We welcome everybody, from any nation. We're open to others. We don't want to be apart from other countries. We want to change this reality . . . I remember, Mr. Obama said, 'We can do it.' So we can do it. Why not? This is our message to the world."

It was hard, listening to Meethaq roll off numbers for oil revenue, describe strategy points for positive change, and articulate the need for sectarian and regional cooperation, to not be swept along in his progressive dream. I could imagine a coalition government defeating incumbent Prime Minister Maliki's State of Law party in the elections on April 30, bringing peace to Anbar, investing oil money in public infrastructure and education, and opening Iraq to intercultural exchange. As I looked around at the gathering crowds at the Mansour Mall, in a food court that could be anywhere in the capitalist world, Meethaq's hopes seemed not only possible, but plausible.

This was a very different Iraq from the one I'd known as a private in the US Army ten years before, although I remembered a lot of hope then, too. But the closest thing I saw to the Mansour Mall in 2004 had been an open-air market in the Green Zone where vendors sold watches bearing Saddam's face and little kids hawked ficky-ficky DVDs. Back then, I never talked to anyone like Meethaq, although odds were good we stopped people like him at checkpoints and forced cars full of people like him out of the way of our convoy. The only Iraqis I talked to back in 2003 and 2004 were day laborers who helped us recover abandoned munitions, a few terps we worked with, and a handful of soldiers and police who pulled gate guard with my unit at FOB Falcon.

I had gotten Meethaq's email address secondhand, from a sociologist who did research on interpreters. I had written Meethaq describing my project, asking if we could talk, and also asking if he knew any Iraqis in Baghdad who'd worked as terps for the US during the war. He was among some dozen or so Iraqis I reached out to before arriving, most of whom seemed cagey at first, unwilling to put their trust too easily in an American journalist. Meethaq, however, was enthusiastic to meet me; he was my first appointment, on my first full day in country. It seemed like a good omen that the first place I'd go in Baghdad would be the mall.

My pitch for the story had been straightforward: Send me back to Iraq. The fall of Fallujah to ISIS in January 2014 had shocked a lot of American veterans and provoked a lot of soul-searching. As Iraq slid into a new civil war, it became harder and harder to make sense of our sacrifices there. For most Americans, that sacrifice had been something distant and abstract: po-faced ceremonies, jingoistic action films, sentimental commercials for real estate and insurance. For myself and my fellow veterans, though, that sacrifice was personal, gut-deep, concrete. Many of us had lost friends, brothers, sisters, parts of ourselves, and parts of our souls in the eight-year-long mess called Operation Iraqi Freedom. The names in the news that winter—Fallujah, Ramadi, Abu Ghraib, Mosul— resonated deeply with American soldiers and marines, triggering memories of fear, violence, and loss, calling up complex feelings of pride and sorrow. To see an al Qaeda splinter group take over a third of Iraq, with daily life there wracked once again by terrorist violence, while the central government fell increasingly under the control of a corrupt and brutal ruler, was to see the props holding up one's sense of honorable service fall away. It meant having to give up the fragile illusion that we might have done some good in Iraq. It meant having to let go of the tenuous belief that we had left the country stable, democratic, and better off. Most troubling of all, it meant having to confront the possibility that we didn't just leave Iraq, we lost Iraq.

Of course, that depends on what you mean by lost. And with the enfeebled state of the American news media today, especially when it comes to international coverage, it was all but impossible to get a sense of what was actually happening on the ground. It seemed that Iraq was nothing but explosions and death, but was it really that bad? Surely there was another side to the story. And what about the upcoming election, Iraq's first real independent parliamentary vote since the 1950s, when the country had been a constitutional monarchy untangling itself from the grip of British colonial rule? Was it free? Was it fair? What would happen? What would it mean?

Thus I found myself, ten years after flying out of Baghdad International Airport on a US Air Force C-130, flying back in on a Royal Jordanian A320, sleep-deprived, jet-lagged, nervous, and feeling trapped.

I had seriously considered bolting during my layover in Amman, just not getting on the plane, giving up the whole trip. Why was I risking my life again? For what? And what the fuck did I think I was doing? I didn't know anybody in Baghdad, just the translator and driver I'd hired; I didn't have any idea of how to be a "foreign correspondent"; I didn't speak any Arabic; I had no insurance, no security team, no backup, and no idea what would happen if I got kidnapped or injured. Meanwhile, Iraq was being torn apart by the most intense violence it had seen in years. Nearly three thousand people had died since January 1, 2014, on top of almost nine thousand killed in 2013, in a rising tide of political murders and suicide attacks. Residents of Baghdad were enduring several car-bomb attacks a week, and the Karrada neighborhood—where I'd gotten my hotel—was a special target, since it happened to be home to many of Iraq's new Shiite elite.

The good news was that most of the violence was limited to just such car bombs, or to fighting between the Iraqi Army and ISIS, outside the city in Anbar and Diyala provinces. Getting killed in Baghdad these days was largely a matter of bad luck. This was a far better situation than the worst years of the civil war, between 2005 and 2008, when on top of IEDs and VBIEDs going off regularly, kidnappings and street assassinations were common occurrences, gun battles between militias and the US Army were an everyday affair, and Westerners were targeted specifically. As I forced myself to line up for my flight from Amman to Baghdad, I kept reminding myself that I would be safer there today than I had been in 2003 and 2004, when the US Army fought sporadic battles with Baathist holdouts, disgruntled locals, and foreign insurgents. Although being a soldier had meant I had armor, a rifle, and twenty heavy dudes backing me up, it also meant I was a target. This time, I wouldn't have the firepower or the backup, but at the same time I wouldn't be a walking symbol of colonialist oppression. Or not as blatantly, anyway. I was still the only palefaced motherfucker on the flight.

We landed a few hours later. The familiar scent of Baghdad hit me as soon as I stepped off the plane: Oil, diesel smog, and a whiff of sulfur. Late at night and early in the morning, when the air is cleanest, this is what Baghdad smells like. As the day goes on, the odor thickens and turns metallic, until darkness falls and the fires start, filling the air with a pungent mélange of kebab and melted plastic. When I was here ten years ago, the smell was mixed with the stench of corpses.

A week before, I'd been in a seminar room at Princeton, talking with my students about the Cold War, Don DeLillo's *Underworld*, and Whitney Houston's version of "The Star-Spangled Banner." The campus outside softly exhaled magnolia.

My driver, Ahmed, was to meet me at the parking lot at the edge of the airport. The cabbie at the terminal told me it'd cost $35 to get out there, then $40, then $45, then $50, the fare changing in as much time as it took him to figure out I was an easy mark. Rolling out to the parking lot on the road we used to call Talladega, I saw the cluster of dull, squat buildings that once marked the American command center at BIAP (Baghdad International Airport): the mayor's cell, Hotel California, the PX. Once upon a time, for me, these unremarkable administrative offices and warehouses had been my closest connection to home. Now they were just random airport infrastructure. Bob Hope DFAC (dining facility) was gone, and so were the hundreds of tents that had housed transient units. We passed the backside of the warehouse where I'd lived with three hundred other men, then our motor pool, the small mosque that had always been off limits, and the area where I used to go jogging when I needed some time alone, a verdant maze of palms and ponds where the Rangers kept their hooches.

In the parking lot, I met Ahmed. I had worried, before coming, about who this guy was, since I would be trusting him with my life, and it had been impossible to tell anything about him from his brief and cryptic emails. When I saw him rise up out of his white Kia, though, a barrel-bellied, patient man with a canny smile, I knew I'd be in good hands.

As we left the airport, it seemed beyond believable that we were driving out into hostile territory, at night, with no protection. We passed the winged statue marking the airport entrance, which in 2003–4 had represented the edge of friendly territory and the beginning of the "red zone," Indian Country. We would lock and load as we passed beneath the statue's wings. I came to think of it as the angel Jehovah had sent to guard, with a fiery sword, the gates of Eden.

To see a place that has become mythical to you changed is to see it diminished. Yet at the same time as the myth diminished in scale, it became human again, and mine. It was just a place, my memories just memories. The stories I'd turned the place into, the impressions that had escaped the realm of self and come back at me like fables from a distant land, fell to earth. They were *only* mine, and nothing more. The place, BIAP, Baghdad . . . it had gone on without me, and my memories hadn't touched it. Everything was coming loose.

It wasn't hostile territory anymore, it wasn't Indian Country. It was just a city. But while I knew that in my head, my body remembered the bad old days. The smells, sights, and feel of Baghdad activated all my old alert mechanisms, the danger focus, the threat assessment matrix. Not knowing what the threats were, or where they came from, I skipped status yellow and went straight to full-on freak-out. Everything was a potential threat. Would the hotel clerk sell me out to ISIS? Would somebody launch an RPG at my room? Was I being followed?

When I met Meethaq at the mall the next day for my first interview in country, after a restless, jet-lagged night, he was vague about which floor to meet on, then late, and, when he finally arrived, sweating and nervous. I found his earnestness difficult to credit and his assertions of goodwill excessive. He was working very hard to get me to trust him, which didn't make any sense. What did he want from me? Who was he? What was I doing here? I couldn't shake the sense that Meethaq was hiding something, and I was puzzled by his idealism. Nevertheless, I had a story to report, so we made plans to meet at the mall again the next evening, when he would bring his friend Ali with him. Ali had been an interpreter for the US Army, and I wanted to ask him about his memories of those days and what he thought now about the legacy of the American occupation in Iraq.

When I woke in the middle of the night, I knew he wanted to kill me. That's why he wanted to meet back at the mall, at six, when the food court would be packed. That's why he took my picture, so the bomber could identify me. It explained him asking me if I'd told the American embassy I was there. It explained a thousand inexplicable details, things he'd said or not said, his strange manner, his self-contradictions, the way he refused to talk about what he'd been doing in Amiriya in 2006 and 2007. The way he'd assured me the mall was totally secure, I wouldn't be targeted there, it was completely safe.

Nowhere was safe. The day I'd arrived, ISIS extremists had hit a campaign rally in northern Baghdad with three separate bombs, killing thirty people and wounding many more. Thaier Al-Sudani, a photographer for Reuters, captured incredible photos of the bombing: giant balls of orange light, dust, and shrapnel. These images seized my mind in the dark of my hotel room, as I came to see the danger I had put myself in. I remembered I'd told Meethaq the name of my hotel—of course I'd have to move, now. I also needed to email *Rolling Stone* and have them advance me some expense money. If things went sideways, I would need to get out quick, and that would take cash.

While I'd been talking with Meethaq and then driving around

Baladiyat, a car bomb had gone off in al-Nasir and there'd been a drive-by in al-Amil. Nine bodies, riddled with bullets, had been found in the Sunni neighborhood of Adhamiya. Meanwhile, the leader of al Qaeda, Ayman al-Zawahiri, had called upon his followers to kidnap Western journalists. The campaign-rally bombing was obviously just the beginning. I knew with absolute certainty that if I went to Mansour Mall again, it would be the last thing I ever did.

2.

At the American Embassy the next morning, over coffee and cookies, one of the first questions Jane Arraf asked the US ambassador was about the rise of Asaib Ahl al-Haq. Jane was an old Baghdad hand, having covered the region since 1991. Utterly charming, sparky, petite, funny, and brimming with sympathetic curiosity, she'd been covering the Asaib Ahl al-Haq rally in Baladiyat for Al Jazeera English on Friday when the three massive bombs had gone off. When she started snapping photos, an armed guard grabbed her camera and smashed it, screaming at her, "Why are you taking pictures?"

"Because we're journalists," she'd shouted back.

Jane's question to the ambassador about Asaib Ahl al-Haq seemed important. During the last few years of the US occupation, General Ray Odierno had considered Asaib Ahl al-Haq the most dangerous Shiite militia in Baghdad. Its name means "League of the Righteous," and the group was known for its brutal history of kidnappings, assassinations, and torture, as well as for its strong ties to Iran's elite Quds Force. But Asaib Ahl al-Haq didn't just have ties with Iran. When the group's leader, Qais al-Khazali, was captured after staging a raid on a US military base in Karbala that killed five soldiers, Prime Minister Nouri al-Maliki protested his detainment and later negotiated his release as part of a cease-fire deal. In exchange, Asaib Ahl al-Haq turned over a British contractor it had held since May 2007, along with the corpses of four of his co-workers. Nearly as soon as Qais was released, however, al-Haq broke the cease-fire and kidnapped an Iraqi-American contractor working for the US Department of Defense, whom it exchanged for four more al-Haq prisoners held by the Iraqi government. Since 2011, Asaib Ahl al-Haq had gone legit, adding a political arm to its militia, which over the last few years had begun fighting alongside the Iraqi army in Anbar and Diyala and sending men to the civil war in Syria. Its campaign posters, plastered all over Baghdad, were readily identifiable by the faces of the armed martyrs who looked down from them.

The group represented the militant wing of Baghdad's energetic Shiite political majority, which comprised several rival factions. The main parties competing in the election were Prime Minister Maliki's State of Law coalition, centered around the Shiite nationalist Dawa Party; the Islamic Supreme Council of Iraq, or ISCI, joining very conservative Islamist cultural politics with a technocratic appeal to middle-class stability, backed up by its bloody-handed Badr Brigades; and Muqtada al-Sadr's populist Al-Ahrar bloc, appealing most explicitly to poor Shiia in Baghdad's slums and the rural south.

These were only the most prominent of the 107 "political entities" and coalitions representing 9,964 candidates competing for 328 seats in the national election. Most of them I'd never heard of, and it was difficult keeping track of even the two dozen most important. Iraqi national politics was a bewildering congeries of politicians, coalitions, outsiders, proxies, and allegiances: in addition to the thousands of candidates, every major regional player had interests and influences, especially Iran, Saudi Arabia, and Turkey; there were five major Shiia clerics involved, whose fatwas could send voters running from one candidate to another; Russian and Chinese oil companies had a stake in securing their investments in the south; Kurdistan, as a semi-autonomous state, had its own politics, and would act as a powerful arbiter of national leadership; the government itself, almost entirely under Maliki's control, functioned nearly as its own political party; and the country was in the midst of a civil war that was its own hornet's nest of allegiances and proxies, involving Sunni tribal leaders, the Sahwa militias that had worked with the US in 2008, al Qaeda, ISIS, and factions from the Syrian civil war, which wasn't, in truth, a completely distinct conflict. Finally, and not least, Uncle Sam was involved—although merely, of course, as a disinterested observer.

When I'd heard that the US Ambassador to Iraq would be giving a "deep backgrounder" to Western journalists on Sunday morning, I jumped at the chance. Not only would it make it possible for me to go into the Green Zone and see the US Embassy, otherwise a challenging prospect, but it would give me the opportunity to hear the official US position on the election, see the Baghdad press corps in action, and maybe come to understand the complexities of Iraqi politics a little better. That I'd never talked with a US ambassador before or been to "a deep backgrounder" didn't really concern me. I was more worried about managing the nagging certainty that I was going to die at the Mansour Mall later that evening. My fear gave the day a buzzsaw edge and turned everything a little desperate, even the imperial bonhomie at the US Embassy and the relaxed intensity of the four journalists who showed up for the briefing.

I'd expected a crowd and had planned on being to be able to fade into it. Instead, I found myself cozily seated across the table from US Ambassador Robert S. Beecroft. On my left was Tim Arango, from the *New York Times*, who with his scruffy beard, disheveled hair, and sleepy manner wouldn't have been out of place at a hipster party in Brooklyn. Prashant Rao, AFP bureau chief, was on my right. Jane, sitting next to him, complimented him on his new jacket, and everyone wanted to know about his fancy recording pen. On Jane's far side sat newly appointed Reuters bureau chief Ned Parker, wearing a baseball cap. Beyond Ned were the embassy press attaché and the head of Public Affairs.

The journalists I found myself among were every one of them

experts on the region, serious reporters with long careers covering Iraq and the Middle East for major outlets. Their talk was all inside baseball, professional shorthand, and old histories. They were there to get into the nitty gritty on Iraq's first postoccupation election, which Arraf suggested was Iraq's "weirdest" election yet.

I was no journalist, no regional expert—this was precisely the second time I'd been to the Middle East in my life. I was a PhD candidate in English at Princeton, working on a dissertation about the politics of sacrifice in American literature about World War II. I was supposed to be working on a chapter about silence and community in the poetry of Kenneth Koch and George Oppen. My only training for all this was having once read Evelyn Waugh's *Scoop*. Sitting in the US embassy in Baghdad didn't make any goddamn sense.

It made some sense, actually. Since getting out of the army, I'd published a few articles and essays about my experience in Iraq and as a veteran, most notably a five-part series in the *New York Times*. I started going to a writing group for veterans at NYU, where I met people who would become close friends, some of whom would go on to become successful writers. It was there that Jacob Siegel, Phil Klay, Perry O'Brien, and I decided together to produce an anthology of veterans' fiction, *Fire and Forget: Short Stories from the Long War* (we brought Matt Gallagher on board later).

With the publication of *Fire and Forget*, I found myself, disconcertingly, one of the central players in an emerging scene: the veteran-writer racket. There was money to be made talking vet (not a lot, but some), a certain celebrity to be won, and a lot of support and respect from audiences, especially if you suggested you had PTSD. But the best part was that you got to keep being special.

The problem with being a veteran is that the aura you have coming home fades as soon as you do something else. Once you stop making your identity all about the war, you lose your connection to world-historical events. People quit asking you to explain the nature of human suffering, international politics, and the essence of truth.

You lose your moral authority. It's hard to let that go, of course, and the best way to keep the aura shining is to keep reminding people that you're a veteran. Keep reminding them that you saw or did some fucked-up shit, maybe you had nightmares, maybe you lost a friend. Keep reminding them that you have something they don't, and keep reminding them that it's something you only get for going. For many of us, the military was the most intense experience we'd ever had, and it offered the most trustworthy form of social validation we'd ever achieved. We were veterans. And for a shiny dime, we'd sell you our story.

Four months earlier, in the icy dregs of January, I'd been deep into my fifth beer with Matt Gallagher at Pete's Candy Store, a neighborly bar on the border between Williamsburg and Greenpoint, when it came to me I had to get out of the scene. Matt was dishing over his Guinness about who'd been sleeping with whom (small gossip in the vet writer community), speculating as to whether or not a writer we knew worked for the CIA, and complaining about how some of the younger vet writers seemed merely ambitious, merely hungry for fame, and seemed not to care about literary craft or the truth of experience. Matt, a waggish, pallid Irishman with perpetually uncombed black hair, had recently been interviewed in his Brooklyn apartment by CBS. They'd knocked on his door after the fall of Fallujah and wanted him to tell them what it meant. Did it change how you thought about our sacrifice? Had our soldiers died in vain?

We'd been at Pete's for an event I had organized, the fourth annual "Bringing the War to Brooklyn" reading. The first time, we'd done it just to give ourselves a chance to read. Since then, I'd worked to find fresh voices. Our reading that night had featured a young poet from New Jersey, a former marine named Johnson Wiley; an MFA fiction student at Columbia who also happened to be a West Point grad with six years in the army, Ravi Venkataramani; and a female National Guard captain, journalist, and blogger, Kristen

Rouse. We'd filled the room with fellow veteran writers and friends, including a literature professor from West Point who blogs about contemporary war lit, an anthropologist at the New School who works on resilience and PTSD, and Meehan Crist, a science writer. The reading had gone well, response was good, and everybody had a fine time. After the event, several of us hung around drinking, trading stories, then brainstorming strategies on how I should handle going back to Baghdad. Matt thought I definitely needed to bring a handgun. I wasn't so sure. Meehan seemed delighted by the conversation: while the streets outside were thick with ice-crusted snow, here we were huddled in a hipster bar arguing about whether or not I needed to pack heat in Iraq.

It was only later, after everyone had left Matt and me to our cups, that the evening took on a sour taste. I had never wanted to be a professional veteran. I had wanted to use my experience, certainly, turn my war into a kind of cultural capital, an investment in my writing career just as the GI Bill was an investment in my education. If I had a special experience, a unique point of view, then people would listen. Some writers get their break because they were drug addicts or because their mom died of cancer. Publishing is a bleak, degrading hustle, like most hustles in this economy, and you sell the story you have. So okay, I'd hustle, flipping the "authenticity" of my war for a chance to keep writing. And it worked. I published an anthology. I did a book tour. I was on *Fresh Air* with Terry Gross.

But it wasn't all just hustle. In the early days, when there were only a few of us, it felt like we were genuinely exploring new territory. Iraq and Afghanistan were different from the Persian Gulf War, Vietnam, and World War II, and it was up to us to see how, to understand in what ways the *experience* differed, to figure out how the world had changed and, in changing, had changed us. As well, we happy few—at least those I knew and talked with—operated under a trust that we would keep each other honest. Our time overseas and in the military was still raw. Even as we were pulled by the expectations of civilian readers toward satisfying lies and drawn by the influences of literary convention toward familiar fables, we could check each other and remind each other of the ways our experiences had belied those expectations and conventions. Finally, there was a profound shared desire for knowledge, maybe even wisdom. We wanted to *make sense* of our experience. We wanted to understand. Sure, we were ambitious. Of course we wanted to succeed. But the conditions for success weren't just worldly acclaim and a publishing contract: we wanted to learn something about what our experience was, how the world worked, and who we were.

All that was gone now. The focus shifted over time from trying to plumb the depths of experience to something else: trying to convey something to audiences, trying to relate something you knew to something they knew, trying to make a connection. As we'd gone on, we'd created our own set of conventions and expectations, shorthand tropes and easy frames that dulled questions and blurred complexity, because that's what's necessary for translating lived reality into language other people can comprehend. What I realized talking with Matt in Pete's Candy Store, over my last beer of the night, was that I had long ago stopped learning anything new about my war. I had gone from being someone who asked what it meant to being someone who explained what it was like.

The truth is, I'd always been ambivalent about being a veteran. On the one hand, I was proud of my service. I'd done something difficult that few Americans show the courage or wherewithal to do, and I'd come out stronger for it. My year in Iraq with the First Armored Division was spent mainly on two kinds of missions: For the first six months of our tour, in 2003, we picked up artillery rounds all over Baghdad. We kept Iraqi kids from blowing themselves up and denied insurgents weapons. For the next six months, I drove a Humvee around a Sunni neighborhood in south Baghdad called Dora, and then down the highway from Baghdad to Karbala and Najaf, looking for roadside bombs and snipers.

On the other hand, the war was the most dehumanizing experience of my life. Inside the wire, we lived like prisoners, staring at the same walls and the same faces, lifting weights, watching DVDs, killing time until we got to go back home. Outside the wire, we moved in an alien, hostile world luminous with adrenaline and danger. Over time, as we were shot at, mortared, and sometimes blown up, fear and rage built up in us like toxins, until we were praying for reasons to shoot—but not people, mind you, just fucking hadjis. We harassed and intimidated hadjis on the street. We humiliated hadjis in their homes. We ran hadji cars off the road when they got in our way. We locked hadjis up for being in the wrong place at the wrong time. Some of us did worse. Some of us did a lot worse.

Meanwhile, the war itself never made any sense. Like many veterans, when it came to my role, I relied on a rhetoric of professionalism and camaraderie and a narrow focus on personal experience to help me ignore heavy questions about the US invasion and occupation of Iraq. Later, I let the relative peace following America's 2011 withdrawal confirm the official narrative: we had made mistakes, but the surge had worked, and we'd left Iraq a functioning democracy. I had my doubts, but it was a story I wanted to believe. Over time, I took up a mantra of comforting phrases that numbed those doubts and fuzzed out my connection to the big picture:

"I'm proud of my service, but it's complicated."

"I did the best I could in a bad situation."

"The war was fucked, but I did my job."

After Fallujah fell, though, I found myself beginning to think that either we *hadn't*, in fact, done our job, or that the job we'd *actually* been sent to do was so reprehensible that even if we were successful, there was no way I'd want to claim it. What if the US military hadn't been sent to Iraq to create a democracy, stabilize a failed state, or even establish a bastion of secular capitalism in the Middle East, as

we'd been repeatedly told, but rather to oversee the sectarian parti-
tion of a sovereign nation, install a weak authoritarian ruler whose
regime would be justified by carefully stage-managed elections, and
turn Iraq into a cockpit for regional sectarian and political blood-
letting? What if the main US interest wasn't regional stability but
rather regional instability, with just enough infrastructure in place
to keep oil flowing out and American-made weapons flowing in?
This was undoubtedly what US policy had accomplished, through
countless deliberate decisions over many years, and what if it hadn't
been a mistake—what if it had been intended?

I couldn't ask Ambassador Beecroft to verify an American policy
of divide and rule, but I decided I could ask him to square America's
promise of democracy in Iraq with what looked like its support for
a developing autocracy. Nouri al-Maliki had been picked by US
Ambassador Zalmay Khalilzad to succeed elected Prime Minister
Ibrahim al-Jaafari in 2006, after Khalilzad had orchestrated Jaafari's
ouster. Then, in 2010, Maliki lost the election to Ayad Allawi, but,
with US support and the threat of violence, managed to hang on to
power. Over the years since, Maliki had worked to bring the organs
of state power under his direct control. Now, he controlled the most
important ministries, the judiciary, the military, and the police.
He ignored parliament when it went against him. He tortured and
assassinated his rivals. He had banned Al Jazeera and the Iraqi TV
station Baghdadiya from broadcasting or reporting in Baghdad.
He ruled over one of the most corrupt governments in the world
and had been manipulating the conditions for the current election
for months. The Supreme Court, alleged to be acting at his behest,
struck down a law passed by parliament that would have limited
the prime minister to two terms. The Independent High Electoral
Commission (IHEC)—the supposedly independent body that man-
ages and monitors elections in Iraq—was widely held to be staffed
by Maliki loyalists and showed its colors by disqualifying numerous
opposition candidates because of alleged Baathist connections.

Another win for Maliki seemed like a defeat for real democracy in Iraq. Was *this* what we had fought for?

"I have what may seem like an unfair question," I said to the Ambassador. "It seems like the best-case scenario is a peaceful transition to a new, democratically elected government. If that *doesn't* happen, what does that mean for the legacy of the American intervention and occupation of Iraq?"

Reporting the conversation that followed is difficult, since the conditions for the briefing were that it was "deep background," not for attribution, quoting, or paraphrase, and the embassy press attaché, Donald Maynard, declined to approve any of the quotations I sent him. Thus I'm limited to describing what other people said and the general outlines of the conversation.

At first, the conversation focused on the credibility of the upcoming elections, then began to move around the question of whether or not the previous Iraqi national election, in 2010, had been fair and credible. I suggested that it wasn't. There was some lively back and forth, and the conversation stalled in a difference of interpretation.

What happened with the 2010 elections was this. As the votes came in, showing that Ayad Allawi's secular, multisectarian Iraqiyya coalition had won a slight majority over Maliki's State of Law coalition, ninety-one seats to eighty-nine, Maliki launched three challenges to the election results. The first was to demand a recount, backed up by the veiled threat of military force. On March 21, the day before the final election results were confirmed, Maliki held a press conference and made his position clear: "I demand, in my capacity as the direct executive authority responsible for the formulation and implementation of state policy and in my capacity as commander in chief of the armed forces, that the Independent High Electoral Commission respond immediately to the demands of these blocs to safeguard political stability and prevent security from deteriorating and violence from increasing."

Reminding people of his role as commander in chief of the armed forces in this context was taken as a veiled military threat. Maliki's second challenge was to lean on the Iraqi judiciary to disqualify winning Iraqiyya candidates because of alleged Baathist ties. The third challenge also involved the judiciary, and especially Supreme Court Chief Justice Medhat al-Mahmoud: Maliki asked for a ruling from the court on Article 76 of the Iraqi Constitution.

The article reads: "The President of the Republic shall charge the nominee of the largest Council of Representatives bloc with the formation of the Council of Ministers within fifteen days from the date of the election of the President of the Republic." As written, it is straightforward: the nominee of the winning bloc forms the government. Maliki saw a loophole, however, and had his office ask the Supreme Court whether "largest bloc" meant the coalition that won the most seats in the election, or the coalition that put together the most seats *after* the election. Maliki's office made their request on March 21, the same day he threatened military force to ensure a recount; the Supreme Court took four days to decide that Article 76 meant the largest bloc *either* before *or* after the election. In their book *Cobra II: The Inside Story of the Invasion and Occupation of Iraq*, Michael Gordon and General Bernard Trainor write, "The ruling appeared to be a blatant reinterpretation of the framers' intent."

Having gotten his recount, disqualified fifty-two candidates from other parties because of "Baathist ties," and succeeded in revising the Iraqi constitution so as to make an electoral majority essentially irrelevant, Maliki then merged his State of Law party with other Shiite groups to form the National Alliance coalition, which commanded 159 out of 325 seats, shutting out Iraqiyya and taking the right to form the next government.

Meanwhile, the Obama administration stood by watching—with upwards of fifty thousand US troops still on the ground. The official line was that it was an Iraqi election and an Iraqi process.

The Americans were deeply involved in the process of forming a government, however, through a shady series of backroom deals that took almost nine months. Against the opposition of the Kurds, Sunni politicians, Shiites in ISCI, and even CENTCOM commander General Jim Mattis, Vice President Joe Biden and newly appointed Ambassador James Jeffrey pushed through a Maliki government, in part through soliciting various promises from Maliki that, after he took power, fell to ashes. But there's more: the real story behind Maliki's 2010 win wasn't just about how the US worked to engineer his victory in the face of widespread opposition, but also about how Iran brokered a deal between Maliki and Muqtada al-Sadr to secure Sadrist support for State of Law. The real story, that is, was how the US and Iran worked together to ensure the continued rule of a sectarian autocrat.

When I asked Ambassador Beecroft more specifically about this problem and the disturbing parallels between Saddam's brutal regime and Maliki's increasingly repressive and violent rule, the conversation grew very lively. The journalists got involved, especially Ned, Prashant, and Jane, and a distinct gap opened up between what Iraq looked like from inside the Green Zone and what it looked like from outside. Ned, Prashant, and Jane had all talked to Iraqis who saw parallels between Maliki's presidency and Saddam's dictatorship, and even more emphatically, had talked to many Iraqis who thought their lives had been better and safer under Saddam's regime than they were now. Working to clarify their positions in what had become an energetic exchange, Ned, Prashant, and Jane tried to make it clear that *they* weren't asserting such parallels between Maliki and Saddam, but merely saying that they had talked to thoughtful, educated, intelligent Iraqis who did so. In the end, no agreement in perception could be reached.

I was left to wonder, over the rest of the afternoon, whether the problem of perception I'd seen at the embassy was intentional or circumstantial. Sometimes we see things a certain way because we don't know better; other times we assert a specific vision of the world because it serves us. I was impressed and fascinated by the lack of official interest in what Jane, Ned, and Prashant had been saying. As I was to discover myself, many people in Iraq saw their lives as being worse today than they had been under Saddam, less stable, more threatened, less free. You would think the US Embassy would want to hear about that perspective. That the ambassador seemed not only uninterested in the truth but outright hostile to it was striking. The situation brought to mind a quote attributed to Karl Rove, which seemed, looking back, as prescient as it was arrogant: "We're an empire now, and when we act, we create our own reality. And while you're studying that reality—judiciously, as you will—we'll act again, creating other new realities, which you can study too, and that's how things will sort out. We're history's actors . . . and you, all of you, will be left to just study what we do."

Ten years ago, I'd been among history's actors, a bit role but nonetheless on the stage, a minor piece in a great game. And I'd spent the decade since then studying, trying to make sense of what I'd seen and done. Making sense meant more than just under-standing, though; making sense also meant explaining what had happened in a way that fit with the kind of life I wanted to lead and the kinds of people I wanted to be around.

Over time, three main narratives had developed in American culture through which most veterans explained their experience of war in Iraq and Afghanistan: pride, trauma, or "it's complicated." All three were undergirded by an ideology of professionalism, in which the defining feature of military service was having "done your job," which, as an article of faith, was detached from any serious political consideration by others of what that job was or what it meant in a wider context. In a way, this was a positive turn away from the Vietnam era, when draftees were sometimes identified with a war they'd been forced to fight and held responsible for political and strategic decisions made in Washington or Saigon. On the other hand, the focus on professionalism that divided the war from the warrior suggested a political compartmentalization by which Americans could disavow democratic responsibility for the actions of our government overseas. If the American army is seen as a citizen army, then even an all-volunteer force represents, symbolically, the American public. To detach military service from the ends to which it is put, to "hate the war but love the warrior," as some would have it, is to disconnect the American people, represented by the citizen army, from the government that acts in its name.

One of the reasons I joined the army in the first place was to bridge that disconnect, to put myself physically at the service of the United States government, and to see what the "global war on terror" and the "new American century" actually meant in concrete terms. And something similar had driven me back to Baghdad now, as a journalist, to observe but also to participate—to insert myself back into history. Perhaps I wasn't so different from the ambassador, in a certain way, in shaping reality to match my perception; since I was part of reality, and part of history now, as a veteran, putting myself out in front meant changing the very situation I was trying to understand. I attracted stares, attention, interest. I was, in fact, despite what I'd first thought, a target. People could die because they talked to me.

I thought about those possibilities as I sat over sweet tea that afternoon talking with Naseer Hassan, a fifty-two-year-old Iraqi poet, about life under Saddam, which topic included Hassan's 1979 arrest by the government and the state executions of his Communist uncles—and also the books of poetry he'd written, Hamlet, existentialist philosophy, and the virtue of hopelessness. Naseer was a translator of Arthur Schopenhauer, Emily Dickinson, and Jorge Luis Borges, a radio host at Radio Free Iraq, and a loyal Maliki supporter. He was a lively, egotistical soul, a convivial conversationalist, and something of a Shiite chauvinist. For Naseer, nothing could match the brutal repression of the Saddam years, and if the present-day security situation was untenable, what Iraq needed was a strong leader like Maliki to clamp down.

Naseer sat rumpled and twisted in his chair, in constant back pain, leaning and swooping over his tea to emphasize a point or suggest a philosophical *mise en abyme*. He saw the American occupation as a "necessary surgery, but a very bad, bloody surgery. The patient has been left bleeding for years . . ." He jabbed at the table. "But that doesn't change the essential fact that America replaced a dictatorship with a democracy . . . Of course, there are those peace activists who think every anti-American thing is right and every pro-American thing is wrong. They look for anti-American sentiment wherever they can, decrying the human cost, smooth killers decrying the occupation, this detail or that detail, like Abu Ghraib. But you know what I call them? Peace statues, not peace activists: stiff, ideal, lifeless, glorious. They're happy when a car bomb goes off in the market and kills a dozen people, because it makes a point that America's bad."

He had been ecstatic in 2003, he'd wanted to dance naked in the streets, but ever since that day in Firdos Square when Saddam's statue fell, he had watched his hopes wither. "I'd had hope for a new era, but now, I see it's just the same battle from birth to death. After 2003, Saddam was gone, but his remnants and orphans ruined everything after. Now there's ISIS, these terrorists—it's the same battle, with no triumph. The happiness of freedom and democracy was stolen from us. I wondered sometimes, can history be that cruel? But history has no conscience. If you're still alive, that's just because its foot hasn't stepped on you yet."

I asked him if he still had any hope at all for Iraq, and he leaned in, as if to explain a great secret: "Hopelessness is the limit and beginning of a new kind of hope. You have to keep going: not to achieve dreams of beautiful mountaintop forests, but because life is more powerful than death. Hopelessness makes possible a new hope that is more modest, a faith in the basic tissue of life that is stronger than any disaster. This is how humanity survives. This is the strength that keeps us going."

As Naseer talked about hopelessness, I thought about my upcoming meeting with Meethaq and Ali at the Mansour Mall, which I was putting off, letting my talk with Naseer go long. My surety that I was going to die, coming at the level of gut fatalism, was stronger than any skepticism, stronger than any faith in the basic tissue of life, but weaker than my shame: when Aziz, my translator, came in to remind me a third time that we needed to go, I couldn't put it off any longer. I shook Naseer's hand, telling him with rather more force than I intended that I hoped I would see him again.

As we headed for the mall, I asked Aziz and Ahmed to stay alert. I hadn't been able to properly explain my fear to them, but I thought maybe they would spot something before I did. There was always a chance. I tried to feel sharp, ready, like a survivor, but instead felt fated and numb. The image of the Asaib Ahl al-Haq campaign rally explosion kept cycling through my mind—a blast of orange light, dust, and blood. My dread deepened, minute by minute, as we passed through the crowded streets of Mansour.

3.

Three days later, the streets were empty and silent. The vibrant crowds of shoppers that thronged Mansour were gone. Stores and restaurants stood shuttered. You could almost hear the heat baking off the concrete and reflecting back into the clear blue sky. Somewhere a voice shouted, "Hey, Ameriki!" I didn't look back.

I followed Aziz across the road, headed for a gaggle of soldiers and police who were, that day, the public face of Baghdad. I showed them my IHEC badge, they patted us down, and then one of them led us toward the school that was being used as a polling center. More soldiers stopped us at the entrance. A police captain came out to greet us. He began asking some questions, then a tense exchange broke out. On the one side stood the tall captain in his black fatigues, pistol on his hip, Iraqi Federal Police eagle on his chest, backed by a half dozen surly men in blue and gray camouflage, with armored vests and Kalashnikovs, while on the other stood Aziz, my translator, a fifty-four year-old former diplomat who had worked as an interpreter for Lieutenant Colonel Ralph Kauzlarich, commander of 2-16 Infantry, during the surge. Aziz was my slouching Virgil, in a purple-and-mauve-striped polo shirt tucked fastidiously into stonewash jeans, with thinning hair and a chronic smoker's cough. He stood facing the soldiers like a bent stick planted in the sand against the tide. I heard Aziz say *"Rolling Stone"* and *"sahafi Ameriki"*—American journalist—and saw the captain get a funny look on his face. A quick back-and-forth broke out, capped by Aziz saying *"La. La. La."*—No. No. No.

His face was grim, but then, Aziz rarely smiled. Like almost every Iraqi I met, his life story was a transcript of disaster, suffering, and crushed hopes. He had worked for Saddam's regime for decades, through the Iran-Iraq War, the Persian Gulf War, and the embargo years, but in 2000, fearing for his life, he'd fled to Lebanon. When he returned to Iraq three years later, after the American invasion, his daughter asked her mother, "Who is this man?" During the occupation, he had a successful career as an interpreter, first with a private security firm, then with the US Army, and then worked as a stringer for the *Washington Post*. After his daughters were injured in a car-bomb attack near his apartment in the Karrada, he decided to apply to come to the US, through the International Organization for Migration Iraq mission. Iraqis who worked with Americans during the occupation have two main routes to the US, the Special Immigrant Visa (SIV) program through the US Embassy, and the International Organization for Migration (IOM), an NGO that works to resettle Iraqi refugees internationally. Aziz chose IOM, because it made more sense for his family, and applied in 2010, but his IOM application was rejected only months later. "They gave me no reason, no justification," he told me. "Just rejected." When I asked him if he'd appealed the rejection, he told me that David Finkel, who knew him from his time with 2-16, had hired a lawyer to work the case but that now, three years later, he wasn't optimistic.

The captain said something, almost grinning, and the conversation went back and forth again between him and Aziz before seeming to founder. The soldiers watched me expectantly. The captain stepped back and gestured into the school. "You are American?" he asked. "*Nam*," I said, "*Aana sahafa Ameriki.*"

"You are welcome," he said, waving toward the door, eyes flashing. A soldier inside smiled.

I looked to Aziz, whose eyes were watching his feet. He moved slightly away from the door, into the shade, and nodded at the space next to him. "Come wait over here," he said.

It's one thing to be traveling in a country where you don't understand the language, customs, and culture. To be a stranger in a strange land can be as exciting as it is exhausting, as ecstatic as it is alienating. It's something else entirely to be somewhere that can turn evil in a heartbeat—where a clear path can grow suddenly precipitous, overshadowed by cryptic threats, unstable in its footing.

I had to trust Aziz. I didn't have any choice. I stood with him by the wall. The captain said something sharp, he and Aziz had another back and forth, then Aziz said, "C'mon, let's go."

"What happened there?" I asked him as we walked quickly back toward Ahmed's white Kia. "What was that?"

He lit a cigarette. "Those guys are a bunch of fucking assholes."

It wasn't the first time we'd gotten static at a polling center. Election day had begun for us in Sadr City, the Shiite ghetto on the north side of Baghdad that had been a dangerous, restive neighborhood even under Saddam. For the entire eight years of the American occupation, the neighborhood had remained beyond the military's control. At the height of the surge, in 2007 and 2008, JSOC (Joint

Special Operations Command) commandos and Iraqi special forces made almost nightly raids there, but General Petraeus's "clear, hold, build" counterinsurgency never got more than a couple blocks in. As the name Sadr City suggests, the neighborhood was a stronghold for the cleric Muqtada al-Sadr and his Jaish al-Mahdi—a fact in evidence as soon as we turned off the Canal Expressway (Omar bin Al Khattab Street) and were greeted by giant orange banners emblazoned with al-Sadr's face.

Security at the edges of Sadr City would turn out to be some of the most intense we would see all day. There was a vehicle ban in place throughout Baghdad, except for government vehicles and registered observers like ourselves, and the usual gauntlet of checkpoints had been reinforced by military hardware and extra troops. Sadr City was something else entirely. In addition to the standard tan Humvees and blue-and-white APCs (armored personnel carriers) belonging to the Federal Police, black-masked Iraqi Special Operations Forces (ISOF) storm troopers manned the checkpoints, supported by giant black SWAT MRAPs (mine-resistant ambush-protected vehicles).

While the Iraqi Army was a bit of a joke, these guys were something else. The Iraqi military had ballooned during the occupation—the army Paul Bremer disbanded in 2004 comprised a mere four hundred thousand men, while Maliki's present-day security force, including the army, federal police, and other units, numbered somewhere between eight hundred thousand and a million. Many of these were paper soldiers, no more than names on forms, and most of the rest were the hypertrophied bloat of a militarized oil state: poorly trained schmucks pulling perpetual guard duty at government offices, public parks, mosques, political party offices, and the hundreds of traffic checkpoints around Baghdad, in what was one of the most reliable forms of gainful employment, while their less well-connected peers were out in Diyala and Anbar, defending the approaches to Baghdad against ISIS, getting ambushed and blown up by IEDs. Within the Federal Police and the regular army, though, and also set off outside, was another group of operators: well-trained, well-supplied elite fighters. The most notorious of these groups were the SWAT teams and the Counter-Terrorism Bureau's various ISOF units, which reported directly to Maliki. On the street, they cut fearsome figures: uniformed in black armor and fatigues, festooned with weaponry and tech, their helmets decorated with Punisher skulls, their faces hidden by Wiley-X ballistic goggles and fang-embossed black masks, they moved with the assurance of easy violence. As a former soldier, someone who got used to being surrounded by burly dudes with assault rifles, who was himself for a time one of those dudes, I can tell you: these were some serious motherfuckers.

They had bigger prey to track than an American journalist, though, so after giving us the stinkeye, they let us through. We drove deep into Sadr City, rolling down side streets looking for a polling center, finally leaving Ahmed and the Kia behind to walk alleys, searching for the Sector 13 polling station.

Throughout my entire tour in Baghdad, I'd driven through Sadr City one time. There was a period of two weeks in the summer of 2003 when my unit was clearing an ammo cache to the northwest of the neighborhood, and our route from Camp Dragoon in Baladiyat to the cache took us along the edges of the neighborhood twice a day. We took the route fast, blasting through traffic at fifty miles an hour, practically daring Iraqi cars to get in our way. It was on this route that we'd had an accident between two of our trucks that gave Corporal Fisher whiplash. It was also on this route that one of our lieutenants started shooting into a crowd because he thought he saw someone with a gun. One day, we drove through the neighborhood on recon, looking for an ammo cache. We didn't find the cache, and we didn't linger.

I never went on a foot patrol. My unit was field artillery and we did everything mounted: I drove Humvees all over Baghdad, and outside the wire, I was never more than twenty feet from my truck. Now, walking through an alley in Sadr City with no more armament than a camera and a notebook, with no more backup than a middle-aged Iraqi in a polo shirt, seemed like a surreal inversion of reality—my own private Bizarro Baghdad. Every vestigial sense of wartime boundaries from ten years ago flashed red, screaming "You shouldn't be here."

Aziz led me down a dirt alley, past poor Iraqis whose stares flickered between gawkery and bitterness, and as we rounded a corner, a young Iraqi came up to me grabbing at my hand and saying "*Sabah hel hyeer*," pulling me toward him into the usual greeting between friendly Iraqi men, kissing each other on the cheek, which I did. Then he asked me for my ID.

I reached for my passport and IHEC card, but Aziz told me not to, then the guy said something else and grabbed my head, pulling me toward him again. "Come here," Aziz said, heading back to the last checkpoint. I pushed Grabby back and broke away, following Aziz, and once we got back past the checkpoint our new friend fell behind, held up by the police. Aziz explained that the guy was just mental.

The hostility came later, from the IHEC staff. The soldiers at the gate checked our IDs and let us in, then brought us through a courtyard to the local commander, a major in the Federal Police. He was sitting in a small room with his shoes off, watching TV while on the phone to his girlfriend. When our escort handed him our IDs, he took them with barely a glance and held them for the several minutes he took to finish his phone call. When he finally turned his attention to us, he didn't get up or put his shoes on, but sat contemplating us with bored irritation.

He asked us what we were doing here and who had told us we were authorized to come here. When Aziz explained that we were journalists authorized by the Independent High Electoral Commission to cover the elections, including interviewing people at polling centers, the major cut him off. "I don't give a shit what IHEC says. I'll decide whether or not you talk to anybody here." Then he asked Aziz what outlet I was with and what kind of story was I doing. Aziz explained that I was an American journalist doing a feature story about life in Baghdad today, and especially about the election. They talked back and forth a bit; then the major decided to escort us in. "No photos," he said.

The major put on his shoes and heaved himself up, threw on some sunglasses, and lumbered out of his cave, snapping for a soldier to follow. We followed too, and he took us out through the courtyard and around to the polling center. Hangdog residents of Sadr City passed in and out as if ashamed. The major took us to the door of an office and went in, closing the door behind him. When the major opened the door again, a young woman in an ornate but demure ochre-colored scarf and robe, her eyes hidden behind massive silver aviator lenses, stood in the center of the room scowling at us. After a brief back and forth between Aziz and the major, Aziz explained to me that this young woman was the local IHEC representative, and that she wasn't going to talk to me. At all. And she wasn't going to allow us to see the polls.

"But we can still talk to people, right?" I asked.

"Sure, okay," Aziz said, and we went out away from the office and stood in the path of the voters coming into and leaving the polls. The major and his soldier stood next to us, and an IHEC monitor hung back near the office, watching. We tried to talk to a few people as they passed, a family, an old man, a woman in an abaya, but everyone took one look at the major, then shook their heads and walked on. Finally, a hardy looking laborer with a proud face stopped and agreed to talk to us. Rahim Ahmed was his name, and he ignored the looks the major was giving as he told me about his hopes for the election.

"We're looking for change," he said. "To change the faces in power. Two elections have gone by, and they haven't done anything

for the people. We want to see new faces." He told me his most
important concerns were security and services, and that things were
so bad now that life was worse than it had been under Saddam.
"Life used to be better," he said, "and we need the new government
to serve Iraqis, not just talk." When I asked him if he thought that
would happen—if he thought Maliki would lose the election—he
shrugged, then nodded. "I can't say for sure. Maybe. Maybe when
one of the Grand Ayatollahs speaks, asks the people to make a
change—then the answer is yes. But if we want all of Iraq to change,
we only need twenty or thirty percent of the seats: that will do
something. That will achieve something."

I was so involved in my conversation with Rahim, following
his body language and Aziz's translations while scribbling down
notes and trying to think of the next question, that I didn't notice
two more soldiers and three IHEC staff surrounding us. One of the
IHEC guys interrupted Aziz, shouting at him, and another IHEC guy
started shouting too. Aziz argued back, then two more IHEC guys got
involved. Things got loud, and one of the IHEC guys grabbed Aziz
by the arm and started pulling him toward the office. Aziz stood his
ground. The IHEC personnel said we weren't allowed to interview
people; Aziz asserted that we were international journalists accred-
ited by IHEC to cover the elections, and that we were following all of
IHEC's guidelines. As the guy tugged again at Aziz's arm, I readied
myself to do something physical, not knowing what, if anything,
would be needed or prudent. The IHEC volunteer told us we had
to come with him, or else. Then Aziz broke away from the IHEC
volunteer's grip and walked off.

"We need to go now," he said to me, and I followed him out.

So much for a transparent election.

———

There were actually two elections. The first had been held on
Monday, the "private election" for security forces. They had been

given their own voting day because they would be so busy enforcing the vehicular ban and guarding poll centers that they wouldn't have a chance to vote during regular hours on Wednesday. This seemed a reasonable solution to a potentially serious problem, and a good way to make sure that all eight hundred thousand–plus state security personnel got to vote, even the ones who existed only on paper. As we drove around the city on Monday, we saw trucks full of police and soldiers speed screaming through the streets, the men waving their guns in the air like bandits.

"They will vote," Ahmed muttered.

The way voting worked was that you went to the polling center with your voter ID card, collected your paper ballot, put your ID card into a card-reading machine, let the machine take your digital fingerprint and read the UPC box on your ballot, had an IHEC staff member cross-check your name on a paper list of registered voters, went behind a cardboard shield to mark your ballot, then folded up the ballot and put it in a sealed plastic box. At that point, you dipped your finger in a bottle of purple ink and returned to life proud at having participated in the sacred ritual of democratic self-determination.

An interesting rumor I'd heard, from a young Sunni engineering student, was that many soldiers and police had two separate voting cards, one for each election. Aziz had heard the same thing himself and told me he personally knew a police officer who had two cards and planned to vote twice and might be willing to talk to me after the election. I was fascinated and infuriated by the rumor, puzzled that I hadn't seen anything about it in the Western media, and curious whether or not it was actually true. Even if only half the military and police voted twice, that would still be four or five hundred thousand votes—which, since most (though not all) police and military supported Maliki, could make a significant difference. With around twenty million registered voters, an extra four hundred thousand votes for State of Law might seal the election.

As we went from polling center to polling center, I asked each IHEC spokesperson who would talk to me about the double-card problem and what IHEC was doing about it. All of them admitted that double cards had been issued, and all of them assured me that IHEC knew about the problem and had solved it. One IHEC rep, in the Karrada, told me that only 21,000 doubles had been issued, and that 19,000 had been withdrawn, so the 2,000 remaining cards wouldn't have a significant impact even if they were used—but, he told me, if somebody did try to use one, the card reader would reject it, since the cards would both have the same information and the reader would know that the person had already voted. The IHEC rep we talked to in Sadr City (at the second polling place we visited there) told me the same. Another, in Zayouna, told me that IHEC had a list of the people who'd received duplicate cards, and that they'd sent letters to them demanding that they turn the duplicates in. All of the voters with duplicate cards were then required to bring a letter that they were supposed to have gotten after they turned in their duplicate cards, without which they wouldn't be allowed to vote. If they didn't have their letter, they wouldn't be allowed to vote. The IHEC rep at the second polling station we visited in Mansour told me that the duplicates had already been collected, but that if somebody did try to vote twice, the IHEC staff would know because of the ink on their finger. I asked him if they had a list of the names of duplicate card holders, and he told me no. I asked him if the machine would read duplicates, and he said probably, yes, but that it didn't matter because of the ink. The IHEC rep at the third polling station in Mansour also told me that the duplicate cards had already been withdrawn, and that IHEC policy was to fine anyone who voted twice.

During the election and just after, I talked to four different police officers about the duplicate-card problem. Two said they had dupli-cate cards; two said they themselves didn't, but they knew lots of others who did. One policeman I talked to on Tuesday told me he'd already voted Monday and planned to vote again on Wednesday, both times for Maliki. The other police officer, who I talked to on Thursday, after the election, told me he voted both days, both times for Maliki. Then he showed me his cards: one for the private election, one for the public. I asked him about the ink; he showed me his finger, which looked clean. "You just dip the tip of your finger in, then you wash it off. No problem." I asked him about the machines—did he encounter any issues with the card readers? No, he told me, no problems at all, then he pointed out that his cards were identical except for one minor difference: his grandfather's name on one card started with a "da," on the other card with a "ra." I asked him if he'd received any kind of letter requiring that he turn in his card, or if he'd had to take a letter with him to the poll center, and he shook his head and laughed. No. Nothing like it.

What happened, he told me, was that a bunch of officers in his unit had received duplicate cards, and on the day of the public election they were given a couple hours off to go vote again. They went home, changed into civilian clothes, voted, changed back into uniforms, and went back to work. He told me that he personally saw forty or fifty people he knew voting twice, and that he'd heard of many more. I asked him if he had been told whom to vote for or if he'd been paid extra to vote twice. "Nobody told me how to vote," he said, "but most police and military follow Maliki. Maybe one thousand out of every hundred." About the extra pay, he denied that he'd been paid extra during the voting period, but said that the army had been. Other police had said the same, and Aziz told me that he'd overheard some soldiers talking about how nice it was to be getting paid extra. This was consonant with other rumors that Maliki was buying votes all over Iraq, promising people land and cash in exchange for support.

There were also rumors of a widespread trade in voting cards, but the problems with the election weren't limited to extra cards and vote buying. Many people claimed not to have gotten voting cards at all, and some reports suggested that IHEC failed to distribute cards to more than two million registered voters. Moreover, the voting machines themselves were subject to mechanical failure. One IHEC representative I talked to told me that they'd been having trouble with the machines whenever they were plugged in, but when they left them unplugged (the machine runs on an internal recharge-able battery), they were fine. Another representative told me that the machines malfunctioned when they got too hot—which, given temperatures in Baghdad, was fairly often. The level of compe-tence shown by IHEC representatives varied widely from station to station. One representative in Mansour didn't seem to know how many registered voters there were in his district, and when I suggested that the number he first told me seemed low, he revised his estimate upward by 150 percent. Allegations of electoral fraud, obstruction, and malfeasance from journalists, bloggers, and oppo-sition candidates were common, including reports from *Asharq Al-Awsat*, *Niqash*, Ned Parker and Ahmed Rasheed at Reuters, Struan Stevenson at *The Hill*, Middle East Monitor, and Al Jazeera.

Perhaps most troubling of all was the limited access granted the media and the paucity of international observers. We visited nine polling stations that day, in five different neighborhoods, and saw a strong media presence at only one—a high-profile center in wealthy Karrada. Except for Karrada, we saw one other journalist all day, a newspaper reporter, in Zayouna. And while every polling center had at least a few internal observers from various political parties monitoring the voting, we saw not a single international observer all day long. Not one. Of the nine polling stations we visited, we'd been forced out of one (in Sadr City) and weren't allowed to enter two (in Mansour and Karrada). Two other polling stations let us come in but refused to let us take pictures, then pressured us to leave (in Mansour and Saydiya). Given that Baghdad had just over two hundred polling centers, meaning we barely saw 5 percent, it would be injudicious to conclude from this small sample that nobody was really watching the elections or that IHEC was actively suppressing media coverage. That was just my experience. I know there were international reporters out there. I talked to them later. I know Iraqi TV and journalists had cameras at predetermined, officially approved sites. I saw the news. I also know that outside of the officially scripted, managed box, IHEC was sometimes obstructionist, occasionally secretive, and largely unwatched as it went about managing Iraq's first free postoccupation elections.

———

Some voters were restrained and noncommittal, nervous about talking to me, and apt to speak in TV-echoing sound bites about the need for security, safety, and stability. Others were more forthcoming. Overall, the impression I got throughout the day was that Baghdadis were tired of politics as usual, anxious about the security situation, and committed to change. What change meant, however, depended on their perspective. For some people, it meant getting rid of Maliki and his Dawa cronies. For one police officer in Sadr City, it meant clearing out the obstructionists in the parliament he saw constraining Maliki's ability to get things done. For most, the constant refrain was "*tahrir*"—liberation, freedom, relief, salvation. They'd had enough corruption, violence, and suffering; they wanted a change for the better. At the same time, most people expected that Maliki would stay in power. Some avidly desired it.

Hassan Ali Asim, a police officer in Sadr City, thought Maliki was the only candidate strong enough to beat ISIS and keep the country safe. Asim had been wounded by a roadside bomb during the civil war, on June 24, 2006, and hated to see the country being torn apart again by sectarian violence. If Iraq could achieve stability, he was sure it could be as peaceful and prosperous as any of its neighbors. "We want our country to be like other countries, like Jordan. Look how stable and comfortable it is there. I'm not talking about America—America is a great nation. I'm talking about our neighbors. Honestly, I wish America had stayed. Not in the city, too many people had problems with them there, but on their bases and on the borders. They would have helped us with stability."

Amaya Faleh, a housewife in Sadr City, was vehement about the need for a new government and the importance of deeds over talk. She was also proud of how many women were active in Iraqi politics. "It's a good thing. Iraqi women need to vote. We're not illiterate. We're not ignorant. We are Iraq." She was appalled by recent attempts in parliament to pass a new Ja'fari law regulating female behavior, legalizing child marriage, and allowing religious courts to take precedence over civil courts on domestic family issues. "This is awful. It's not right at all."

Jodet Marja Jodet, a fifty-six-year-old veterinarian, thought the most important thing was to get past the sectarian violence still bleeding Iraq dry. "We need a strong government that can control the militias," he told me. "Over politics, over infrastructure, even over poverty, the most important thing is to end the sectarian fighting. It has taken too many innocent souls."

Haider Hassan, twenty-eight years old, had brought the problem of sectarian violence home with him. Aziz spotted him before I did: a young man in shorts, flip-flops, and a camouflage T-shirt, limping down the hallway of the grade school polling center on Al-Falah Street in Sadr City. I would have missed him among the bustling voters, but when Aziz pointed him out to me, I immediately saw why. Bandages on the young man's head covered a recent wound, and bloodstains on his T-shirt suggested something more serious than an accident around the house. He was beautiful, too, with the kind of piercing, unrelenting gaze you see in mystics, sociopaths, and traumatized soldiers.

It turned out he was among the latter. He'd been in the Iraqi Army four months—barely out of basic training. Not even a week ago, his unit had been on foot patrol in a suburb west of Baghdad when a roadside IED went off. ISIS forces opened fire from the surrounding houses and date groves, then retreated. Haider had been wounded in his head, leg, and torso, but survived and was evacuated. He was now recovering and had struggled out of bed to vote. He considered it his patriotic duty, just as he considered his military service a duty. "People should be volunteering to protect our country," he told me. "It's our responsibility."

Haider expressed some of the usual desires Baghdadis expressed for security and stability. But as he went on, he waxed passionate: "We want to be like before. When we had pride. We don't want other countries interfering in Iraq, like Qatar and Saudi Arabia. We want to be our own people." For Haider, change meant a strong military and strong borders. As I watched him limp away, I wondered what he would have said if I'd told him I'd been an American soldier. In 2003, he would have been seventeen. His entire adult life had been lived under an occupation, and now he was fighting a battle America had helped to create. We'd promised him democracy, but what we gave him was a life at war.

———

As the afternoon passed, I began to feel the need to go somewhere dangerous. Nothing had blown up all day, and with the heavy security presence on the streets, I figured even a bad neighborhood would be manageable—or at least more manageable than it would be normally. I'd gotten a tingle in Sadr City, a sweet taste of old danger, and I wanted to try my luck one last time. Aziz and Ahmed suggested we head back to the hotel, then go to the central polling station in the Karrada. I suggested instead Baladiyat, Ghaziliyah, or Dora, in response to which Aziz and Ahmed were silent. I waited, then Aziz told me he didn't think we'd be able to get into Dora. He might have been right; we'd had trouble getting in before. A sometimes-rough Sunni neighborhood with a bloody history, the police were fond of shutting down its checkpoints in and out.

"What about Saydiya?" I asked, naming a neighborhood near Dora that was widely considered the most volatile area in Baghdad. It had been the scene of vicious fighting during the civil war, and unlike most other neighborhoods, it had remained mixed Sunni and Shia. Saydiya could turn nasty in a heartbeat.

Ahmed smiled. "You don't go to Saydiya."

"It's election day. They're voting too."

"We can't get in there," Aziz told me.

"Well, why don't we go see. If we get in, we'll hit a polling center, then call it a day."

"My family lives there," Aziz said, "and my cousin is in the police. Even he tells me not to come to Saydiya."

"We'll just check it out," I insisted.

We didn't have any problems getting in. And although there was a palpable anxiety coming off Ahmed and Aziz, the neighborhood didn't look any worse than anywhere else we'd gone. It wasn't as poor as Sadr City or Baladiyat, and it was mostly empty, like everywhere, because of the vehicle ban. It was coming on to the hot part of the afternoon, when most people went home to rest, so there were even fewer voters on the street than we'd seen earlier. Trash blew across vacant streets; I half expected Ennio Morricone music to start playing.

"Here is your Saydiya," Ahmed said, as I snapped some pictures with my phone. A teenager on the corner, one foot on a soccer ball, glared as we went by.

It didn't take us long to find a polling center. Ahmed parked on the street, while Aziz and I went through the outer checkpoint. While the police were checking our IDs, a six-truck convoy of machine-gun-mounted pickups roared by, each one filled with black-masked ISOF. They didn't give us any trouble at the checkpoint, nor at the entrance to the school, where, as a security precaution, they collected voters' cell phones.

One of the guards brought us into the school and took us to

the principal's office to meet the security detachment commander. He was coolly friendly and completely professional, asking me a few questions in superb English. He looked at my ID and passport, writing my name into a log book. "Is this your first time to Baghdad?" he asked me.

"Yes." I lied.

"And how do you find it?"

"Complicated. The people are very friendly. Of course it depends on the neighborhood."

He smiled. "Yes. And you are with a newspaper?"

"A magazine, *Rolling Stone*."

"And what kind of magazine is this *Rolling Stone*?"

"It mainly covers music and popular culture, but it also does long stories on politics, international events, different things."

"Yes. Well, you are most welcome to Iraq. You will not take any pictures here."

I thanked him, then went out to meet the IHEC representative. He was a short, stern man, with a closed face. With exceedingly efficient movements and remarks, he guided us through the entire center, showing us each polling station and giving us the most up-to-date numbers for voter turnout. His answers to my questions were polite but curt. They'd had a few minor problems with the machines, which they'd resolved. They'd found forty-four duplicate cards in their district, which had been withdrawn. Security was good. Voter turnout was good. When I asked him if any other media had visited this polling station, he told me that the media were prohibited from coming here, but they'd made an exception for me. I asked him if we could talk to some people, and he considered it for a moment, then agreed.

He stationed us in the main hall, near the exit. Traffic in the poll center was light—few voters were coming in, and those who did looked distracted and glum. They avoided looking at me, and avoided the IHEC rep as well, keeping their eyes down and scuttling through the hall as if they wanted to disappear. The reek of fear in the polling center was so thick you could taste it: an acrid tang in the back of your throat, bitter as myrrh. Aziz watched his feet. The few people that the IHEC rep approached shook their heads vigorously no, then sped away.

At last, the IHEC rep stopped a middle-aged man walking by who agreed to talk to me, though his eyes bulged in fear. His name was Ahmed Abdul-Rajid. He was a sixty-one-year-old professor of English, and although he spoke to me in that language, he communicated only terror. His answers pinched out of his mouth as if he hoped each one would end the interview; each word he spoke made it clear he wanted nothing to do with me and wished I would leave him alone. He grinned as he talked, but it was a rictus of desperation. The IHEC rep stood beside us, staring into the distance but noting every word that was said.

When I asked Dr. Abdul-Rajid what his hopes were for the election, his answer was "For the good." When I asked him what he meant by "good," he told me "Security, safety, and stability," the same mantra I'd been hearing all day. I asked him if there were any other issues that were important to him in the election, and he said "No, mostly security, safety, and stability." Did he have any worries about the election? "No, none." Did he think Maliki was going to win a third term? "Nobody knows. It depends on the results." What did he think would happen if Maliki won a third term? "I hope for the good." What did he mean by that? "Mostly security, safety, and stability." Was he positive about Iraq's future? "Definitely."

When I thanked him, Dr. Abdul-Rajid nodded with obvious relief, glanced at the IHEC rep, then fled. The interview left me with a bad taste in my mouth, but I pushed on, trying to talk to more people as the IHEC rep shepherded us toward the exit. Nobody else would speak with me. On the way out, though, the IHEC rep introduced me to a soldier manning the exit. Jasim Mohammed Alwan, a sergeant major in the Federal Police with ten years in service, looked capable, intelligent, and young for his responsibilities. He stood at parade rest, with his hands clasped behind his back, and answered my questions crisply, directly. The IHEC rep stood at his elbow, but the young sergeant major ignored him.

His responsibilities included managing two ballot centers in Saydiya, and he told me that everything was going fine. There hadn't been any security problems all day. Asked about his hopes for the election, he told me he was hoping for change—I heard the word *tahrir* again—along with an increase in security and stability. "What kind of change?" I asked, and he told me that he wanted to see a change in government. "People are looking for something better. Somebody needs to fix what has been destroyed, take care of the people who just suffer now."

The IHEC rep stepped between us, ending the interview. He said something to Aziz and then something else to the sergeant major, who turned on his heel and walked off. The IHEC rep turned a grim smile toward me. Aziz said mildly, "We should go now."

4.

Back in the war, I'd dreamed of Mutanabbi Street. I'd heard it was a place they sold books, a famous street market where intellectuals gathered and talked about ideas. I fantasized sometimes about going there on my own, sneaking off the FOB somehow, hiring an orange-and-white Iraqi cab to take me. I could switch into the one set of civilian clothes I'd brought with me, leave my rifle, leave my boots. I'd still look unmistakably American, of course, and I couldn't read or speak any Arabic, but at least I'd be able to *feel* what it was like, be able to see and hear real Iraqis and authentic Baghdad culture. Not the pidgin we talked with Iraqi soldiers on gate guard, not the guarded, pro-American talk we got from our terps, but the real literary, philosophical, and political pulse of a city with traditions going back thousands of years. *Civilization* had been invented here. They'd invented *writing* and *math*. Iraq was the birthplace and motherland of Western culture, older than the Romans, older than the Greeks, as old as the Egyptians and even more important, and in my dream you could brush up against that living history on the street, there on Mutanabbi.

I had naively supposed that, after the US won the war in 2003, things would settle down and we'd start rebuilding. Combat missions would transition to stability-and-support operations, and we would move out into the communities. The US occupations in Germany, Japan, and Korea were the most prominent examples I had of how it might have worked, but the more recent American military intervention in the Balkans seemed a plausible model as well. These operations were all within living memory and continued to have material, concrete historical existence. My unit, First Armored Division, was stationed in Germany, as American units had been since 1945. American units trained with German units. American bases hired German workers. American soldiers dated German girls. The Balkans were different, but when we deployed, to Iraq a few of our Humvees still had KFOR (Kosovo Force) painted on the side, and old sergeants liked to tell us stories of their misadventures there. I imagined something like that would happen in Baghdad. We would *meet people*. We would *mingle*.

In the very early days, I even fantasized about going to Ur or Babylon to see ziggurats and ruins; visiting a mosque; eating kebab, mezze, and flatbread with locals; maybe going to the National Museum. Of course none of that ever happened. Stability-and-support operations were sidelined in favor of force protection, which meant pulling security on isolated American bases and letting looters plunder the country's infrastructure and heritage.

Our life settled into a strange, sequestered version of garrison existence, on bases initially primitive but increasingly Americanized.

Burger King was the first franchise to arrive at BIAP, and American fast food soon became a staple of our diet. There were some efforts at integration: vendors were allowed to open shops selling knickknacks and rugs, and some FOBs contracted with Iraqis to run laundromats, shawarma restaurants, and cafés instead of the American companies and third-country nationals de rigueur on the larger bases. Despite these minor efforts, the basic conditions of the occupation were segregation and mutual distrust.

For my unit, as for most Americans in Iraq, you only ever went off post on mission, with at least two trucks and eight soldiers, loaded for bear and ready to fight. Until Petraeus took over in 2007 and implemented his counterinsurgency doctrine, pushing units out into small neighborhood posts, American policy was defensive, centralized, and isolationist. According to General John Abizaid's "antibody theory," which guided policy before 2007, the more our soldiers interacted with Iraqis, the more we'd be attacked. That may have been true, in a crude statistical sense, but it created a situation that allowed racism and suspicion to flourish, making it easy for Iraqis to see Americans as distant, alien occupiers, and for Americans to view Iraqis as backward, hostile primitives.

Officially, Iraqis were "local nationals." Mostly we called them hadjis. The word is a term of respect in the Muslim world; it's a title signifying that its bearer has completed the hadj, the pilgrimage to Mecca. We didn't mean it like that. We meant it more like Hadji from the 1960s Hanna-Barbera cartoon *Johnny Quest*, Johnny's turbaned brown Hindi sidekick. It wasn't quite as derogatory as some of the things soldiers called Iraqis. At its very best, it was merely patronizing.

Over and over during my tour, I dreamed of crossing the wire. I hated seeing myself reduce human beings to caricatures and threat assessments, as I did every day, and I wanted to have a human encounter with the people whose nation we'd invaded, occupied, and upended. I was also driven by curiosity, a sense of adventure, and a desire for a richer cultural palette than FOB life offered.

Mutanabbi Street came to represent for me not just the storied Iraqi culture with which we weren't engaging and of which we were almost entirely ignorant, but literary and intellectual culture itself: the resilience of humanistic inquiry and debate in even the most inhospitable conditions. I imagined seeing it, feeling it around me, connecting in even some small way with this manifestation of the human spirit. I carried that dream for years, out of time and out of place, always thinking of it as a symbol of a history that should have been.

———

Two days after the election, security was still tight, but everyone was in a festive mood. There was a certain giddiness in the air, too, connected to a sense of having escaped a baleful fate: everyone had thought that the election would be wracked with violence, and while there had been a few minor attacks outside the city and in the north, Baghdad had been serene. Now Mutanabbi Street was packed with readers, book buyers, kids, and journalists, out as if on holiday.

Aziz guided me down the street, pointing out the spot where a car bomb had gone off in 2007 and killed twenty-six people. The physical scars of the bombing were barely visible; among the milling shoppers, you could almost believe that someday even the memory would fade. Today the street thrived. Old books and new books, hardbound and paperback, books in Arabic and English and French and Chinese, romance novels and Korans and *Mein Kampf* and programming manuals and dusty issues of *National Geographic* lay in mosaics on the sidewalks and stacked the shelves of tiny shops back off the street. The Abbasid poet Abu at-Tayyib Ahmad bin al-Husayn al-Mutanabbi, whose majestic bronze figure overlooks the Tigris at the end of street, once bragged that his poetry was so beautiful that it was heard even by the deaf and read even by the blind; just so, the street that bore his name would have broken through any resistance with its cheerful vitality. Juice sellers stalked the crowd in yellow bibs, ringing brass saucers to attract attention. Old friends, tufts of white hair ringing bald heads, stood drinking at tea carts, smoking and arguing about the election. Oud and lute music wove through the chatter, and a singer's voice keened over our heads like a scarlet ribbon. In a courtyard off the street, poets versified, their voices thrown by Pignose amps. And although the crowds in the street were overwhelmingly male, some women browsed too, some in hijab, some not. Aziz ran into a friend of his, an Iraqi newspaperman. I ran into the Colombian TV crew who were staying at my hotel. And while I took everything in, I kept an eye out for some of the people I'd talked to earlier whom I expected to see there, like Soheil Najm, a poet and translator, and Hanaa Edwar, head of the leading Iraqi NGO for human rights and women's issues, Iraqi Al-Amal.

I had spoken with Hanaa Edwar in her home office the morning after the election. Her living room was warm and welcoming, decorated by her many awards for humanitarian activism, and her three white dogs barked and nipped and cowered like fluffy courtiers. With her steely, short-cut hair and forthright gaze, Edwar sat on her sofa like a baroness, regal and determined. She had been fighting for a better world since her student days in the 1960s, when she joined the General Students Union, the Communist Party, and the Iraqi Women's League. After earning a law degree at Baghdad University, she had been nominated in 1972 to represent the Iraqi Women's League at the Secretariat of Women International Democratic Federation in East Berlin, and lived there for ten years before returning to Iraq—not to Baghdad, however, or to her native Basra, but to Kurdistan, where she joined the Communist partisan resistance against Saddam. She lived there for three years, until Saddam Hussein's use of chemical weapons against the Kurds in 1988 forced her to flee to Damascus, where she founded Iraqi Al-Amal (Iraqi

Hope). In 1996 she returned to Kurdistan, and finally came home to Baghdad after the American invasion in 2003.

Despite her lifelong resistance to Saddam's tyranny and her tireless efforts to bring modern, cosmopolitan values to Iraq, Edwar saw the American invasion as a disaster for the Iraqi people. In Edwar's view, the United States' interest in toppling Saddam was political, military, and economic, and had nothing to do with avowed commitments to human rights or democracy. From the beginning, United States policy worked to divide Iraq, founding the national government on a sectarian-ethnic quota system from the Iraqi Governing Council (IGC) onward.

"This was the wrong basis. No democracy can be built on religious or sectarian difference. And as we have seen, the system in Iraq is very weak because of this. It has produced crisis after crisis without any solution, and increased conflicts between the Iraqi people. It's not just elements from outside, like al Qaeda, but it's spread through the whole of Iraqi society . . ." Edwar frowned and shook her head. "It was a big mistake for Americans to support religious parties, like Maliki's Dawa. There was an opportunity to break this kind of rule in 2003, but I believe there was always an intention to keep Iraq weak, make Iraq a weak state, so there's no chance for solid change for development, no chance for real democracy. I can say now, after ten years, that we are not living in a state. We are living in a non-state. There is no rule of law, no real institutions, impunity for the militias, rule of tribes and religions over the rule of law, and pervasive corruption. This was another thing the Americans did—the American money lost in Iraq, still missing, and where did it go?"

What I'd seen myself seemed to bear out her judgment. Things were better now in Baghdad than they had been in 2004, economically, but the lack of political stability was heartbreaking. In 2004, Iraq was nearly at its nadir. It had suffered under ten years of American sanctions and sporadic bombing that had crippled its economy, caused the deaths of tens of thousands of infants, led to starvation and malnutrition for millions of children, and given birth to a violent criminal underclass of gangsters and black-market smugglers. Then Iraq had been hit by a "shock and awe" bombing campaign designed to demolish critical dual-use infrastructure like the electrical grid, water treatment systems, and communications networks. The invasion that followed the bombing was relatively restrained, compared to what it could have been, but the peace that followed the invasion was more destructive and violent than anyone could have imagined. Paul Bremer disbanded the Iraqi Army, sending four hundred thousand armed men out onto the streets, while General Tommy Franks ordered American soldiers to stay on their bases and ignore the looting and chaos that swept the country like wildfire.

My first weeks in Iraq were spent at an old ammo depot tucked away on farmland between the airport and the village of Abu Ghraib. Every night the skies sang with fire and the stars were laced with gleaming streaks of magnesium scarlet and barium green. Explosions lit the horizon in dull mahogany flashes. We huddled behind the wire, protecting the thousands of Iraqi Army artillery rounds, rockets, and grenades cached in the bunkers at our depot, watching for thieves, shooting wild dogs, and staging gladiatorial battles between scorpions and camel spiders. I had thought then that the storm of violence blowing around our tiny, beleaguered island was the natural aftereffect of war. In fact, as I learned later, the catastrophe that destroyed Iraqi civil society was an effect of American policy, a policy consonant with American practices in the Middle East and elsewhere: a political and cultural adaptation of radical economic liberalization (Milton Friedman's "shock policy").

When I left Iraq in 2004, things had calmed slightly from the postinvasion chaos, but it would have been difficult to say things had improved. Fallujah had become a battleground, Muqtada

al-Sadr's Jaish al-Mahdi was in open revolt, and the electricity
was still on for only a few hours a day. The streets were lined with
garbage and flooded with raw sewage. The American military
controlled its bases and its transportation routes, but little else.
Meanwhile, as Iraqis turned to neighborhood religious authorities
for security and gangs took to the streets, the sectarian conflict
that would explode into civil war with the Samarra mosque
bombing of 2006 was already simmering. I was happy to get out.
I never expected to go back.

Now, ten years later, there was more electricity. The power still
failed several times a day, but the outages usually only lasted a few
minutes. There were new shops. There was more money around.
There were police in Baghdad now, everywhere, and an army. Things
were better—except for the daily threat of car bombs. Except for
ISIS. Except for the civil war that had erupted again in Anbar and
Diyala. Except for the widespread poverty outside the capital, the
broken schools, the increasing illiteracy, and the increasing influence
of religious extremists. Except for the increasingly authoritarian
rule of Nouri al-Maliki, who jailed and assassinated opposition
leaders, attacked dissidents, and gave a long leash to proxy militias
like Asaib Ahl al-Haq.

Yes, there was an election. But as Hanaa Edwar told me, "Democracy is not only elections, not just voting. Democracy is about
building civil institutions, transparency, accountability, the separa-
tion of powers, the peaceful transfer of power. We don't have any of
that. We don't have the rule of law. Instead, everything is in ruins.
Baghdad is in ruins. My hometown, Basra, is in ruins. They don't
have clean drinking water. I was shocked. Shocked . . . And now,
again, we see Daesh or al Qaeda in Anbar and the north, and they're
moving toward Baghdad. They're in the suburbs, in Abu Ghraib.
So what kind of state is this, that was built and is still supported by
America? What were the intentions? What is behind it? To divide
this country into three states, like Biden said in 2007? . . . You lost

five thousand soldiers to bloodshed in Iraq, and spent so much money, and to what purpose? To create a sectarian state?"

Despite her grim analysis of the political situation, Hanaa Edwar would not stop fighting. Even though international NGOs and the Western media lost interest in Iraq after 2011, especially after the Arab spring, Edwar still worked to connect with organizations and activists outside Iraq. Even though Maliki had tried to dissolve Al-Amal and had used police, government regulations, and proxies to threaten and attack journalists, arrest protestors, and undermine activists, Edwar continued to speak out publicly against what she saw as a new dictatorship. Even though conservative and extremist religious forces were turning Iraq into an Islamic republic, she continued to work for women's rights, secular government, and freedom of speech.

Hanaa Edwar was a physical embodiment of the spirit of Mutanabbi Street. So, in another way, was Ali Adad, the friend of Meethaq Waleed's who I'd been convinced was going to blow me up at the Mansour Mall. In the end, we never made it to the Mansour Mall, because it had been closed in advance of the election. And Ali hadn't tried to kill me. We'd had coffee on the top floor of a nearby Maximall, and as far as I could tell, Ali wasn't a member of ISIS, but an intelligent, highly motivated, proud young man who had worked his way up from humble origins into the Foreign Service Institute, where he now studied with Meethaq.

One of the first things Ali had told me after introducing himself and showing me some pictures from his seven and a half years working as an interpreter with the US Army was that he was a man of literature and a poet. Later, he showed me some of his work, darkly passionate poems in English, influenced by the British Graveyard Poets, such as Edward Young and Thomas Gray, touched by notes of Blake, Whitman, and Donne. His writing showed a masterful command of rhythm and idiom, and a sophisticated sense of rhyme, playing with internal assonance and slant rhyme in complex ways. He told me that what he really wanted was to be a university professor, but that he had entered Foreign Service school in the hopes of securing a career that would let him take care of his family while doing something valuable for his country. Although he saw a difficult road ahead for Iraq, estimating that it would take decades for the country to recover from the bloodshed and trauma of the American invasion and the sectarian civil war it had unleashed, he was committed to making things better.

Ali had come to the US in 2012 on a Special Immigrant Visa, bringing his wife with him, but after three months, he and his wife decided to return to Iraq. He had been working on an assembly line at Hewlett Packard, earning minimum wage, and when his wife got pregnant, they both questioned whether or not they wanted to raise their child in the US.

"She said, I want to go back, I don't want to give birth here," he told me. "And I said, that was just on the tip of my tongue. I would rather have my baby here than there. I don't want him to feel different. Because it's different there. It's hard. I wouldn't say it's easy here, but I would say it's better . . . I asked myself hundreds of times, what am I doing here, what was my purpose, why had God created me to be here, on that spot of the earth? And for the record, I'm very patriotic. I am a patriot. I love this country. I hope when the end comes, I would die and be buried in this country. So I asked myself many times, what is my being, why am I being created and why here . . . I wanted my son to be born here, to feel what I have felt. But I don't want him to go through all the difficulties that I have gone through, because I have seen many difficulties. Here, I can make a difference."

Making a difference and helping people were, according to Ali, two of the main reasons he had started working with the Americans in 2003. Nineteen years old then, Ali had learned his English from movies and music videos. He started talking to American soldiers in his neighborhood on Haifa Street, telling them where to find hidden caches of munitions, then helping them hand out medicine and first aid to people in the area. With his last year of high school interrupted by the invasion, and as the only child of a single mother, Ali didn't have much to tie him down, and the tall, powerful American soldiers who had so easily conquered Saddam must have filled some need in Ali for a surrogate father, as his own father had disappeared when he was four years old.

He took a few months to finish high school in 2004, then started working for the army in August. Over the next seven years, he worked with combat units on patrol, Rangers, the Coalition Provisional Authority, military transition teams and police transition teams, and liaison officers. He was as proud of his time in the field as a "combat interpreter" as he was of his work in Baghdad with senior staff and Iraqi Army generals. While with Bravo 2-15 FA in 2004 and 2005, pulling patrols in the suburbs west of Baghdad, he collected sixty pieces of shrapnel from IEDs his patrols had encountered. He saw one of his units completely replaced, when the first sergeant and commanding officer of the unit he'd been assigned to were found selling confiscated weapons on the black market and running whorehouses in collaboration with local Iraqi Army units.

Ali had been a trusted and valued part of the American occupation. Along the way, he married, divorced, married again, and managed to complete a bachelor's degree in English Language and Literature at Mustansiriya University. All while his country was wracked by war.

Ali told me he admired Ralph Waldo Emerson, and in many ways he seemed an exemplar of Emersonian self-reliance. He'd been a soldier and a scholar, and was now training to be a diplomat, having pulled himself up from the streets. He was independent, high-minded, earnest, proud, and thoughtful. I realized that part of what had disturbed me with Meethaq was just this quality of earnest idealism that the two men shared. On the one hand, I had gotten so used to the cynicism infecting American society, I didn't know what to make of these young men who showed no trace of it; on the other, I'd expected Iraqis to be uniformly pessimistic and bitter. Meethaq and Ali had been through dark times, but they weren't embittered; they saw the troubles they had faced as challenges they had overcome. As Meethaq told me, quoting a French proverb, "Difficult times make strong men."

I asked Ali what he thought of working with the American army, and he gave me a complex, thoughtful reply. It was clear that the experience, over seven and a half years, was one of the defining aspects of his life. Yet at the same time, he had taken a certain philosophical distance on it and measured out both the good and the bad.

"Generally, the army is a society. Just like any other organization. It's an organization that's governed by rules, that has a lot of discipline, but sometimes rules can be obstacles. Sometimes rules are broken. Sometimes justice is lost in the rules. That's the way I see it. My overall assessment of the army is that it has something to offer, other than advantages and privileges on the social level. It has something spiritual to offer. You have the core values, you have the discipline, you have the mind-set that you learn. That will get you somewhere. For me personally, it helped defining my skills . . . I find all kinds of people in there. People from the ghettos. Crackheads. They have some crackheads in the army. They do. They have some people that inhale the aerosol cans, just to get high. I mean, c'mon, that'll give you cancer. Why would you do that? They have some pretty good examples and some pretty bad examples . . . I was in a long time and took a lot of it . . . Being in the army is hard. When you work for the army, it's even harder. When you don't have the privileges and the advantages they have, it's even harder. There were some times when we suffered a lot. But if you can take it, you will come out with something. It's not wealth, but it's an intellectual gain."

After a long conversation at the Maximall, we had arranged to meet again after the election, on Mutanabbi Street. Aziz and I found Ali and Meethaq eating lunch at a shawarma place, and I was unexpectedly happy to see them. When they were done eating, we walked around the Ottoman Kishle, looked at Baghdad's oldest clock, and listened to some poets read, then met up with some friends of theirs. We all took a boat ride on the Tigris. They joked among themselves and took goofy pictures. Ali explained to me the different varieties of traditional Iraqi musical instruments, then the different kinds of traditional Iraqi boats. I reached into the Tigris and felt the water flow over my hand, watched it split and come back together, while the boat puttered in a slow circle. I felt for a moment like I was anywhere. I felt for a moment like a tourist, among friends.

Remembering my panic and suspicion Saturday night and Sunday, I felt guilty, even ashamed. How could I ever tell them I'd thought they were going to kill me? That I'd assumed—that I'd believed, ardently, for a whole day, that they were both ISIS terrorists? The gratitude I felt toward them for having given me this moment of tranquility in a place I had for ten years associated with terror and violence was complicated, through my suspicion, by a feeling of deceit. I would never be able to discharge the debt I'd incurred by doubting their trust. I'd never be free of the guilt I felt for having assumed these men were terrorists.

When we said goodbye, I gave Ali some books of poetry I'd brought from the US and told him and Meethaq that I hoped to see them again, although I wasn't sure if I'd have time. Already, the profound expanse of days that had opened at the beginning of my trip was closing in as my flight home rushed inevitably nearer. Every connection was already diverging. Soon I would leave again, and Baghdad would go on, and what would happen in the years before my next return, if I ever came back at all? I could see nothing good in Baghdad's future except its people, and they would go on living and suffering as they had before.

Over the next few days, I talked to many people who had suffered deeply during the occupation, but few of them directly at the hands of American soldiers. Despite our bombing, invasion, torture, and heavy-handed occupation, the American army didn't commit the worst acts of violence that went on during those years. What the US did was to foster the conditions that allowed horrific things to happen, allow those things to go on unchecked for years, and support the people who committed them. Then we left.

The policeman I'd talked to who'd shown me his duplicate voter ID cards told me he'd lost twenty-three family members in the sectarian civil war. "Iraq has lost a son a day since the US came," he said and assured me that things had been better under Saddam. Much better. "With Saddam, if you try to touch his chair, he'll attack you. Otherwise he'll leave you alone." Now all his hopes lay with Maliki, whom he saw as the only leader in Iraq strong enough to beat ISIS and end the sectarian violence.

A spice-shop proprietor named Sedrad, in Baghdad's busy Shorja market, told me how his father had been martyred during the civil war, and showed me a picture he'd hung in his stall of his nephew, Ahmed Sadr, killed six weeks ago by a VBIED. "We lost this one, but we're going to keep the rest," he said. "It didn't use to be like this. We didn't know what sect our neighbor belonged to. We didn't care. I'm a Shiia, my friend Othman is a Sunni, and when I was sick, he carried me to the hospital on his back. There was no difference. We're brothers. Now, if you're not safe, you can't work on the street. You have to expect a knife in your back—like Ahmed, when they blew up his store."

When I met Raad al-Azzur, I knew nothing about him except that he drove a van for St. George's Church in Mansour. I offered to go to his church to meet him, but it was easier for him to come to me. I received him in the ostentatiously modern lobby of the Coral Boutique Hotel, whose plate-glass windows overlooking Jadriya Street seemed to invite VBIEDs, and asked the Turkish-vested and pantalooned bellboy to bring us some tea from the dining room. Bland Western classical oozed in the background. Raad was a dour, middle-aged man with a limp, in cheap but clean clothes.

He was out of place at this hotel catering to high-rolling Iraqis and foreign money, but I tried to make him comfortable. Seated on giant striped sofas, with an American cop show blazing behind us on an enormous HD TV, I began to ask him the basic introductory questions I normally started with—where he was from, his age, what he did, and so on.

"Did you know my son was killed?" he interrupted.

I didn't. Raad began to explain, then reached into his pocket to pull out a small cloth bag. From the bag he withdrew two plastic-coated photographs. Each showed one of his children lying in a pool of blood, shot in the head. The boy, Aziz, was four and a half. The girl, Ranin, fifteen.

It had happened just over ten years ago. Men with guns forced their way into his house one night, threatened him and his wife, then shot their two children. The men didn't say who they were or why they came, except that they were "supporters of Islam." Raad didn't know why he was targeted. It may have been because for a month or so that winter, he'd helped a friend sell liquor. It may have been because he was Christian.

Over the years, eleven members of his family had been murdered, and he'd heard of more among his congregation. His cousin in Mosul had recently been killed—a stranger knocked on his door, asked him his name, then put a pistol in his mouth and shot him. Many others had been kidnapped or threatened with letters or text messages. There were almost no Christians left in Baghdad, he told me. Most of the ones who hadn't been killed had fled.

After his children were murdered, Raad had tried to escape, too, taking his three remaining children and going to Jordan. He applied to the UN for refugee status, but they rejected him. He tried again in Syria and was again rejected. So he came back to Baghdad, to the same house in which his children had been killed, where he lives today.

He worked for a time in the Ministry of Displaced People and

Immigration, under a Christian supervisor, but he was fired after his supervisor was replaced by a Muslim. Then he got a job at the Baghdad Provincial Council, but he was fired there too when they found out he was Christian. He lived now on the little money he earned driving a van for the church and a disability stipend he got from the government: he pulled up his pantleg to show me the artificial limb he'd been given to replace the leg that had been blown off in Iraq's war with Iran.

"Life was better under Saddam," he told me. "Nobody attacked Christians then. When somebody did, Saddam's police would find the killer and punish them. Now, you can see, ten years and I'm still looking. When they cut the power under Saddam, you knew when and how long. Now, you never know. In the old days, people did their work and handed out rations because they were afraid of what would happen if they didn't. Now, nobody does anything, and the corruption is so bad you don't get anything . . . Nothing is going to change now. The faces you see in the election are the same faces that came in on the American tanks."

I looked at the pictures on the table. Here, I thought, were images that would connect with readers, images that could make the suffering real. Yet what could these pictures of pictures do that hundreds of pictures over eleven years hadn't? Images of suffering, sorrow, and grief inspired pity for the world's down-trodden, but almost never engaged real sympathy. How could they? How could a photograph communicate the empty heaviness a man like Raad carried with him, coming home every day to the same rooms in which his children had been murdered, knowing that there was no one who could help him, looking ahead to a future without hope, a future always shattering in the echo of remembered gunshots? I could show you a picture, or a picture of a picture, but the picture can't show you the ghosts that haunt people's lives, the memories of sudden violence, the abysses hiding behind desperate efforts at normality. Maybe you can imagine living in a war for a day, a week, or even a year. Maybe you're sympathetic and brave and willing to take the trouble. Now imagine that war goes on your whole life.

I asked him if I could take pictures of the pictures of his dead children. It seemed necessary but inadequate, and when he agreed I felt like a vulture. I had to keep retaking the pictures again and again from different angles, shifting the photos around the table. My reflection kept getting in the way.

————

The dream I had of Mutanabbi Street was a dream that life could win out over death, as the poet Naseer had said a few days ago: a faith that the tissue of existence was stronger than the ravages of imperial politics or religious violence. I wanted to believe it was true, and I wanted to believe that even in the darkest days, some flame flickered. Before coming to Baghdad, I had been lucky enough to meet Hassan Blasim, an Iraqi writer whose short-story collection, *The Corpse Exhibition*, took the perverse cruelty of thirty years of war and tyranny and turned it into art. The collection's title story is about just what it says, a corpse exhibition by an artist who sculpts death, murdering people and arranging their bodies in grotesquely aestheticized positions. Blasim's work isn't the kind of redemptive bullshit you often get when people "turn suffering into art." His stories are as cruel as the cruelty they portray, and they redeem no one and nothing. Yet somehow, even though his work offered no redemption, the mere fact of its existence, the fact that the human imagination had transformed horror into something beautiful was some kind of testament to the human spirit. Blasim's work isn't redemptive but rather tragic, and like the best tragedy, affirms life even at its most awful.

But Blasim had escaped. He lived in Finland now. There were artists, writers, and poets who hadn't, still living in Baghdad, still writing and working. Indeed, while I was there, the Iraqi novelist

Ahmed Saadawi won the 2014 International Prize for Arabic Fiction for his gothic novel of wartime life, *Frankenstein in Baghdad*. The novel's plot is a metaphor for artistic life in Iraq today: a scavenger named Hadi begins to collect pieces from the unidentified corpses of bomb victims, stitching them together into one body so that they could be properly buried. Before he has a chance to bury the monstrosity, however, it comes to life, and begins a rampage of vengeance, hunting down the killers who had murdered the various people its body was now composed of.

Another artist I met, a playwright and sculptor named Sarem Dakhel Ahmad, who had spent seven long years in the Iraqi Army during the Iran-Iraq War and the Persian Gulf War, thought of his art not as cruelty but as catharsis. "The curse of war has polluted my life . . . but after getting out of the army, I started making art as a way to purge the pollution. I think of my art as a practice of purification." Under Saddam's regime, he had been investigated for staging Samuel Beckett's *Waiting for Godot*, and had had a play of his own, *The Night of Murder*, banned. After the fall of the regime, he was threatened by religious extremists. One day he received an envelope with a note and a bullet. The note read: "Stop making sculpture." He kept on making art, though he did take advantage of a fellowship offered by a Russian art institute to spend some time outside the country. The fellowship had been awarded because of a series of sculptures he'd made using American shell brass. After the invasion (in which the Americans had accidentally bombed his house), Ahmad began collecting spent American brass wherever he could find it. He melted the brass down and shaped it into several stark, Giacometti-like sculptures: a man and a woman on a boat, a three-headed minotaur figure, two women lifting a body overhead.

For all the stories of individual artists struggling to show an affirming flame, like Saadawi or Ahmad, there were as many stories of flames being choked out and smothered by religious fundamentalism. Haider Hashim, owner of the Akkad Art Gallery in the Karrada, told me how the art scene in Baghdad had been all but obliterated by the war, and that now, neglected by a government focused only on weapons and oil and under attack from religious zealots, it was breathing its last gasp. In 2002, Haider told me, there had been more than fifty art galleries in Baghdad. Today, his was one of two.

Ahmed Farouk Lafta, who under the name J-Fire was one of the most celebrated contemporary musicians on the Baghdad scene, used to perform rap and nü-metal, inspired by bands such as Linkin Park, P.O.D., Limp Bizkit, and Korn. When Islamic extremists threatened to kill him if he kept on using Western styles, he switched over to more anodyne Middle Eastern pop. The Baghdad music scene itself now existed almost entirely online: people were afraid concerts and dance clubs would attract bombs, and xenophobic religious conservatives opposed any youth culture that swerved from traditional lines—which meant anything that's not Islamic, Arab, and segregated by sex.

Meanwhile, in Baghdad's universities, departments were rife with sectarianism and corruption was eating away at educational and scholarly standards. I talked to professors and students at Baghdad University, Mustansiriya University, and the Academy of Fine Arts, and the system was failing everywhere. Students bought their way into college, then bought their way through it. Religious and sectarian pressures were forcing academic committees to limit what professors could teach and sometimes even intervene directly in professor's courses. Nadia Faydh, a professor of English language and literature who quoted Matthew Arnold's "Dover Beach" to me to describe the current situation in Iraq ("And we are here as on a darkling plain / Swept with confused alarms of struggle and flight, / Where ignorant armies clash by night"), was banned from including Marxist literary criticism on her syllabus, and chastised by her department chair for "causing trouble" by teaching Percy

Bysshe Shelley's "A Defense of Poetry," a canonical text of English Romanticism. Students had been offended by Shelley's equation of love and poetry with religion, as when he writes:

"Love became a religion, the idols of whose worship were ever present. It was as if the statues of Apollo and the Muses had been endowed with life and motion, and had walked forth among their worshippers; so that Earth became peopled with the inhabitants of a diviner world. The familiar appearance and proceedings of life became wonderful and heavenly, and a paradise was created as out of the wrecks of Eden."

The dream I'd had of Mutanabbi Street wasn't just about cultural tourism, escaping the spartan constraints of military life, or even connecting with Iraqis. The dream I'd had was about finding common ground in a cosmopolitan humanist vision of intellectual freedom, self-development, learning, and collective cultural exchange. But such exchange depends on a free and open culture, and on engagement that goes deeper than military occupation and political manipulation.

I had visited Mutanabbi Street, as I had dreamed of doing for so many years. I talked to poets, artists, musicians, teachers, students, and philosophers. I walked among the people as they voted. I searched for every hopeful flame I could. But the spirit I found in Baghdad was broken, corrupted, or threatened where it wasn't already dead—and we had caused the damage. We had let loose a grisly pandemonium in Iraq, then walked away and tried to wash our hands of the whole affair.

5.

We blasted along the Tigris, Nicki Minaj ripping out of the speakers over a furious woofer bump, Duraid's Dodge Charger slipping through the traffic on Abu Nuwas Street like a hammerhead through a school of clownfish. The Karkh blazed and streaked across the gleaming black water, streetlights turning the faces of drinkers on the Jadriya Bridge a dull, efflorescent bronze. Duraid slowed to pass an Iraqi police Humvee, then gunned it down a side street, as kids and wary fathers watched us roar through the night. The city slowed around us, blurring into abstractions, statues, swaths of color.

It was my last night in Baghdad. Earlier in the evening, I'd met up with two freelancers working on a story about Baghdad EOD (explosive ordnance disposal) for *Vice* magazine, Ayman Oghanna and Andrea Bernardi, and Borzou Daragahi, a Pulitzer Prize finalist on staff at the *Financial Times*, and we'd walked over to Pizza House to get some dinner to take back to their crash pad at the Internews House, a cheap rental for journalists in Baghdad. I had some beers to finish off before I left in the morning, and Borzou had some vodka and Campari to dispose of before he flew to Cairo, so the four of us made a party of it. Borzou and Ayman dissected the election and Andrea showed us combat footage he'd taken during the Libyan revolution. Meanwhile, firecrackers went off behind the house, setting us all slightly on edge. It seemed like a good omen, though—they were the only explosions I'd heard the entire time I was in Baghdad.

I told them about the brief visit I'd convinced Aziz to make with me to a nearby nightclub, where Iraqi fat cats puffing nargilehs watched glammy young women dance in hip-tight, shimmering dresses. The audience was all men, clustered around tables laden with whiskey bottles and mezze plates, except, oddly enough, two families tucked away in the corners eating dinner. The nightclub had a rocking band belting out Middle Eastern pop too loud to talk over, and during the break the singer came out into the crowd and sat with one of the customers, asking him how he was doing that evening, complimenting him, thanking him for coming. In response, the man at the table tossed a fistful of dinars into the air. This seemed to be some kind of ritual: the singer moved to another table and the same thing happened again. Hundred-thousand-dinar bills fluttered out over the stage like ash after an explosion. Between songs, the girls came out and sat with the men, chatting them up, leaning in. I wanted to stay longer, but the management wasn't encouraging our stay, and Aziz was growing increasingly uncomfortable. "I can't even look at those women," he hissed over the music. "They're diseased."

Borzou whipped out his phone and showed us a story he'd written about a similar club, back in 2010. He'd worked a deal with the management to hang out all night, and even claimed to have sneakily snapped a couple photos with his phone. Borzou had been in and out of Baghdad since 2003, and if there was a story in the city he hadn't heard, covered, or written himself, it probably wasn't worth talking about. And it wasn't just Borzou: for eight years, the city had swarmed with Western journalists scrambling and hustling to scoop each other. You name it, somebody had written it. Baghdad nightclubs? Check. Iraqi rappers? Check. The looting of the national museum? Check. Corruption? Check. Children orphaned by war? Check. The rise of sectarian militias? Check. After the Americans left in 2011, though, the press corps scattered, back to New York and Washington, London, Paris, or settling into regional offices in Cairo, Beirut, or Istanbul—accessible cities with lower insurance premiums. Without any boots on the ground, American interest faded.

A handful of salty journos had ambled back for the elections, and I wandered into the party like a goof. Any story I might scare up had already been hunted, and when it came to finding real news, I was out of my league, poorly equipped, and totally inexperienced. The best journalists had at least some Arabic, could pass for a Middle Easterner on the street, and knew how to work through the sometimes paralyzing Iraqi inertia, the constant "Inshallah" that could stall out even the most motivated investigator. I had none of that, but I had one thing that none of them could put a claim on: an exclusive account of what it was like coming back to Iraq as a veteran, ten years later. As Matt Bradley from the *Wall Street Journal* had observed at a party at the Swedish Consulate, my story was all about putting my fucked-up self into the story.

Now my fucked-up self was leaning back as Duraid fishtailed around a corner, tires squealing. The last time I'd been in a Dodge Charger had been almost exactly a year before, the sun rising slowly behind us as we drove over the misty blue hills of central Texas, headed for the Austin airport after having driven all night from New Orleans. Austin had been the final stop on the *Fire and Forget* book tour, and the five of us behind the project—me, Jake, Phil, Matt, and Perry—all flew down for it, scheduling a quick visit to New Orleans as a kind of last hurrah. The car rental place at the airport had upgraded our rental on account of our being veterans, and so we found ourselves tooling around in a muscle car Jake dubbed Black Betty.

In New Orleans, we stayed at the Café Brasil, a Marigny landmark shuttered by its owner, Adgenor "Adé" Salgado, after Hurricane Katrina, for reasons that remained known only to him. But he was a friend of Jake's, and so he let us stay upstairs. Adé was an enigmatic, hard-edged Brazilian mystic, a curved blade in a silk shirt, and he'd put Jake up for a few months after Jake had come back from Iraq. He welcomed us into the empty upper rooms of the Café and offered us beer, weed, and whatever else we might want. The rooms were musty and haunted, full of old books, clothes, Adé's thickly daubed abstract paintings, sculptural junk, and, for Jake, memories of a strange time.

The next day, before we left, while Jake was catching up with Adé and the other guys were napping, I found a worn copy of Milton's *Paradise Lost* on the mantel of a bricked-up fireplace. I opened the book at random and came to a passage in one of Satan's monologues, a passage that resounded like the striking of a clock.

It echoed through my ears all that day, all night as we drove back from New Orleans, all through the soft blue Texas morning, and onto the plane coming up out of Austin:

> Which way I fly is Hell; myself am Hell;
> And, in the lowest deep, a lower deep
> Still threatening to devour me opens wide,
> To which the Hell I suffer seems a Heaven.

The lines came back to me again in the close darkness of Duraid's Charger, Nicki Minaj singing "I beez in the trap," Baghdad a blur around me. Which part was the story, I wondered, and which part my fucked-up self? Who was a terrorist? Who was a victim? Who was trapped in hell, and who could fly away?

Almost everyone I talked to wanted to leave. The Americans wanted to leave. The ambassador wanted to leave. My translator, Aziz, wanted to leave. My driver, Ahmed, wanted to leave. The English literature students I talked to at Mustansiriya University wanted to leave, and who could blame them? Rania Tawfeeq, a Western-dressed woman with a direct gaze and free-flowing black hair who was finally finishing her bachelor's degree at twenty-five, had spent much of her life in exile in Jordan, Sweden, and Syria. She was "home" now, but felt trapped and dreamed of nothing but escaping with her daughter. "Baghdad streets can't compare to anywhere else," she said, shaking her head. Huda Kadhim, a fresh-faced twenty-two-year-old in hijab, hadn't seen her father since he'd been kidnapped in 2006. One of her cousins had also been kidnapped, and another murdered. The state paid her family a pension from her father's salary for six months after his disappearance, then someone in the ministry started stealing it. Osama Kadhim, twenty-three, moved back to Iraq with his family from

Yemen in 2003, then saw most of his family killed over the next few years. He was an affable, gentle-looking young man, but everything he said spoke of a soul clarified and hardened by violence. "Politics here is just lies and more lies," he said. "I'm afraid to leave my house, afraid to die or be kidnapped." Maysoun, looking even younger than her twenty years with her shy smile and bashful glance, had been forced to move from Saydiya to Abu Ghraib, now on the front lines of the fight against ISIS. Her brother had been kidnapped in 2006, and she hadn't seen him since. She was phlegmatic about the dangers of living in an area being fought over by Daesh and the Iraqi Army, and of having to travel every day into the city for school. "I believe if I'm going to die, I will die," she said, shrugging.

"You're not going to die," Professor Faydh told her, laughing. "They will use you for some other purpose."

"There are worse things than death," one of her fellow female students said, giggling.

Maysoun hoped to leave Iraq, but didn't think she'd be able to, because of the difficulties involved, but also because she didn't think her parents would let her. "I have dreams," she said. "I just can't achieve them because I'm a girl."

Professor Faydh herself, who studied and taught American literature, said that her greatest wish was to come to the United States but she probably never would because she was unmarried and her parents wouldn't let her travel. Professor Ghadah Abdul-Sattar, who taught philosophy of science at Baghdad University, told me she was obliged to wear hijab at the university or risk harassment from fellow teachers and even students. Isma Najm, an idealistic young woman with a degree in chemical engineering and a specialization in oil refining, was unemployed and pouring her energies into Facebook activism, because her parents wouldn't let her move to the south of Iraq where she could get work with an oil company. Wasan Faghel, one of Professor Faydh's most forceful and articulate students, left college in 2004 after getting married, and when she decided to go back to school in 2011, her husband told her she couldn't. Only her mother-in-law's influence convinced him to let her go. Wasan expressed her admiration for Professor Faydh and her desire to be a professor herself but didn't think she'd ever be able to. "When I came back here, I had a dream to be something. I was influenced by a great teacher. She was a great model for me, she has a good character, she is an educated woman, and she is sitting right in front of me. She presents the woman I dream to be. But actually, I don't believe I will be." The other girls laughed. "I dream to be just like her but I don't believe that I can do this, because I'm so tied to my family and my husband."

Many wanted to leave, but few could. The SIV program and the IOM had tight filters and narrow pipelines for getting people out, and the process often took years—and this was for people who had worked with the US and were eligible for special consideration. For most Iraqis, not only was leaving impossible, but even traveling outside Iraq had become incredibly difficult. "The Iraqi passport means nothing now," one of Professor Faydh's students told me. "Nobody recognizes us. You can't go anywhere." Meanwhile, refugees from Fallujah came back to the neighborhoods in Baghdad they'd been forced out of in 2006, where they were threatened by the same militias as before. Refugees who had moved to Syria had become refugees again. Part of the misery of Iraq was the pervasive feeling that the walls were closing in: it was getting harder and harder for foreigners to come in and harder and harder for Iraqis to leave.

For me, leaving the first time was easy. I got on a C-130 at Baghdad Airport and I was gone. When people asked me if I'd ever go back, I'd laugh: "What for?"

My tour in Iraq had been extended past its original end date, after the Jaish al-Mahdi uprising in April 2004, and during our last months there, my anger, fear, and frustration grew into an unbounded hate: I hated the constant threat of violence, the smell of oil, the despicable role I was forced to play as an occupier, and the resentment we drew in performing that role. I hated my commander, who was an idiot. I hated military logic, with its redundancy and regulations, and I hated military culture, with its puffed-up machismo and dumb aggression. I hated the explosions and the gunfire and the mortars. I hated the feel of the air. I hated the sand, the heat, the tents, the streets, the camouflage, the Iraqis, the Americans, the sky, the sun, the wind, and the hands of the clock marking time.

It took about a year before other feelings started filtering in, other memories. As time went on, my memories grew richer and more ambivalent. I remembered standing on the roof of a building at Camp Dragoon in Baladiyat, watching the sun go down a purple sky over Sadr City. I remembered watching people go to ice shops on the street as though there wasn't a war on, envying their vulnerable freedom. I remembered my first Rani peach drink, ice cold, bought at a stand by the side of the road after I'd convinced my commander it was safe to stop. I remembered the water buffalo we passed every day on the way from Baghdad Ammo Depot West to the airport. I remembered the Iraqi who ran the coffee shop at FOB Falcon, who brought his daughters in and let them talk to us. I remembered the local girls who did our laundry there, and how I heard they were murdered just after we left. I remembered two Iraqi boys I took a picture of in Dora, both of them in ridiculous pink pants, and I remembered wondering what their lives would be like. I remembered Waleed, the Facility Protection Services cop who pulled gate guard with us, who taught me and RonRon how to curse in Arabic. I remembered the thrill of danger and how it made me feel alive. I remembered something sweet in the evening air over the Tigris, as the muezzin called out across the city.

And as Duraid downshifted and cut past an SUV back onto Jadriya Street, slamming my body against the door, I remembered hitting a hundred and twenty on the highway back to Austin from New Orleans, feeling something shudder and crack inside as one cycle came around to its end and another began, and I remembered swerving through traffic at the head of a convoy, ten years before, feeling my Humvee slide and grind under my fingers, my foot slipping gas-brake-gas.

6.

Leaving, it turned out, wasn't as simple as all that. The past doesn't fall away but lives on in your flesh, in your habits, in the synaptic weave that makes consciousness out of electrical pulses and meat. I left Iraq in 2004 and the army in 2006, but I found over time that neither one had left me. My year in Iraq made me who I became after, as did my four years in the army, no matter how I felt about it. In the same way, America's eight-year-long occupation there has shaped what America is, whether we want to remember those years or not. Shock and Awe, WMDs, Abu Ghraib, Haditha, abandoned soccer fields, Fallujah, Tal Afar, Karbala, Asaib Ahl al-Haq, the Jaish al-Mahdi, the Green Zone, Sadr City, Sahwah, the Imam Ali mosque in Najaf, the Samarra mosque, al Qaeda in Iraq, and the millions of lives we uprooted, left unguarded, destroyed, and abandoned are all a part of us now. We made them part of America, American identity and American history—Iraq has become flesh of our flesh, Baghdad blood of our blood. We can pretend to forget, try to rub out the image in the mirror, but we can't change what we've done.

When I was in Baghdad in 2003 and 2004, most of the students I talked to in 2014 would have been teenagers. I was an American soldier then, distant and wary, separated from the world I lived in by armor, power, ignorance, and fear. They were hadji kids, worried about school and clothes and the future. Worried about getting enough to eat, not getting blown up, not getting shot by nervous Americans.

I left, they stayed. Over the next ten years, I finished my time in the army, went back to college, then went on to Princeton. I got married and got divorced. I wrote and published and thought a lot about what it means to be a veteran. I went hiking in western Ireland, the south of France, and New Hampshire. Meanwhile, those kids in Baghdad struggled to finish high school in the midst of a civil war. They saw friends and family members murdered and blown up. Some just disappeared. The American surge came and went, stabilizing things for a couple of years, and then the Americans left, taking that stability with them. Meanwhile, Rania, Huda, Osama, Maysoun, and their classmates hid from militias, bandaged wounds, took pleasure where they could, and tried to imagine a life that might be livable.

They stayed, I left. But while I may have left Iraq, Iraq hadn't left me. Baghdad might have been hell, and it might still be hell today, but it wasn't a hell I'd visited and escaped. It was a hell I had helped create.

———

The layers write over each other without erasing what came before but changing it, changing me. All the places I'd been in Baghdad, the psychogeography of FOBs and patrols that had loomed so large for me for so long, diminished in the symbolic scale of my past but took on an existential weight they'd never had before. I went back to FOB Falcon and Camp Dragoon, now Federal Police bases, and found a strange continuity in the up-armored American Humvees guarding the entrances, although they bore the Iraqi flag. I had Ahmed and Aziz take me through the streets of Dora where I'd once driven patrols, which then had been open and full of people. Today, the neighborhoods were a maze of concrete barriers, segregated from the rest of the city by fifteen-foot-high blast walls and military checkpoints. The streets were in better repair; there wasn't as much raw sewage spilling out over the curbs, and the shops seemed renovated, with shiny new signs. Bollards lined the sidewalks of the main commercial avenue, to protect against car bombs. But the streets were almost empty. It felt like a ghost town.

Finally, I went looking for Baghdad Ammo Depot West, "Camp Shithole," the munitions cache between the airport and Abu Ghraib where my unit spent the first six weeks of our tour. We were really "in the field" then, with no running water, no electricity, burning our shit in giant metal tubs, showering with canteens, and eating T-rats (tray rations) delivered twice a day from BIAP. I slept in the open, wrapped in a mosquito net on a cot next to my Humvee, and several mornings woke to wild dogs licking the sweat off my toes. Camp Shithole seemed like the absolute boonies, though in fact we were just a few miles from the city.

Ahmed drove us down the highway to Fallujah, off which a road led that would, I hoped, bring us to the remains of Camp Shithole. As we passed the outskirts of Baghdad, the checkpoints got bigger, more serious, and more frequent. To our south, what had been Camp Victory, the largest US installation in Iraq, now an Iraqi army base, sprawled behind massive concrete barriers. Traffic congestion worsened at the checkpoints, and the farther we got from Baghdad, the more the road filled with beat-up old vans and rattling junkers. When we got into Abu Ghraib, traffic stopped.

This was familiar territory, even ten years later: streams of poor, rural Iraqis with Dorothea Lange dustbowl faces, women in full black abayas, squat stucco buildings with rusty signs. Broiling heat and stalled traffic. Men in vans staring at me in wonder and hostility. The difference was that I didn't have a rifle, a helmet, a machine gunner on overwatch, or three trucks behind me full of bros. It was me and Aziz and Ahmed in a Kia. I didn't even have a hat.

"Do you have a hat?" I asked Ahmed.

"Yeah, sure, I have everything." He opened the center compartment and pulled out a baseball cap and some Wiley X shades. I put the ballcap on, thinking it might hide my hair and face.

"Does this make me look less American?"

"More."

I took off the hat, and Ahmed offered me a cigarette. "Here. Have a cigarette. Smoke and think. Maybe it will be your last."

"Is it dangerous here?" I asked.

"Oh yes," Aziz said. "Very dangerous. There is a lot of fighting out here between Daesh and the army."

I accepted Ahmed's cigarette, and then another, and another, as we slowly rolled through the traffic jam, then made a U-turn to get on the south side of the highway. We came back through more traffic and eventually turned off into the town of Abu Ghraib, rolling down a dirt road past hovels and shacks. We were stopped at a small checkpoint, where Aziz told the soldiers that I was a journalist and we were looking for flooding. The soldiers told us there wasn't any flooding around here and the road went nowhere, but they let us go see for ourselves.

It turned out they were right. What had been Baghdad Ammo Depot West was now nothing but hills of garbage. The road that once would have taken us right into the heart of the camp dead-ended in a mound of trash and dirt. This was probably a good thing, all told, given the likelihood of unexploded munitions lying around, but nonetheless I couldn't help feeling that the place's fate was too ironic. What we had called Camp Shithole was now, literally, a shithole. As a symbol for the American occupation, it was stupidly perfect. I got out and took some pictures. A wild dog lay panting in the sun. Then I got in Ahmed's Kia, and we drove back into the city.

———

I'd seen what I'd come to see, now I was leaving. Duraid whipped the Charger around a corner and drove back behind the Coral Boutique Hotel, dropping us off at the Internews House. The night was buzzy and smooth. Ayman said goodbye to his friends, and we headed in for more vodka. Somehow, Borzou and I got into an argument about America's role in fomenting the sectarian violence in Iraq.

"You have to remember, these are old problems," he told me. "The US didn't create the Shia-Sunni split. But it's not even that. It's all these countries that had once been part of the Ottoman Empire, and then when that comes apart, people fight. Think about it: of all the countries that came out of the Ottoman Empire, did any one of them *not* have some kind of awful violence?"

I tried Turkey, but Borzou brought up the Armenian genocide. I couldn't remember whether the Armenian genocide had happened before or after 1920 (it happened in 1915, it turns out—one of the last acts of the Ottoman Empire, though the Republic of Turkey has persistently denied that it ever occurred), but I could see his point, for which Yugoslavia was the prime contemporary example, that pre-existing ethnic or sectarian differences were, historically, inflamed and exacerbated by political instability. "Okay," I said, "that's true, but the US could have done things differently. It should have done things differently. If you invade a country and change the rulers, that's your responsibility."

"Yeah, sure," he said. "You break it, you buy it. But they were totally ignorant of what they were getting into. And anyway, what could they have done differently?"

"They could have not started the government on a quota system. They could have not backed sectarian leaders like Maliki. They could have not dumped money into the militias. But more basically, they could have not disbanded the army and de-Baathified the government. They basically destroyed what civil institutions there were and left a vacuum that all but invited sectarian violence, which they then fostered by supporting a Shiite government."

"I was here then and I don't remember any quota system."

"No, you know, they divided it up so many seats to Shiites and so many seats to Sunnis, a seat for the Christians, and so on."

"Well, sure, but what are they supposed to do? Not give minorities representation?"

"No. But don't found the political process on sectarian identity. Let people form parties around issues and groups that aren't based in religious or ethnic identity. Republicans, Democrats, Socialists, whatever. Don't *start* with racial or sectarian politics."

"I'm looking at the people on the IGC, and there were some secular Sunnis, and a religious Sunni, and a couple secular Shia, there's Chalabi, and, sure, yeah, some religious Shia. But look, the people you're talking about had helped the US in the invasion. Some of those Shia fought alongside the US army and helped win the war. What were they supposed to do? You have to take care of the people that helped you."

"They could have been bracketed. I just don't think putting people with a grudge in power is the best way to form a stable postwar government."

"That's true, but I'm saying you should be careful about claiming that the US started the sectarianism."

"No, you're right. It was already there. But our policies and our attitudes fed it and helped it grow. And I can't help but think it was intentional."

"That's conspiracy talk. Look, the US just didn't know what it was doing, especially at first. They didn't have any real Middle East experts on the ground; the military didn't know what it was doing, and they didn't have a plan."

"Yeah, I don't buy that anymore. I think 'no plan' *was* the plan. The US *had* experts, knowledgeable people on the Middle East, and they got sidelined. What's more, we came in deciding that the Sunnis were the enemy and the Shia were the good guys. We came in with a sectarian agenda."

"I don't think that's true."

"Man, I remember when we got here in May 2003. We knew fuck-all about Iraq, except 'Kif, oguf,' and that the Sunnis were the bad guys and the Shia were the oppressed underdogs. You look at Fallujah, we killed seventeen people there in May that year, protestors, for nothing. All up until the surge, even during the worst insurgency, Sunni tribal leaders kept reaching out to the Americans to work with them, trying to get into the political process, and every time General Casey was like, 'Fuck those guys.'"

"Casey was an asshole. So was Abizaid."

"Yeah, sure, but the point is, we had decided, going in, that Iraq was divided into Sunnis, Shias, and Kurds, and that the Sunnis and Shias hated each other, and that we were going to support the Shia. Then that's what we did. We knew that the Shiite militias were working with the Iraqi police and government as early as 2005, sending out death squads and torturing people, and the policy was to not do a damn thing about it. We trained them, even. And then we put Maliki in power. And that was all by accident?"

"What do you mean we?"

"I mean commanding generals and policy makers in Iraq. And now, that policy has resulted in a weakened, divided Iraq that can't build an effective, independent national politics, but is still pumping out oil. That seems to fit the needs of the US government very well. I have a hard time believing it wasn't intentional."

"I'm telling you, I was here then. I was talking to generals and to people at the CPA. Nobody knew what the hell they were doing. It was just a complete mess."

"I know. I was here too, for part of it, and what I saw was a total goatfuck. But I can't believe the 'innocent American' story anymore. The US has too much involved, too much power, too much money, and too deep a history in the Middle East to not have a very good idea, at the upper levels, of precisely what the fuck it's doing. I just can't believe in the fairy tale of innocent, fumbling Americans anymore. If we made a mess, it's because we wanted a mess."

In January, when I agreed to the assignment from *Rolling Stone* to go back to Iraq, I took it upon myself to try to understand why we'd lost the war. Beginning from the premise that mistakes were made, I found mistakes: trying to completely reinvent an entire society, ruling by sectarian division, a shallow commitment to nation building, no coherent or well-articulated plan, a high turnover rate for both units and commanders, a consistent inability to adapt to changing circumstances, persistent support for Maliki from 2006 onward, and the general incompetence of the US Army and its leadership all seemed like persuasive reasons for American failure. As I read more deeply in US policy in the Middle East and Iraq, though, it became increasingly difficult to accept my initial premise that American actions in Iraq should be understood as a series of mistakes. Instead, it became impossible not to see the Iraq War as part of a consistent pattern of imperialist manipulation aimed at preventing national independence, populist self-determination, and regional stability. That pattern included our intimate involvement with repressive regimes in Saudi Arabia and pre-revolutionary Iran, CIA support for Iraq's Baathist coup in 1963, our work fomenting and sustaining al Qaeda and the Taliban in Afghanistan in the late 1970s and 1980s, our backing Saddam Hussein during his war with Iran (including tacit support for his use of chemical weapons), our unscrupulous history of selling arms to competing and sometimes warring nations (including, from the 1950s to the present, Iran, Iraq, Saudi Arabia, Jordan, Israel, Egypt, Yemen, Turkey, and Syrian rebels), and our long-term collusion, going back to the early years of the twentieth century, with the efforts of oil companies to weaken nationalist democracies, foster ethnic, sectarian, and religious conflict, and undermine labor organizing and social reform.

To what end? Most simply, to keep Iraq from becoming a powerful, independent regional player. Since Iraq sits on the world's fifth-largest proven reserves of oil, including the second-largest single known oil field on the planet, and sits uncomfortably between the American-supported fundamentalist Sunni kingdom of Saudi Arabia, and the independent, American-resistant Shiia Republic of Iran, the US simply can't afford to let Iraq go its own way. Unfortunately for everyone concerned, though, the US lacks the regional and cultural power to ensure the allegiance of an independent Iraq, and it lacks popular support for the kind of long-term occupation and reconstruction that would be needed to create a stable, Americanized ally, such as what happened with Germany and South Korea. I say "unfortunately" because, with US interests in the region at stake but US options for exercising its power limited, the most sensible choice is to keep Iraq weak and bleeding. The best ways to do that are by promoting sectarian and ethnic conflict, supporting Sunni extremists through Saudi Arabia and the UAE, supporting Shia extremists through the Iraqi military, obstructing any efforts toward stability and peace, and flooding the region with weapons.

Just because this happens to perfectly describe American policy in the region since 2003, however, doesn't *prove* that's what the US *intended*. There's much to be said for the narrative that describes a fumbling but well-intentioned America. It's a familiar story, after all: We meant to do well. We really meant to spread democracy and peace and freedom. We just fucked up because we're so ignorant of other cultures and so committed to American exceptionalism. It was just imperial overstretch. Sorry! Our bad! While US diplomats and oil company agents had been working intimately with locals in the Middle East for more than a century, it was good old arrogant stupidity, personified by Donald Rumsfeld, that sidelined all that institutional knowledge and just made a big doody-poo. Who could have known? If it so happens that the bloody conflict and immense human suffering we "accidentally" caused when we opened the lid on "ancient sectarian quarrels" serves American political and corporate interests, well, gee whiz, that doesn't mean we *meant* things to go that way.

But as I sat over my vodka on my last night in Iraq, looking back at my service there and considering what I'd seen and what I'd heard, especially from Iraqis themselves, I realized it didn't matter what we'd intended. What mattered was what we'd done. We'd invaded a sovereign nation on a pretense, fucked up the lives of thirty million people, started a bitter, bloody civil war by pitting one religious sect against another, then left and pretended it had nothing to do with us. We'd helped strengthen fundamentalist religious extremists in the Middle East and put intellectuals, journalists, and activists at risk. A few people made a whole bunch of money, and a whole nation was left in shambles. Whether or not breaking Iraq into pieces had been a deliberate plan from the beginning, as some evidence suggests, the war had been nothing but a murderous hustle. The politicians who ran the war had shown no higher ideals than robbery and plunder, and I'd been nothing but their thug.

As an historical agent in the vast, crooked enterprise that was the Iraq War, I had helped cause immense suffering, and I had profited by it. I had let it happen, and I had made it happen. And when I thought of the pride I'd taken in my service, the combat pay I'd spent vacationing in Paris, London, and Berlin, and the blood money that had bought my college education, holding them up against the lives I'd seen shattered by violence, the hopes I'd seen trampled, and the dreams for a better future I'd seen starved by neglect and choked by frustration, I could feel nothing but disgust and shame for having been an American soldier.

———

The night was growing late. Ayman brought out his bottle of arak and I poured myself a shot for the road, then stumbled out through the gate and back to my hotel. When I woke in the morning, still wearing my clothes from the night before, it took me a while to register where I was and what I was doing. Blue predawn light filtered through the gap in the curtains. I was leaving Iraq again.

Ahmed picked me up downstairs. Traffic was light and the city quiet. As we drove to the airport, we passed the winged statue marking its entrance.

I pointed out the statue to Ahmed: "I always remembered that angel."

"Abbas ibn Firnas," he said.

"What?"

"That's not an angel. That's Abbas ibn Firnas."

Abbas ibn Firnas, it turned out, was a Berber-Andalusian inventor, poet, and musician who lived in the Caliphate of Córdoba—what is now southern Spain—in the ninth century. He had made the first recorded attempt at glider flight in Europe, using wings fashioned from vulture feathers. Firnas had built his wings, Ahmed told me, to escape prison.

As my plane rose into the sky, I watched Iraq fall away below. Five thousand years ago, this precise stretch of land, the fertile crescent running west along the Tigris and Euphrates rivers, had been the birthplace of Western civilization. Twelve hundred years ago, it had been the heart of an empire spanning from Kabul to Tunis. Two hundred years from tomorrow, after the fifth-largest proven oil reserves in the world have been pumped dry and burned, it may finally see peace. [2014]

The Fantasy of American Violence

For a long time after I came home from the war, fireworks made me jumpy. They sounded like what they are, shrieking rockets and exploding gunpowder, and every Fourth of July set off Alert Level Yellow. I'd crack another beer and try to laugh it off, even as the friends I was with turned into ghosts of the soldiers I once knew.

Thirteen years ago, I spent the Fourth of July on the roof of a building in Baghdad that had once belonged to Saddam Hussein's secret police. Our command had suspended missions for the day, set up a grill, and organized a *Star Wars* marathon—the three good ones—in an old auditorium. But George Lucas's lasers couldn't compete with the light show playing out across Baghdad, and watching a film about the warriors of an ancient religion rising up from the desert to fight a faceless empire seemed, under the circumstances, perverse.

So instead of *A New Hope*, I watched scenes from Operation Iraqi Freedom: tracers, helicopters, distant explosions in a modern city under an increasingly senseless occupation. I could see the United Nations compound that would get bombed later that summer. I could see the memorial to the soldiers who had died in the Iran-Iraq War in the 1980s, a giant turquoise teardrop sliced in two. I could see Sadr City, the wire-crossed slum that would give birth to Shiite death squads, and the Green Zone, where American proconsuls forged a new Iraq.

I was a Bicentennial baby, born in 1976; *Star Wars* was the first movie I saw, strapped in a car seat at the drive-in, and the film implanted deep in my infant subconscious a worldview, an idea of justice, and the desire to wield a light saber, all growing entangled as I grew older with the Bicentennial celebrating the American Revolution—another story of scrappy rebels fighting a mighty empire.

Star Wars managed a remarkable trick. Two years after the fall of Saigon and America's withdrawal in defeat from a dishonorable war, Mr. Lucas's Wagnerian space opera recast for Americans the mythic story so central to our sense of ourselves as a nation.

In this story, war is a terrible thing we do only because we have to. In this story, the violence of war has a power that unifies and enlightens. In this story, war is how we show ourselves that we're heroes. Whom we're fighting against or why doesn't matter as much as the violence itself, our stoic willingness to shed blood, the promise that it might renew the body politic.

The literary historian Richard Slotkin called this story the myth of regeneration through violence, and he traces it from the earliest Indian captivity narratives through the golden age of the Western, and it's the same story we often tell ourselves today. It's a story about how violence makes us American. It's a story about how violence makes us good.

Looking out over Baghdad on the Fourth of July, I saw the truth that story obscured and inverted: I was the faceless storm trooper, and the scrappy rebels were the Iraqis.

Did it really take going to Baghdad to learn this? Hadn't I read about the campaigns against the Cherokee, Nez Percé, and Sioux, the long war against Philippine independence, and the horrors of Vietnam? My grandfather served on a Swift Boat in the Mekong Delta, though he never talked about it; hadn't trying to fill in his silence taught me about free-fire zones, My Lai, and hospitals full of napalmed orphans? The bloody track of American history, from slavery to genocide to empire, is plain for all to see. But reckoning with the violence itself was the appeal: I thought I could confront our dark side, just like Luke Skywalker, and come away enlightened.

Veterans and pundits often talk about the military-civilian gap. So few Americans serve, they say, that most of the nation doesn't have any sense of what that service means. This is superficially true. The military is a professional subculture with its own rituals, traditions, and jargon. There's a military-civilian gap, just as there's a police-civilian gap, an oil rigger–civilian gap, a barista-civilian gap. But that's not what these vets and pundits mean.

What they're really claiming is that veterans know something civilians don't understand or can't imagine, and that this failure of imagination is a failure of democracy, a failure of dialogue, a failure to listen. What they mean is that veterans have learned something special through their encounter with violence, and civilians need to hear that sacred knowledge. This is where talk about the military-civilian gap goes awry.

The truth is, most Americans understand what our soldiers do very well. They understand that American troops are sent overseas to defend American political and economic interests, wreak vengeance on those who have wronged us, and hunt down our enemies and kill them. There is no gap there. The American military has a job, and most of us, on some level, understand exactly what that job is. The American soldier or marine is an agent of American state power.

The real gap is between the myth of violence and the truth of war. The real gap is between our subconscious belief that righteous violence can redeem us, even ennoble us, and the chastening truth that violence debases and corrupts.

After the attacks on September 11, 2001, American troops were deployed throughout the Middle East and Southwest Asia for reasons that were confused then and remain dubious today, but on some unconscious level the myth of violence was at work, promising that waging war abroad would heal the wounds borne that day. We might have to get our hands dirty, but that trial itself would prove our commitment to American values. As George W.

Bush said when we invaded Iraq (even though it had nothing to do with 9/11), "We will pass through this time of peril and carry on the work of peace. We will defend our freedom. We will bring freedom to others. And we will prevail."

That's not how things would turn out, as wiser heads warned at the time, but in the frightened months after 9/11, the myth of violence was more powerful than the truth of war. As an American soldier in Iraq, I was both caught up in that myth and released from it: I could see what "the work of peace" really looked like, what American violence did to Iraqi homes and bodies, yet it remained my job to be an agent of that violence—a violence that neither redeemed nor enlightened.

On this Fourth of July, amid a crucial presidential election campaign, while American violence continues to rain down on Iraq, Syria, Afghanistan, Pakistan, and Yemen, as we continue to support violence in Saudi Arabia, Nigeria, Equatorial Guinea, and elsewhere so as to get a better price on oil that we then burn and dump into the atmosphere, precipitously heating the planet, we should ask ourselves what we're really celebrating with our bottle rockets and sparklers.

There is another version of America beyond the noise our fireworks make: not military strength, but the deliberate commitment to collective self-determination. Perhaps this Fourth of July we could commemorate that. Instead of celebrating American violence, we might celebrate our Declaration of Independence and Constitution, and the ideals those documents invoke of an educated citizenry deciding its fate not through war but through civil disagreement. Instead of honoring our troops, whose chief virtues are obedience and aggressiveness, we could honor our great dissenters and conscientious objectors. And instead of blowing things up, maybe we could try building something.

It's our choice. We make our myths. We show by our actions what our holy days mean. Forty years after the American Bicentennial, thirteen years after standing on a rooftop in Baghdad and ten years after getting out of the army, I won't be out under the fire, cheering our explosions. I won't be watching *Star Wars*, either. My America isn't an empire or a rebellion, but an ideal; it's not a conquest, nor a liberation, but a commitment. [2016]

III.

VIOLENCE & COMMUNION

The Terror of the New

In 2001, German avant-garde composer Karlheinz Stockhausen caused an international scandal when he made the following remarks about the September 11 attacks on the World Trade Center:

> Well, what happened there is, of course—now all of you must adjust your brains—the biggest work of art there has ever been. The fact that spirits achieve with one act something which we in music could never dream of, that people practice ten years madly, fanatically for a concert. And then die. And that is the greatest work of art that exists for the whole Cosmos. Just imagine what happened there. There are people who are so concentrated on this single performance, and then five thousand people are driven to Resurrection. In one moment. I couldn't do that. Compared to that, we are nothing, as composers.[1]

Critics denounced these remarks and sought to explain them by reference to Stockhausen's characteristic megalomania, his occasional claims to have been educated in the distant star system Sirius, and the many controversies marking his long career as one of the most important composers of the twentieth century. Anthony Tommasini of the *New York Times* took a more theoretical tack, charging Stockhausen with a failure to distinguish between art and

life: "Art may be hard to define," Tommasini wrote, "but whatever
art is, it's a step removed from reality." He went on:

> A theatrical depiction of suffering may be art; real
> suffering is not. Because the art of photography often
> blurs this distinction, it can make us uncomfortable.
> Real people, sometimes suffering people, have been
> photography's unwitting subjects. That's why we have
> photojournalism, to keep things clearer. The image of a
> naked, fleeing, napalm-burned Vietnamese girl is truth,
> not art. Images of the blazing twin towers, however
> horrifically compelling, are not art.[2]

Tommasini's argument, though expressing a common sentiment,
remains unconvincing. Kenneth Goldsmith's *Seven American Deaths
and Disasters*, which includes among its documentary transcriptions
radio reports of the attacks of September 11 and was inspired by
Andy Warhol's 1962–1963 series of painted silk-screened photographs of car crashes, disasters, and suicides, is only the readiest
example of "real suffering" that is also art. Nina Berman's photographs of Marine Sergeant Ty Ziegel's horrifically disfigured face
and crippled body—you may remember her iconic photograph of
Ziegel and his bride—are another. Berman's photos of Ziegel were
featured in the 2010 Whitney Biennial and have been exhibited
widely in galleries and museums across the world. Whatever their
putative truth content, Berman's photos are both "horrifically
compelling" photographs of an actually suffering person *and* aes-
thetically crafted objects exhibited in museums for the pleasure and
edification of audiences. They are both "real" and "art."

Anthony Tommasini is a prestigious critic and has written for the
New York Times for many years. It is unimaginable that he is ignorant of the robust, long-lived tradition of innovative art practice
that works to blur the line between reality and art. He may well not

consider the work of Chris Burden, the Viennese Actionists, Karen Finley, and Marina Abramovitch to be art, but he must know that others do. Thoughtless Tommasini may be, but not naïve. Rather than consider him merely thoughtless, however, I would argue that Tommasini is stretching his argument not because he really believes art is divorced from reality, nor because human suffering is a forbidden subject, but because Stockhausen's comments reveal discomfiting resonances between modern ideologies of art and the use of political violence.

Stockhausen had the sort of ego that would have scorned the idea that between artists and audiences there is any kind of equivalence. Such a genius *knows better* than his or her readers, listeners, and viewers, and moreover has an obligation to educate them, even and especially if this includes shocking them out of their preconceptions. The creator leads, the audience follows. Moreover, the artist's role is explicitly rebellious, revolutionary, anticonventional—if not to *épater les bourgeois* or transform consciousness, at the very least to "think outside the box." Stockhausen was right, in his way, to connect the violent resistance of al Qaeda to the Luciferan—or Satanic—rebellion so central to modern conceptions of aesthetic production. There is a line from Blake to Baudelaire to Kathy Acker, and that line connects de Sade, Duchamp, Stephen Daedalus, Wagner, Nietzsche, Dada, Andy Warhol, and *The Threepenny Opera*.

While I do not think anyone could reasonably argue that this tradition of Satanic modernism leads directly to Osama bin Laden, Stockhausen's understanding of 9/11 as a work of art fits within a broadly high-modern conception of innovative aesthetic production. Theodor Adorno's analysis of aesthetic autonomy buttresses this. For Adorno, the work of art—and especially the *new* work of art—manifests an immanent presence that by its very existence performs a negation, critique, and transformation of the social world from which it is created. Consider the following:

The act of repulsion must be constantly renewed.

Art is the social antithesis of society.

Among the dangers faced by new art, the worst is the absence of danger.

Scars of damage and disruption are the modern's seal of authenticity; by their means, art desperately negates the closed confines of the ever-same; explosion is one of its invariants.[3]

Such statements are characteristic of a *terror aesthetic* in which art opposes contemporary society with formal and conceptual, if not physical, violence. Stockhausen, indeed, was not the first to suggest kinship between terrorism and art. In Don DeLillo's 1991 novel *Mao II*, the novelist Bill Gray asserts, "There's a curious knot that binds novelists and terrorists . . . Years ago I used to think it was possible for a novelist to alter the inner life of the culture. Now bomb-makers and gunmen have taken that territory. They make raids on human consciousness. What writers used to do before we were all incorporated."[4] Nor were Stockhausen and DeLillo the last. Hilary Plum's novel *They Dragged Them Through the Streets* addresses this very question, in its lyrical meditation on the limits of both writing and bombing as ways of "altering the inner life of a culture."

It remains doubtful whether early twentieth-century avant-gardes, much less DeLillo's novelist's "raids on human consciousness," ever achieved the spectacular power Stockhausen dreamed of or the philosophical force Adorno attributed to them. Art, innovative or not, does or does not make anything happen, on a scale of decades, and in ways so complex and difficult to pin down it might take a master artist to depict them. Gertrude Stein, in *The Autobiography of Alice B. Toklas*, describes the infamous opening night of *The Rite of Spring* by focusing on Guillaume Apollinaire and the way he held his handkerchief. A seminal moment of aesthetic innovation is represented not as a spectacular *event*, but as background to a functionally metonymic detail. Modernism is condensed into a gesture. The part is the whole, and vice versa.

The whole of *our* parts is the so-called global war on terror. We, meaning you and me and all of us, are and are not part of that war. It concerns us in terms of aesthetics because we live and breathe aesthetic production and consumption. And it concerns us in terms of politics because it affects us politically, more or less. Mostly less, to be honest—few of us will feel the chill touch of Big Brother on our shoulder. But we sense—we know—we believe we ought to be concerned with what the US does, both abroad to others and at home to us, from trivial acts of degradation like forcing us to remove our shoes at the airport to not-so-trivial acts of torture and totalitarian surveillance.

As aesthetic producers and consumers, we operate within a cultural logic that fetishizes novelty. As political beings, we are responsible to a greater or lesser degree for shaping our collective life. What do these things have to do with each other? The answer is not clear. Certainly there are traditions in which the artist's responsibilities include cultural critique and social intervention. Innovation in this domain is a technique for subverting preconceptions and conventions and making space for utopian possibility. As Adorno understands aesthetic production, it is through innovation itself that the artwork achieves its social reality as a negation of society. Yet if the cultural logic of commodity capitalism is itself one of constant innovation, how can innovation possibly be understood as the form of its critique?

It has been twelve years since the attacks of September 11, twelve years since Stockhausen's comments, and we have had twelve years of aesthetic responses to terror and to the global war on terror, some innovative in the way we mean by the word *experimental,* some innovative in other ways, but most fairly conventional. From James Cameron's *Avatar* to Kenneth Goldsmith's *Traffic* and *Seven American Deaths and Disasters,* from Deborah Eisenberg's *Twilight of the Superheroes* to Joss Whedon's blockbuster *Avengers,* from PJ Harvey's album *Let England Shake* to Sinan Antoon's novel *The Corpse Washer,* from the numerous soldier-posted YouTube videos of songs like "Fobbit Rap," "Hadji Girl," and "The Homecoming Song," to Jena Osman's *Public Figures,* Philip Metres's *Abu Ghraib Arias,* and Hilary Plum's *They Dragged Them Through the Streets,* a staggering amount and variety of aesthetic production has responded to diverse aspects of what we're calling the global war on terror.

But what do we even mean, finally, by this term—this whole of our parts—the so-called global war on terror? Do we understand it? It is not an event, or even a series of events, or even a network of events, but rather maybe something like a lifeworld, an era, a Zeitgeist. Like the Sixties, the Cold War, or even modernity, the global war on terror is an abstract index, a very thin question mark in place of a robust complexity. It is part of a bigger complexity we used to call globalization, which is itself interwoven with other great complexities of the present: the digital revolution, the great recession, and global climate change. It is difficult, if not impossible, to see where or when one complexity ends and another begins. Even before the NSA started monitoring our Facebook posts, Google searches, and cell-phone calls, the war on terror had already stained the very fabric of our lives.

Which is to say that responding to the phenomenon is like responding to capitalism, or society, or the atmosphere. It is our environment. It is our world. It is not just a war, or an event, or a moment, just as modernism is not only *The Rite of Spring.* Part of our problem is that we cannot even see our world, our moment, as it is happening, or even as it has just happened. Always already caught up in the next thing, we are distracted from the present by the new.

Returning to Stockhausen and Adorno, what their terror aesthetics suggest is that innovation is not a solution, but a symptom.
We have been laboring for a century under the tyranny of the
modern demand to "make it new," under an idea of art as innovation, as the social antithesis of society, as shock therapy for
conventional thought, an idea that bears disturbing affinities
with both terrorism and the commodity logic of the empire that
ostensibly makes war against it. What was truly scandalous in
Stockhausen's statement about 9/11 was his thoughtless exposure of the revolutionary utopian claims of modern aesthetic
production, and the fact that the new always demands not only
the destruction of the past, but the annihilation of the present.
[2013/2014]

The Trauma Hero

Every true war story is a story of trauma and recovery. A boy goes to war, his head full of romantic visions of glory, courage, and sacrifice, his heart yearning to achieve heroic deeds, but on the field of battle he finds only death and horror. He sees, suffers, and causes brutal and brutalizing violence. Such violence wounds the soldier's very soul.

After the war, the boy, now a veteran and a man, returns to the world of peace haunted by his experience, wracked by the central compulsion of trauma and atrocity: the struggle between the need to bear witness to his shattering encounter with violence and the compulsion to repress it. The veteran tries to make sense of his memory but finds it all but impossible. Most people don't want to hear the awful truths that war has taught him, the political powers that be want to cover up the shocking reality of war, and anybody who wasn't there simply can't understand what it was like.

The truth of war, the veteran comes to learn, is a truth beyond words, a truth that can be known only by having *been there*, an unspeakable truth he must bear for society.

So goes the myth of the trauma hero.

This myth informs our politics, shapes our news reports, and underwrites our history. It dominates critical and scholarly interpretation of war literature, war movies, and the visual culture of war. It shapes how we understand Iraq, Afghanistan, Vietnam, and World War II, and it affects whom we vote for. Like all myths, this story frames and filters our perceptions of reality through a set of recognizable and comforting conventions. It works to convince us that war is a special kind of experience that offers a special kind of truth, a truth that gives those who have been there a special kind of authority.

The trauma-hero myth also serves a scapegoat function, discharging national bloodguilt by substituting the victim of trauma, the soldier, for the victim of violence, the enemy. Take Clint Eastwood's recent adaptation of Chris Kyle's memoir, *American Sniper*. The story, as everyone knows, is of the life and death of Navy SEAL Chris Kyle, who as a shooter in Iraq racked up more confirmed kills than any other sniper in American military history. Kyle served four tours in Iraq as a trigger puller, then retired and began to work with disabled and traumatized veterans. One day one of these veterans shot him.

The opening scene sets the moral stakes. Our hero, played all lockjaw, thousand-yard stare, and darting eyes by Bradley Cooper, must decide whether or not to shoot an Iraqi child whose mother gave him a grenade to throw at an American convoy. Never mind the tired Vietnam-era trope of the bomb-wielding child, a fiction that Eastwood grafted onto Kyle's less sensational autobiographical account of shooting a woman. What's important here is that we're being shown what extremes of psychological torment our hero must endure—and this is only the beginning. Such suffering is the upshot of the whole narrative, which is an account of Kyle's increasing combat stress and the toll that takes on his family, layered over with a simplistic dueling snipers plot, both of which culminate in a climactic rooftop battle scene.

In this scene, Kyle draws on his years of training and warrior wisdom to make an "impossible" shot, killing the sniper "Mustafa." As a gibbering horde of Iraqi insurgents descends upon our American heroes, Kyle calls his wife by satellite phone and tells her he's ready to come home. A dust storm envelops the battle and the Americans fight their way out, barely escaping, in a visually striking chaos that serves as a symbolic baptism: Kyle is sucked into the whirlwind and only barely makes it out, leaving his weapon and his lucky Bible behind him. He has been reborn.

The last scenes of the film intimate Kyle's recuperation. Cooper loses his thousand-yard stare and lets his jaw relax, revealing a man who has learned how to turn the lessons of war into the lessons of peace. Instead of helping endangered soldiers by killing Iraqis, he has learned to help wounded soldiers by talking with them and mentoring them in shooting-range therapy. The final scene, before the documentary footage of Kyle's flag-bedecked funeral, is of Kyle as father and husband, warm, joking, engaged with his wife and children.

American Sniper focuses in tight on one man's story of trauma, leaving out the complex questions of why Kyle was in Iraq being traumatized in the first place. The Iraqis in the film are villains, caricatures, and targets, and the only real opinion on them the film offers is Kyle's. The Iraqis are all "savages" who threaten American lives and need to be killed. There's some truth in this representation, insofar as this is how a lot of American soldiers thought. Yet the film obviates the questions of why *any* American soldiers were in Iraq, why they stayed there for eight years, why they killed thousands upon thousands of Iraqi civilians, and how we are to understand the long and ongoing bloodbath once called the "War on Terror." It does that precisely by turning a killer into a victim, a war hero into a trauma hero.

———

The myth of the trauma hero, like all great myths, has a history. It goes back to the birth of Romanticism in the eighteenth century and is first seen taking shape in Stendhal's *The Charterhouse of Parma* and Tolstoy's *War and Peace*. The myth achieved its mature form in twentieth-century war literature and is often now read as the very definition of war literature itself, even though as the twentieth century wore on, the myth became increasingly conventional and self-referential. Tracking this myth through the poetry of Wilfred Owen, the prose of Ernest Hemingway and Tim O'Brien, and Kevin Powers's Iraq war novel *The Yellow Birds* can help us see how the myth works, how it has been used by writers eager to capitalize on the moral authority it offers, and how it has turned from being a frame for understanding reality into a mirroring surface that reflects back only our own expectations.

In June 1917, while recuperating from shell shock at Craiglockhart War Hospital, British lieutenant Wilfred Owen wrote the first draft of a bitter poem describing the death of a fellow soldier in a gas attack. This draft was dedicated "To Jessie Pope," a widely published female civilian poet known for her patriotic poems. Owen's dedication, later amended "To a certain poetess," was as facetious as the poem's now famous ending is ironic: the vividly depicted horror of a comrade's choking death was intended to chasten prowar civilians like Pope and repudiate "the old Lie: *Dulce et decorum est / Pro patria mori.*"

Owen begins his poem in the perspective of marching soldiers, identifying a speaking "we" that shifts between subjective sensation and close description of physical suffering: "Bent double, like old beggars under sacks, / Knock-kneed, coughing like hags, we cursed through sludge . . ." Vivid images paint a scene as if out of Bosch, and details such as the caliber of the artillery rounds help establish the narrator's authority. The men come under gas attack, and we, with our narrator, helplessly watch one die choking, drowning in air. We see through the narrator's eyes, through the "misty" lenses of his gas mask. This shift via perceptual detail into the narrator's subjectivity is pushed further in the next stanza's free-standing couplet, where the death recurs as a traumatic repetition within the narrator's dreams: "In all my dreams, before my helpless sight, / He plunges at me, guttering, choking, drowning."

In the final stanza, the narrator turns from his dream to the reader's, indicting the one who doesn't know the experience of war: "If in some smothering dreams you too could pace / Behind the wagon that we flung him in . . ." The details press on, one after the other, but now instead of describing the scene itself, or even its memory, Owen describes the dream that you, the reader, *would* be tortured by—*if* you'd seen what he'd seen and felt what he'd felt. If you could see, the narrator tells Jessie Pope, if you knew *what it was really like*, then you wouldn't write poems supporting the war.

The Latin tag ending the poem, from Horace's *Carmina* 3.2, translates roughly as "It is dear and honorable to die for one's nation." This tag stands for what Owen is aiming to attack, to dispel, to silence: the "old Lie" taught in English schoolbooks and put forth by civilian poets. I know the truth, Owen claims, not because I read about it in Horace, but because I've seen it, heard it, and felt it. Owen means to malign war, but according to his logic, it is his very experience of war that gives him privileged access to moral truth beyond anything civilians like Jessie Pope can ever hope to achieve. Owen asserts that war's truth is the truth of the soldier's experience, which puts the issue of war beyond debate.

The Israeli military historian Yuval Harari has argued that the practice of hallowing the experience of war as trauma grows out of a larger historical shift from recording external deeds as evidence of valor to recording internal experiences as evidence of developing sensibility. Revolutions in military technology and organization in the early seventeenth century created the conditions for detaching personal glory from military experience. In the eighteenth and early nineteenth centuries, the growth of sensationalism, the cult of sensibility, and Romanticism combined with increasing literacy and a more professionalized and middle-class officer corps to make "war as revelation" the predominant frame for interpreting the individual experience of war in the West. Once a field of accomplishment, war became a kind of sentimental education.

In the US, this interpretive frame has led to contradictory

attitudes about war. On the one hand, Americans denounce war as something uncivilized and exceptional, something only other countries do, something America does only under duress. On the other hand, Americans indulge in what historian David Bell has described as "an unabated fascination with war, considering it a test of their society's worth. They treat members of the armed forces with respect verging on reverence and take for granted that no one who has not been in combat can ever really understand 'what it is like' or how it changes a person."

Most Americans seem to believe that war can be known only through direct, physical, sensory experience on the battlefield, such as the moment of vision Owen describes in "Dulce et Decorum Est." Ernest Hemingway, who in contrast to Owen's long frontline service lasted only a few weeks as a noncombatant before being wounded and returning to the US, stands in American letters as the high priest of combat gnosticism. In Hemingway's work, the emphasis on physicality, embodiment, and materiality we see in Owen's representations of the soldier's truth opens into a metaphysical bias against representation itself. In Hemingway's novel of World War I, *A Farewell to Arms*, Lieutenant Frederic Henry delivers a famous denunciation of martial ideals and abstract language, founded in the moral authority of his earlier wounding, that makes this point explicit.

During a conversation between Lieutenant Henry and an Italian ambulance driver named Gino, in an area of the front that had recently been taken back, Gino comments that the summer fighting "cannot have been done in vain." Lieutenant Henry silently disdains not just Gino's patriotism, but the very words he uses:

> I was always embarrassed by the words sacred, glorious, and sacrifice and the expression in vain. We had heard them, sometimes standing in the rain almost out of earshot, so that only the shouted words came

through, and had read them, on proclamations that
were slapped up by billposters over other proclamations, now for a long time, and I had seen nothing
sacred, and the things that were glorious had no glory
and the sacrifices were like the stockyards at Chicago if
nothing was done with the meat except bury it. There
were many words that you could not stand to hear and
finally only the names of places had dignity. Certain
numbers were the same way and certain dates and
these with the names of the places were all you could
say and have them mean anything. Abstract words
such as glory, honor, courage, or hallow were obscene
beside the concrete names of villages, the numbers of
roads, the names of rivers, the numbers of regiments
and the dates.

For Hemingway's Lieutenant Henry, the soldier's truth becomes
a formal truth: it determines not only who can speak, but what
words can be spoken. Gino, after all, has seen as much or more
war than Lieutenant Henry has. The difference between them is in
their sensibility. For Hemingway, Gino is a crude nationalist who
thinks and speaks in clichés, while Lieutenant Henry is a refined
and sensitive soul who knows the true words for war. Those words
must be concrete, sensory, metonymic: place names, regimental
numbers, and dates must stand in for the battles that were fought
there. Any recognition of social value, any judgment of character
or worth, Hemingway finds repugnant. War and combat can be
properly addressed only by invoking the temporal and geographic
markers by which those who were present will remember them.

Upping the literary stakes, Tim O'Brien's influential collection
of linked stories *The Things They Carried* pushes beyond Hemingway's repudiation of idealism and abstraction to a repudiation of
civic discourse and truth as such. Where Hemingway still allows

invocation to retain the dignity of battlefield presence, O'Brien refuses any connection at all between social norms and combat. Where Hemingway insists on the concrete, O'Brien avows the obscene. "A true war story," he writes in *The Things They Carried*, "is never moral."

> It does not instruct, nor encourage virtue, nor suggest models of proper human behavior, nor restrain men from doing the things men have always done. If a story seems moral, do not believe it. If at the end of a war story you feel uplifted, or if you feel some small bit of rectitude has been salvaged from the larger waste, then you have been made the victim of a very old and terrible lie. There is no rectitude whatsoever. There is no virtue. As a first rule of thumb, therefore, you can tell a true war story by its absolute and uncompromising allegiance to obscenity and evil.

The Things They Carried is presented as a series of reminiscences, partly fictionalized, ambiguously true, from O'Brien's time as an infantryman in Vietnam. In "How to Tell a True War Story," much as in Owen's poem, O'Brien offers the voyeuristic drama of watching a fellow soldier die as evidence against "a very old and terrible lie." On patrol in the jungle, two infantrymen, Rat Kiley and Curt Lemon, are playing catch with a smoke grenade when Lemon steps on a booby trap and gets blown up. Like Owen, O'Brien revisits the moment of death again and again. Whereas Owen's choking soldier comes back first as a dream, then as the reader's dream, O'Brien's exploding Curt Lemon comes back and back and back in a fictional model of traumatic repetition.

What O'Brien ultimately works toward, in this story and throughout *The Things They Carried*, is the assertion of an encounter with truth that transcends communicability—not only for his characters, but for the writer. The knowledge Tim O'Brien claims to have experienced in Vietnam can't be understood or even discussed, but only felt.

> For the common soldier, at least, war has the feel— the spiritual texture—of a great ghostly fog, thick and permanent. There is no clarity. Everything swirls. The old rules are no longer binding; the old truths, no longer true. Right spills over into wrong. Order blends into chaos, love into hate, ugliness into beauty, law into anarchy, civility into savagery. The vapors suck you in. You can't tell where you are or why you're there, and the only certainty is overwhelming ambiguity. In war you lose your sense of the definite, hence your sense of truth itself, and therefore it's safe to say that in a true war story nothing is ever absolutely true.

For O'Brien, a true war story is about the failure of language to communicate experience altogether, which is an assertion that the soldier's truth is a mystic truth. Illumination here takes the form of negative theology, apophatically denying that the experience of war can be described, thereby denying both the truth of prior descriptions and the possibility that the experience can ever be communicated at all.

Confronting O'Brien's total negation of language, Kevin Powers's 2012 Iraq War novel *The Yellow Birds* flips the script by representing war trauma as the font of poetic transcendence: instead of negating language, the experience of war inspires it. Through flashbacks, *The Yellow Birds* tells of privates John Bartle and Daniel Murphy, a wartime George and Lennie who deploy to Iraq under the tyrannical rule of one Sergeant Sterling. While downrange, Murphy loses his mind and goes AWOL; Bartle and Sterling eventually find his mutilated corpse. In the novel's present, Bartle has returned to the US, struggles with PTSD, and is wrongly imprisoned by the military's Criminal Investigation Division for his alleged involvement in an atrocity committed by Sergeant Sterling, who has in the meantime committed suicide. What redeems Bartle in the end is the novel itself, his story, his voice: the novel dramatizes the transformation of Bartle's trauma into Powers's poetry.

Powers's literary ambitions are signaled in the novel's first lines, a lyrical meditation on war that builds metaphor upon metaphor into a surreal montage of sensation beyond meaning, extending from its tortuously elaborate sentences through its melodramatic plot to its hyperconscious symbolism of hyacinths. Private Bartle's narration is a perpetual cry of pain, a constant ache of swollen language that breaks into traumatic revelation when he commits violence:

> I moved to the edge of the bridge and began firing at anything moving. I saw one man fall in a heap near the bank of the river among the bulrushes and green fields on its edges. In that moment, I disowned the waters of my youth. My memories of them became a useless luxury, their names as foreign as any that could be found in Nineveh: the Tigris or the Chesapeake, the James or the Shatt al Arab farther to the south, all belonged to someone else, and perhaps had never really been my own. I was an intruder, at best a visitor, and would be even in my home, in my misremembered history, until the glow of phosphorescence in the Chesapeake I had longed to swim inside again someday became a taunt against my insignificance, a cruel trick of light that had always made me think of stars. No more. I gave up longing, because I was sure that anything seen at such a scale would reveal the universe as cast aside and drowned, and if I ever

floated there again, out where the level of the water reached my neck, and my feet lost contact with its muddy bottom, I might realize that to understand the world, one's place in it, is to be always at the risk of drowning.

Noctiluca, I thought, *Ceratium*, as the tracers began to show themselves in the sifted twilight.

Powers ascends from description to meditation, from simple declarations to disordered hyperbaton, from the concrete names of rivers now turned foreign to the abstract stymieing of pluperfect desires ("until the glow of phosphorescence in the Chesapeake I had longed to swim inside again someday became a taunt against my insignificance"), and finally to esoteric Latin terms deployed in a telling inversion of Owen's rhetorical move ending "Dulce et Decorum Est." Where Owen marshals sense data to controvert the authority of Latinate literariness, Powers takes flight from materiality into literature. Where Owen inscribes a vision, Powers poetizes: "*Noctiluca*, I thought, *Ceratium* . . ."

For Powers, the conventional tropes of war lit are not a means of conveying truth, but the truth of war itself. The transformation of experience into literature is here characterized as a dissociation from one's own embodied memory ("I disowned the water of my youth"), a process of evacuation in which concrete facts, Hemingway's "names of rivers," become not only interchangeable but also alienated, pure signs operating in a closed economy of literary signification in which Powers (or Bartle) is an interloper (they "all belonged to someone else, and perhaps had never really been my own")—an economy we might read as the system of MFA programs and New York publishing circles that shaped *The Yellow Birds* and its reception. Powers's climactic turn from *experience* to *literature* rather than the other way around suggests that the conventions of traumatic revelation have become purely formal expectations of an audience more interested in war as myth than in war as reality or even as literature.

————

In one of the most substantial recent articles on contemporary war lit, George Packer in the *New Yorker* reads the genre as a set of variations on the trauma-hero myth, focusing on the Owen-Hemingway-O'Brien lineage while ignoring works that don't fit that frame, such as John Dos Passos's epic *U.S.A.* trilogy, James Jones's masterful combat novel *The Thin Red Line*, John Horne Burns's acidic portrait of American-occupied Naples, *The Gallery*, or Stephen Wright's surreal, elusive novel about media and surveillance in Vietnam, *Meditations in Green*. Shoehorning more recent war lit from Iraq and Afghanistan into his narrow rubric, Packer extends his interpretation from the literature of those wars to the wars themselves, writing, "The wars in Iraq and Afghanistan fully meet [Paul] Fussell's description of the ironic: they were worse than expected. Both began with hubris and false victories, turned into prolonged stalemates, and finally deserved the bitter name of defeat." This is, we should note, a partial view. Packer was one of the liberal hawks calling for an American invasion of Iraq in 2002 and 2003, against the advice of State Department officials, Middle East experts, UN weapons inspector Hans Blix, and the US Army chief of staff. Only after spending time on the ground in Baghdad, "seeing what it was really like" and realizing that wars are messy, bloody, dumb, and wasteful, did Packer recant his earlier jingoism.

In light of his own experience, as understood through the lens of Fussell's canonical reading of World War I poetry in *The Great War and Modern Memory*, Packer sees the novels, poems, and stories coming out of Iraq and Afghanistan as bearing the truth of a traumatic and disillusioning revelation. He reads Kevin Powers's rather banal poetry as "meditative and convalescent," evincing "the poet's mind reopening after a great shock," and finds "one of the best distillations of combat" he'd ever read in a dull comparison *The Yellow Birds* makes between combat and a car accident. Packer interprets Benjamin Busch's lyrical memoir *Dust to Dust* as the formal embodiment of PTSD, writing, "Fragments are perhaps the most honest literary form available to writers who fought so recently." It's difficult to know what it would mean for a *literary form* to be "honest," unless you are predisposed to understand experience as having a certain shape. Brian Turner, the pre-eminent American poet of the Iraq War, fits rather more easily into Packer's trauma-hero reading, for Turner's poetry is already deeply Romantic in sensibility. For Turner, poetry itself is experience as revelation; the fact that he is a war poet is practically accidental, except insofar as we seem to expect our war poets to write precisely that kind of poem. Packer ends his essay by considering Phil Klay's award-winning short-story collection *Redeployment*, lauding the book as a paragon not of literary sophistication and suspended judgment, which it is, but of "rigorous honesty" and, of course, irony. Klay's virtues are, for Packer, the essential virtues of war literature: not art, but experience. This itself is ironic, considering that Klay spent his war behind a desk as a public affairs officer—what the military calls a publicist.

By focusing strictly on writers who happen to be veterans, Packer misses not only some of the most interesting novels published so far about the wars in Iraq and Afghanistan, including *Billy Lynn's Long Halftime Walk*, by Ben Fountain, *The Watch*, by Joydeep Roy-Bhattacharya, and *They Dragged Them Through the Streets*, by Hilary Plum, but also essential work in translation by Iraqi writers, such as Sinan Antoon's elegiac novel *The Corpse Washer* and Hassan Blasim's devastating, surreal short stories in *The Corpse Exhibition*. What's more, Packer ignores veteran writers who don't fit the conventions of the trauma hero myth. A stirring diversity of short stories, novels, poems, essays, and memoirs by a growing community of writers are effaced and reduced to a handful of works that conform to expected conventions.

Where Packer missteps most precipitously, however, is where he considers war literature in its historical and political contexts.

> Journalists and historians have to distort war. In order to find the plot—causation, sequence, meaning—they make war more intelligible than it really is. In the literature by veterans, there are virtually no politics or polemics, in stark contrast to the tendentious way in which most Americans, especially those farthest removed from the fighting, discussed Iraq. This new writing takes the war, though not its terrible cost, as a given.

This isn't just wrong, it's dangerous. It presumes that journalists and historians adhere to conventions of understanding ("causation, sequence, meaning") whereas novelists and poets do not, which not only offers a patently nonsensical way of approaching literature but also makes extravagant demands upon it: how could a writer possibly communicate *any* experience without making it "more intelligible than it really is"? Making experience intelligible is just what language does. Furthermore, Packer makes the specious assumption that ignoring the causes, background, and motivating forces for a war represents an *absence* of politics, rather than seeing it for what it is—a politics of forgetting that actively elides the question of what US soldiers were fighting for and the bigger problem of whom they were killing, in favor of a narrower and more manageable question, "What was it like?"

Packer's tendentious argument highlights the most troubling consequence of our faith in the revelatory truth of combat experience and our sanctification of the trauma hero: by focusing so insistently on the psychological trauma American soldiers have had to endure, we allow ourselves to forget the death and destruction those very soldiers are responsible for. Consider the title story of Phil Klay's *Redeployment*. Klay's collection opens with a US Marine reflecting on his experience in Iraq as he returns home, declaring, "We shot dogs." This short, powerful sentence, while factually true, offers readers a comforting moral lie. "We shot dogs" is as accurate as "We built schools" or "We brought democracy," and works much the way we seem to want our war literature to function: by foregrounding a peripheral detail, it obscures much more significant big-picture realities. By focusing on the fact that we shot dogs, Klay allows American readers to ignore the fact that we shot people.

The story "Redeployment" tells is of a traumatized marine veteran, Sergeant Price, who returns home from Iraq to his wife, Cheryl, and his dog, Vicar. Vicar, he finds, is terminally ill. As Sergeant Price adjusts to peacetime life and processes his experience of the war, he is troubled by Vicar's worsening condition, and eventually decides to take the dog out to the river and shoot him.

Klay's *Old Yeller* narrative of masculine hardening is layered over with a deliberate conflation of Iraqis and dogs. It is telling that Sergeant Price's dog is named Vicar. A vicar is a representative or substitute, as the pope is the Vicar of Christ, and in "Redeployment," the tumorous Vicar is a substitute for the narrator's trauma and guilt. Yet Vicar also stands in as a substitute for the thousands of Iraqis killed during the American occupation. The comparison is made explicit at the story's end, as Sergeant Price is preparing to shoot his dog, when he remembers his marines killing an insurgent in Fallujah. The insurgent had been found in a cesspool, "hiding beneath the liquid and only coming up for air . . . like a fish rising up to grab a fly." The insurgent has no face, no name, no body: he is no more than a mouth breaking the surface of a fetid pool.

The sad fact Klay plays on is that most American readers will care more about a dead dog than they will about a dead Iraqi, and in this way "Redeployment" opens up an emotional conduit for those readers to feel the pangs of grief and guilt that come with killing, but without having to connect that feeling to the political reality of the war in Iraq. Whereas an Iraqi victim would have to be reckoned with as a fellow human being, with all the complexity that entails, a dog can simply be pitied and his killer simply empathized with. This moral simplification comes at a cost.

Klay, embodying the moral authority of a veteran, assures American readers that a dead Iraqi needn't trouble them any more than a dead dog would. And since most of us already feel that way, his story provides a much-desired release, freeing us from the worry that we ought to feel guilty about the havoc the American military unleashed and the blood American soldiers and marines spilled. Sergeant Price is our trauma hero—he pays the "price" for our bloodguilt. Rather than forcing us to face our collective complicity in a brutal war of aggression that has left thousands upon thousands dead, Klay asks us to feel bad for how much psychological pain one sensitive marine has suffered doing what had to be done.

Read in the context of Klay's other stories in *Redeployment*, or with the other stories it was published alongside in the collection I co-edited with Matt Gallagher, *Fire and Forget: Short Stories from the Long War*, Klay's trauma-hero narrative can be read productively and provocatively as one perspective among many. Yet when the trauma-hero myth is taken as representing the ultimate truth of more than a decade of global aggression, we allow the psychological suffering endured by those we sent to kill for us displace and erase the innocents killed in our name. As in Klay's story, the real victims of American political violence disappear under a load of shit.

The Yellow Birds, "Redeployment," and *American Sniper* may portray a loss of innocence that makes the dirty war in Iraq palatable as an individual tragedy, but they only do so by obscuring the connection between American audiences and the millions of Iraqi lives destroyed or shattered since 2003. Focusing on the suffering of Private Bartle, Sergeant Price, or Chief Petty Officer Kyle allows us to forget the suffering of the very people whose land was occupied in our name. There are almost no Iraqis in *The Yellow Birds* or *Redeployment* at all, and where they do appear, they are caricatures. If the point of literature is to help us "recognize [our] own suffering in the stories of others," as George Packer sententiously asserts, rather than soothing our troubled consciences with precisely the stories we want to hear, then novels such as *The Yellow Birds* and stories such as "Redeployment" are gross moral and literary failures. But the failure does not belong to the writers. It belongs to all the readers and citizens who expect veterans to play out for them the ritual *fort-da* of trauma and recovery, and to carry for them the collective guilt of war.

Such an expectation is the privilege of those who can afford to have others do their killing for them. Off-loading the problem of war onto the figure of the traumatized veteran, however, has long-term costs we have yet to reckon. The imperative to see war clearly is persistent, as urgent today as ever, as US military forces return to Iraq and a new kettle of hawks cry for war in Ukraine and Syria. Understanding the problem of American political violence demands recognizing soldiers as agents of national power and understanding what kind of work the trauma hero is doing when he comes bearing witness in his bloody fatigues. [2015]

The Idea of Order
I Can't Breathe

It is extremely dangerous to encourage people to see themselves as exceptional, whatever the motivation. There are big countries and small countries, rich and poor, those with long democratic traditions and those still finding their way to democracy. Their policies differ, too. We are all different, but when we ask for the Lord's blessings, we must not forget that God created us equal.

—**Vladimir Putin,** *New York Times* **(September 11, 2013)**

1. The First Death

This is a story about bodies and texts. Bodies and difference. Texts and difference. Bodies and violence. This is a story about texts and violence. This is a story about violence and reflection, difference and equivalence, universalism and parochialism, capitalism and cosmopolitanism and racism and war and peace, freedom and repression and language and justice and slavery and serfdom, rich and poor, North and South, America and Russia, France and Algeria, America and Iraq, Saudi Arabia, Afghanistan, Germany, Japan, Nigeria, Ghana, Senegal, Cameroon, Namibia, Côte d'Ivoire, Liberia, Guinea, Guinea-Bissau, Sierra Leone, Togo, Benin, The Gambia, Gabon, Congo and Angola and Ferguson and Staten Island and Baltimore and Cleveland and Oberlin and New Haven and Princeton and Moscow and Washington and Brooklyn and ontology and epistemology and aesthetics and ethics.

This is a story about many things, but it begins with a body. Maybe that means it's a mystery, because mysteries always start with a body. But then so do wars, gospels, sacrifices, and autopsies—all stories that begin with a body and end with truth. This story doesn't end with truth, though, so it's probably not a mystery, or a war, or a gospel, a sacrifice, or an autopsy. Capitalism starts with a body, too, the laboring human body, and ends with profit—or revolution. This story doesn't end with profit or revolution, though, but with sorrow and loss. So it's probably not capitalism, either. I suppose if this story is anything, it might be philosophy, because it starts with a body and moves toward spirit. It starts with particulars and moves toward abstractions. It starts with confusion and moves toward understanding. I can't claim it ever gets there—or anywhere near there, for that matter—but it struggles, moves, works, thinks, and tries, even if it moves in circles, even if it thinks in fragments and mistakes, even if it struggles in bits and pieces and gestures and failures.

So, without further ado: the bodies.

On August 19, 2014, an eighteen-year-old man was shot dead by a police officer in Ferguson, Missouri. His name was Michael Brown. He had, with a friend, shoplifted some Swisher Sweets from a corner store. The clerk at the store called the police and the police dispatcher sent out a description. Ferguson Police Officer Darren Wilson, already in the neighborhood, stopped Brown and his friend on the street. Something happened between Wilson and Brown, some kind of scuffle that ended with Wilson drawing his pistol in his police SUV and firing two shots, one of which grazed Brown's hand. Brown ran and Wilson followed, then Brown stopped and turned. Ferguson Police Officer Darren Wilson then pulled the trigger of his Sig Sauer P229 .40-caliber service automatic ten times. Six bullets hit Michael Brown, in the face, neck, chest, and right arm, killing him. Michael Brown may have had his hands up and he may have been saying "Don't shoot."

He may have been moving toward Darren Wilson in a threatening manner. Eyewitness evidence is ambiguous. We do know that Michael Brown was unarmed, that he was more than thirty yards away from Wilson, and that he had just graduated high school. The police let his body bleed in the street for hours.

On Monday, November 24, 2014, a Ferguson grand jury decided not to indict Darren Wilson in the death of Michael Brown, a decision that provoked widespread outrage and days of protests throughout the United States.

About ten days later, on December 3, 2014, a New York grand jury decided not to indict New York Police Department officers in the death of Eric Garner, a grandfather and retired New York Parks & Recreation employee with diabetes and asthma. On July 17, Garner had been approached by two police officers for allegedly selling loosies, individual cigarettes, which is illegal in New York, though loosies are sold in many corner markets. I used to buy them sometimes when I lived in Crown Heights. Eric Garner told the police to stop harassing him, and in response they grabbed him and tried to handcuff him. Garner, a big man, brushed them off, so Police Officer Daniel Pantaleo wrapped his arm around Garner's neck in an illegal hold, and, after a short struggle in which three other police helped take Garner down, choked him to death. Pantaleo's supervisor stood by watching. We've all seen the video. We've all heard Eric Garner saying "I can't breathe" while the police were killing him; we've all heard him begging for air. Another death, another body left lying in the street, surrounded by police. More outrage and protests.

In both cases the evidence clearly showed that excessive police force resulted in the death of a citizen, yet both ruling municipal grand juries declined to indict. These two egregiously unjust grand jury decisions in rapid succession refreshed recent memories of the Trayvon Martin case, in which a vigilante named George Zimmerman murdered a seventeen-year-old boy in cold blood, yet was acquitted by a Florida jury under Old West–style self-defense laws. The two unjust grand jury decisions tore open a wound in the American body politic, brought to national attention a systemic problem of murderously aggressive policing, and catalyzed an atmosphere of outrage, fear, and struggle. Something was happening. A profound, pain-stricken anger had been awakened. Protesting in the streets or watching Twitter, you could see it, you could feel it.

On a cold January morning a few weeks later, while protestors' shouts of "I can't breathe" and "No justice, no peace" still echoed in the streets of American cities, Saïd and Chérif Kouachi entered the Paris offices of the French satirical magazine *Charlie Hebdo* and started shooting. They found their way to the second-floor conference room, where the editors of the magazine were holding a meeting. Saïd and Chérif first sprayed indiscriminately, then executed deliberately. The two brothers killed twelve people that day: maintenance worker Frédéric Boisseau, psychoanalyst and columnist Elsa Cayat, editor-in-chief Stéphane Charbonnier, editor Bernard Maris, copy editor Mustapha Ourrad, cartoonists Philippe Honoré, Jean Cabut, Bernard Verlhac, and Georges Wolinski, festival organizer Michel Renaud, and police officers Ahmed Merabet and Franck Brinsolaro. That same morning, a man named Amedy Coulibaly, suspected of working in collusion with the brothers, shot a jogger in a Paris suburb. The next day he shot and killed police officer Clarissa Jean-Philippe and wounded a street sweeper. On January 9, two days after the *Charlie Hebdo* shootings, police killed Saïd and Chérif Kouachi after a nine-hour siege. Elsewhere in Paris that day, Amedy Coulibaly entered a supermarket, killed four people, and took several others hostage. He was later killed by police when they stormed the grocery.

In Shakespeare the bodies tend to all pile up at the end. Think of *Hamlet*, *King Lear*, or *Othello*. A good tragedy builds inexorably toward a moment of spectacular violence, when all the ratcheting tension is finally discharged in bloody havoc. People often describe real deaths as tragic, real events as tragedies, including the many deaths just discussed, but at the risk of being pedantic I have to say that's not quite right, though it is illustrative of something important that we'll come back to later, the easy confusion in the human mind between fact and fiction, our tendency to rely unreflectively and even unconsciously on certain archetypical structures of narrative. But my point here is that, to be precise, tragedy is a genre of dramatic art, a communal ritual, a narrative form.

Tragedy is a kind of play, inherently artificial because it is made. When a typhoon hits the Philippines, destroys thousands of homes, and kills hundreds of people, that's not a tragedy because it's not a communal ritual but a natural event. When a lone psychotic goes into a suburban school and shoots a bunch of children, that's not a tragedy either, for the same reason. It may be dramatic, theatrical, sorrowful, and horrific, which are some of what we often mean when we use the word *tragic*, but when we call such an event a tragedy we're confusing an event with a kind of narrative form. We mistake history for aesthetics.

Tragedy, as any high school student knows, has its roots in ancient Greece. It began in the annual rituals celebrating the death and rebirth of the god of wine, Dionysus. A community would come together to drink and sing and watch a drama unfold. The drama usually ended with a body.

The word itself, *tragōidia*, or "goat song," gives a clue to the deeper roots of this genre in collective ritual sacrifice. Tragedy is the song of the scapegoat, the sacrificial animal that bears the sins of the community and thereby, in its death or expulsion, expunges them. In coming together to witness, celebrate, and participate in collective bloodshed, the members of a community purge themselves of sin and avow their collective identity—a process Aristotle called *catharsis*. The story of Dionysus, the god in whose name the celebration was held, hints at even deeper, darker roots: the god's dismemberment and rebirth suggests that the origins of tragedy lie not in animal sacrifice, but in human sacrifice—a body on an altar, a body torn to pieces. The body of a sacred offering. Whether the sacrifice is a scapegoat or a martyr turns out to be ambiguous. Both are totemic, both heroic, but one is expelled and the other raised up. Interpretation depends upon the specific social group and their values. Whether the story is a goat-song or a gospel depends on whether they see the sacrificial victim as different from them or the same. It all comes down to a question of identity.

This very aspect of the tragic sacrifice, the cathartic affirmation of collective identity, may be what the voices on the television or in the newspaper mean to imply when they describe an event as a tragedy. What they want to say is that we all come together over the dead. We are unified in their blood. But who are we? What collective is this? Are we the white police standing over Michael Brown and Eric Garner? Are we the black protestors marching in Ferguson, New York, Oakland, and Baltimore, shouting "Black lives matter"? Are we the European and American intellectuals and politicians avowing "*Je suis Charlie*"? Are we the French Algerians struggling every day against racism and Islamophobia, honoring the memory of those who died resisting more than 130 years of brutal colonial rule?

We are the world. But is there any *we* here at all?

2. Russian Reversal

Moscow is a low, wide city expanding in a series of rings out from the Kremlin and Red Square, spreading over some nine hundred square miles of land cleared in a cold northern forest, near where Arctic taiga blends into Sarmatic mixed forests. It's a mistake to think Moscow is part of Europe: the city looks more like Saskatoon than it looks like Berlin, all monstrous boxes built up out of nothing as if to compensate for the puniness of the human animal in the immensity of so much space, and it feels and sounds like something else yet again. To visit Europe is to tour a giant mausoleum dedicated to centuries of war, rich with the booty of global empire: a cemetery turned into a shopping mall. Going to Moscow is like visiting a Turkish moon base built in the 1950s. Cyrillic script and Slavic phonemes mesh in the air with so many *oo*'s, *shch*'s, and *ve*'s, uncannily similar enough to a Latin alphabet to look both familiar and wrong, unbroken by any tourist-friendly English. Like its script, Moscow is at once familiar and strange. Russia and America are siblings in many ways, both countries of the twentieth century, both conquerors of vast spaces, both abstract and callous and massive and dangerous.

How much do we see each other, and how much do we just see negative mirror images of ourselves? The classic late–Cold War American joke about Russia, endlessly variable, was based on a simple reversal of subject and object: "In America, everyone watches television. In Soviet Russia, television watches you!" "In America, everyone drives a car. In Soviet Russia, a car drives you!" . . . "In Soviet Russia, the police call you!" . . . "In Soviet Russia, the party finds you!" . . . "In Soviet Russia, the law breaks you!" . . . "In Soviet Russia, the war wins you!"

My trip to Moscow seemed to be an exercise in such a reversal: I was going to give a paper at an American Studies conference at the Russian State University for the Humanities, which conference was on the topic "War in American Culture." My paper would be about Wallace Stevens, James Jones, and the problem of the hero in American World War II literature, and it just so happened that the conference was scheduled the week after Victory Day, May 9, the holiday celebrating the Soviet Union's victory over Nazi Germany, perhaps the most important anniversary in modern Russian history.

The coincidence was serendipitous, as it seemed likely that the celebration would mark a historical footnote: leaders from Britain, France, and the US refused to attend the anniversary, rebuking

President Vladimir Putin (and insulting the Russian people) for Russian military intervention in Ukraine, while NATO staged military exercises in Latvia and Estonia and the US deployed paratroopers to Kiev to train soldiers in Ukraine. German Chancellor Angela Merkel was the only Western leader to break the boycott, though she skipped Victory Day proper and came a day late, to lay a wreath at Moscow's Tomb of the Unknown Soldier. While Barack Obama and David Cameron turned their backs on Putin, India's President Pranab Mukherjee and Chinese Premier Xi Jinping did not, meeting the Russian president in Moscow on May 9 with open arms, standing with him to watch the traditional parade of Russian soldiers, tanks, and missile launchers. Meanwhile, in the Black Sea, Russian and Chinese sailors trained together in a joint military exercise.

On May 7, 2015, two days before the big parade, I went to the State Museum of the Great Patriotic War, which is what Russians call World War II. The museum sits on the vast grounds of Park Pobedy (Victory Park), across the Moskva River from the old Arbat and the new business district with its hypermodern skyscrapers. A long promenade leads to a towering spire topped with a horn-blowing angel, who hovers high over a plaza framed on the west by the massive colonnaded arc of the museum proper, capped by a great dome. At the base of the spire there is a statue of Saint George slaying a dragon. As with most of Moscow, the scale is gargantuan and theatrical, at once imposing and absurd.

Halfway down the promenade, a line of old women and families shuffled through security checkpoints to wind into a small chapel dedicated to Saint George. Down the hill, a path leads to an outdoor museum of military hardware from the war, everything from T-34 tanks and Katyusha rocket launchers to the torn tail of a wrecked German Messerschmitt. Among the birches and lawns of the park around the museum, sculptures stand honoring the dead. There is a sculpture for the Allies, one for the Spanish Civil War, one for those missing in action. The most remarkable is Zurab Tsereteli's sculpture dedicated to the memory of the victims of the Holocaust, called *Tragedy of Peoples*: enormous naked men, women, and children, bald and emaciated, rise up out of or sink back into a falling line of stones. On one side is a pile of personal goods, shoes, a stuffed rabbit, eyeglasses, and so on.

It was a bright, clear, blue-skied sunny day. The park and the museum were packed, full of families, children in miniature World War II–era Soviet military uniforms, and old women, everyone wearing a black and orange Saint George's ribbon commemorating the war, celebrating their collective unity and patriotism. Groups of students on field trips were led through the Museum's dioramas illustrating the major battles of the war—the Battle of Moscow, the Battle of Kursk, the Siege of Leningrad, the Battle of Stalingrad, and the Fall of Berlin. They stood in the Hall of Memory and Sorrow, where 2.6 million bronze pendants hang from the ceiling symbolizing the 20 to 40 million Russian dead. They looked carefully at the exhibits of weaponry, uniforms, and memorabilia from the war.

Over the next few days of celebration, I would see the same crowds all over the city, with the same enthusiasm, wearing the same orange-and-black Saint George's ribbons. I stood in a surging, endless crowd near the Byelorusskiy train station watching the state military parade thunder down Tverskaya Street, swept up in the crowd's ebullient cheering as armored personnel carriers and tanks rolled by. In the crowd, the red, white, and blue of the Russian flag flew alongside the red and gold Soviet banner. Families carried framed pictures of their dead grandfathers and grandmothers through the streets of the city.

In June 1941 German Panzers crossed the Brest-Litovsk line that had divided Poland in two since 1939, engaging ill-prepared Russian troops and advancing through them at an astonishing pace, replicating the speed and ferocity of Germany's victories the previous year in the Battle of France. By the time winter hit, the German Army had rolled the Russians back more than six hundred miles along a thousand-mile-wide front from the Black Sea to the Baltic. Elements of the Fourth Panzer Army had reached the outskirts of Moscow, barely twenty miles from the Kremlin. Leningrad was under a siege that would last nine hundred days. Kiev, Odessa, Sevastopol, Kursk, Kharkov, Minsk, Smolensk, and Riga had all fallen to the Nazis, who now controlled the Slavic heartlands of Byelorussia and Ukraine. Over the winter the Russians counterattacked and took back small pockets of land here and there along the front, but when the 1942 spring thaw came, the Germans launched a new offensive, in the south, driving another three hundred miles to Stalingrad while simultaneously pushing southeast toward the oil fields of the Caucasus. That winter the tide turned, and Russian reinforcements began to push the Germans back. Over the next two years, the Russian Army killed its way back across the blood-soaked plains of Ukraine and Byelorussia, destroying the German Army and eventually sacking Berlin.

The scale of devastation on the Eastern Front boggles the mind. The Battle for Kursk, for example, was and remains the largest armored battle in history: 940,000 Germans with more than 3,000 tanks and supported by more than 2,000 aircraft faced 2.5 million Russians with more than 7,000 tanks supported by around 3,000 aircraft, in an area about the same size as West Virginia. In that battle alone, the Germans suffered 198,000 casualties (including wounded and MIA); the Russians, 863,000. By May 9, 1945, when the fighting was over, more than 30 million people had died on the Eastern Front, around 26 million of them citizens of the USSR, including around 15 million civilians. Russia suffered more, lost more, and killed more than any other nation in World War II. All told, the USSR had seen between 13 and 14 percent of its population killed—more than one person in ten.

How could anyone make sense of 26 million bodies? Is it a tragedy or a gospel?

To understand what those numbers mean, imagine a conquering army killing more than 43 *million* Americans as it burned its way across Texas, Louisiana, Oklahoma, Arkansas, Mississippi, Kansas, and Missouri. By way of contrast, only 750,000 Americans died on *both sides* of the Civil War, out of a total US population of, at the time, some 31 million: a death rate of about 2 percent, which is very high but nowhere near Russia's in World War II. Most Russians living today had at least one relative within two generations die in the war. To Russians, the war represents incalculable horror and destruction, and the Russian people's greatest moment on the world stage: their stalwart defense of the Russian homeland. The Soviet Union was the primary force responsible for defeating Nazi Germany: without the Russians in the East butchering German soldiers by the thousands, D-Day would have been impossible. As a living memory of suffering, terror, and victory, World War II is for Russians a personal, visceral historical event—both tragedy and gospel—unlike any other.

Much of the war was fought in Ukraine. Today, while hawks in Washington, D.C. and the *New York Times* say that it's Russian president Vladimir Putin who is aggressively pushing into Ukraine, Putin and most Russians see it differently. They see an expansionist NATO, led by the United States, the avowed enemy of Russia for most of the twentieth century, propping up and supporting an anti-Russian regime in Kiev. They see the US allying with Ukrainian fascists, the European Union working to separate Ukraine from Russia's economic and political influence, and American politicians calling for military buildup all along Russia's borders. They see this in a context of fourteen years of unilateral American military aggression in the Middle East, a global American campaign of torture and assassination, political instability throughout Central Asia, and a melting Arctic that promises to ignite a resource war over massive oil fields suspected to lie beneath the ice.

I heard the roar of the crowd wash over me on Tverskaya as

strategic bombers flew overhead like death-metal condors. I heard the cheers drowned out by giant ICBM launchers rumbling past. These people were proud of their military strength, proud of their nuclear force, proud of their nation, their leader, and their history.

Later that day, after the military parade was over, I met a Russian poet and video artist named Kirill Adibekov beneath the statue *The Worker and the Kolkhoz Woman*, an eighty-foot-high stainless-steel monument to the Soviet proletariat built for the 1937 Paris World's Fair. The two figures in the monument, a muscular, hammer-wielding man and a powerfully built woman with a sickle, stand shoulder to shoulder, arms upraised, towering over a traffic intersection, blazing brilliant silver in the sun, striding confidently into a utopian future. Kirill sat beneath them, a thin artist with long, dark hair and a gentle smile. We walked from the statue through VDNKh, the Exhibition of Achievements of the People's Economy, a massive Soviet-era expo and park in the north of Moscow celebrating the economic achievements of the far republics of the Soviet Union: Armenia, Kazakhstan, Kyrgyzstan, Leningrad, Karelia, and the others. He pushed his bike along while we awkwardly weaved through the thick Victory Day crowds. Occasionally we would stop so I could photograph some oddity, like the riding field or the girl on high-tech suspension stilts. We paused for a while at a café beside a lake, which Kirill told me reminded him of the Crimea; we had beer and khachapuri, a Georgian hot cheese bread.

Along the way we talked about state censorship, politics, poetry, the Saint George's ribbon, Russia's current economic recession, and many other things. Kirill was glum about the political and economic prospects his country offered but happy in his work as an artist, connected to a lively art world that, though the artists within it couldn't really come out in direct opposition to Putin's regime, did offer an independent and vaguely countercultural attitude that didn't seem all that different from the apolitical anti-authoritarianism of metropolitan hipsters and much contemporary American literature. He was saddened by how readily his fellow Russians seemed to accept the nationalist propaganda being broadcast on Russian television and websites, but he was philosophical about it. "You have to remember," he said, "Russia was a slave state until the 1860s. I think sometimes that we're still working our way out of that moment a hundred and fifty years ago."

Toward the end of our talk, Kirill pointed out the entrance to VDNKh, an enormous arch, and told me that in the 1950s there had been a giant statue of Stalin between it and the first pavilion. The statue of Stalin had been to scale with the arch, Kirill said, to show that he was a leader on a vast scale, and to turn the entrance to VDNKh into a theater of his power. "So much of Moscow is theater," he said, "the giant spaces, the great monuments—it's all a set for a play."

His comment about theater provoked a moment of realization: "That helps me make sense of this Gertrude Stein quote I've been puzzling over—I'm not sure where it's from—where she says that Americans and Russians are alike because they are both abstract and cruel," I said.[1] "I understand what she means about America being abstract, but I've been trying to puzzle out how that relates to Russia. All these giant figures, they don't seem abstract at all, at least not in the sense of abstract painting. But they *are* abstract, in a figural sense, like an allegory, or theater. They are the giant abstraction of a characteristic, of a character, the idea of a person rather than a person itself."

"What's more," I went on, "what you said about Russia only ending slavery in the 1860s suggests another similarity with America, which reflects back into this problem of abstraction and theatricality, because America was also a slave state until the 1860s. The difference between Russia and America, though, is in the relation between the masters and the slaves. In America, the relationship was seen through race, a concept predicated on the idea of biological, physical difference, fundamentally blood. Skin color

and phenotype were too variable to reliably mark racial identity, so
it always came back to the idea of white blood and Negro blood.
You can't *see* blood, though, and it's all red anyway. This epistemological instability at the heart of the American political order was
a profound problem for the ruling class. How do you know who is
'really' white and 'really' black? We might imagine that ruling-class
anxiety about this problem is part of what gave rise to American
literary and cultural fixations on 'realism,' since the most terrifying
and troubling question gnawing at the soul of the white ruling class
is precisely the question of how you know what is real."

I looked out across the motley Muscovites dressed for a holiday
swirling around the massive architecture, almost all of them wearing
their black-and-orange ribbons. "In Russia, on the other hand, the
masters and the slaves are the same, from the same country, probably looking much the same, sharing a religion and a culture going
back centuries. In Russia, there is no ontological fact separating
the rulers and the ruled, but rather the ruling class must rely for its
power on the *performance* of its role as the ruling class. This explains
the performative anxiety of all this massive sculpture, but it also
suggests a way of looking at the dramatic quality at work in Russian
literature and culture, from Tolstoy to Nabokov. It also helps explain
Putin, it seems to me, and the current impasse in American-Russian
relations, in that Obama's staff seem to take Putin for a player of
realpolitik; they read him by asking themselves what he 'really' wants
or 'really' plans to do, whereas Putin is in a position where he feels
he has to perform tough leadership, perform the reconstitution of
Russia as a world power, perform the thuggery and daring that has
helped him gain power and earned the respect of his people and
the fear of the world."

"That's very interesting," Kirill said. "You know, of course, that
the first actors in Russia were all serfs, right? They put on plays
for the aristocracy."

"Wow," I said. "Like minstrelsy in the US. Blackface dramatizes and discharges ruling-class anxiety about the epistemological uncertainty at the heart of the political order. If race is just a performance, then there's nothing holding up the dominance of white privilege. So race *must* be performed, under the gaze of a white audience, in order to ritually enact the very hierarchy the idea of its being a performance calls into question. Like in Spike Lee's *Bamboozled*. The ruling class has to play with the question of race in order to reassure itself that, at the end of the day, it retains the power to define reality."

3. Gospel

More bodies. History is full of them. Some days it seems that's all history is: piles of bodies, a gruesome wreckage of bones growing ever larger. Some have names. A few are remembered. Most are lost.

In 1781, the captain of a British slaving ship, gone off course on its way to Jamaica and rapidly running out of fresh water, ordered between 130 and 150 of the slaves it was carrying dumped overboard. I say dumped, but I must mean forced. Pushed. The crew must have had swords or guns and must have forced the slaves to jump into the ocean a few at a time. Maybe one at a time. Obviously, you couldn't bring all hundred-some slaves on deck at once and force them into suicide. They would mutiny. No, it must have happened one by one.

The sailors go below into the stinking hold and unchain a slave, drag him up into the first fresh air he's smelled in weeks. Imagine the taste of the salt air and the smell of the sea, the blinding fury of the Caribbean sun after days upon days of darkness and unwashed bodies and bilge, tight and close and hot. The sails crack overhead in the shifting wind while waves crash and split against the hull. You hear the angry calls of gulls. The rocking movement you've been blindly subjected to, the nauseating underwater dip and wobble, is transformed now into the brisk glide of the keel along the water. For a moment you savor the taste and feel of free air.

Then the sailors force you to the gunwale and, just as it dawns on you what's happening, push you over. You probably don't even have time to beg, though you might give a shout before you hit the water. Your hands tied, your body weakened by countless hours of immobility and days of bad food, you still can't give up so you kick, kick desperately—you've probably never swum in the ocean before, certainly never in water so deep, bottomless, abyssal—and you call out, shouting to the men who threw you over, but they have turned away and gone below for the next. You realize that what you thought were the calls of gulls were actually the cries of other slaves: you can see three, maybe four, a line of shouting heads bobbing in the ship's wake. Four, then three. Then two. When their legs give out, the ocean takes them. As the ship sails away, you see another dark-skinned body jerked to the gunwale and shoved unceremoniously over. You kick as long as you can, though you cannot imagine being rescued. You pray. You kick. You inhale salt water and feel the sun bake your eyes.

Aboard the *Zong*, known as the *Zorg* before a mishap painting turned the Dutch word for "care" into noise, the sailors keep working stoically, slave by slave. The job probably took all afternoon. Surely some struggled more than others, some not at all. We must be certain it was easier with the ones who didn't, because they were easier to hate: disgust mingled with contempt kills the sympathy you might feel for those who fight, as you're certain you would if you were in their situation. The sailors on the *Zong* were hard men—only rough and desperate men would risk the uprisings, disease, and other dangers of working on a slave ship—and they would have respected and sympathized with the fighters. Sailing men knew firsthand the taste of the lash. Most would have been impressed—kidnapped into service—at one time or another, and some were probably former slaves themselves. They would have identified with the resisters.

The *Zong* had set sail from Ghana with some 442 slaves on board, about twice as many as a ship its size would normally carry. The ship had been a Dutch slaver, captured by a British gunship during the fourth Anglo-Dutch war and sold to a syndicate based in Liverpool, and it was being steered by a former ship's surgeon, one Luke Collingwood, in what was his first voyage as captain. But Collingwood fell ill during the voyage and command seems to have broken down. After making it across the Atlantic, the crew mistook Jamaica—their destination—for Hispaniola, and sailed three hundred miles out of the way. It was at this point that someone, possibly Collingwood, ordered a number of slaves dumped overboard, ostensibly because the ship was low on water. We know about this massacre because when the *Zong* finally made port, its owners filed an insurance claim seeking recompense for the value of the lost property, and the insurers refused to pay on the grounds that the loss was the fault of the captain.

The *Zong* was only one ship among many, one insurance case among many, though it has become historically important and was, at the time, a landmark ruling in the fight to abolish slavery in the United Kingdom. Historians estimate that anywhere from 9 to 12 million Africans were transported across the Middle Passage to the Americas between 1500 and 1900, and probably around 2 million of those died at sea. These raw numbers of bodies, however, like the 26 million Russian dead in World War II or the 6 million dead in the Shoah, are merely so much information. You can read them again and again every day and feel nothing, learn nothing. About 1.3 million people die in car accidents every year all over the globe, which means that in the past twenty-five years, since 1980, global deaths from automobile accidents must have passed 30 million. So what?

The question here is how we remember bodies and events. How we keep the dead alive, in stories, in art, in history. How we make meaning from death. The story of the *Zong*, like the story of the slave uprising on the *Amistad* or the one on the *Tyral*, which inspired

Herman Melville's story "Benito Cereno," offers a compact, bounded narrative that we might recount easily enough, and which might serve as an allegory or synecdoche for the four-century-long horror of the transatlantic slave trade, or even as a story standing in for slavery as a whole. The treatment of the slaves onboard the *Zong*, dragged across the sea or dumped overboard as deemed necessary, illustrates the cruelty of treating humans as things. The court case deciding whether or not the ship's insurers were required to pay the owners' insurance claim illustrates the inhumanity and callousness of a legal system based in the abstraction of property. Indeed, the case suggests the absurdity and inhumanity of law as such. Where is the place for feeling in this abstruse, arcane language? Where are the voices of the Africans? Where are the spaces for compassion, or even for sympathy and respect? The names of the slaves on the *Zong* were not recorded and are not known. How could a legal system that doesn't even recognize the names of the dead be in any way just or fair?

Yet all the same, even taking the case as it is, retelling the story involves *telling* it, which means making aesthetic and narrative choices. The lack of water could be emphasized, and the story could be told as an illustration of the hard ethical choices people are forced to make in difficult situations. If your ship is running out of fresh water, people are already dying, and you don't have enough water to get your crew back to port, what do you do? How do you decide between letting your crew die, along with all three hundred-odd remaining slaves, and murdering one hundred fifty slaves to save the rest? Is it an economic calculation or a humanitarian one? The *Zong* could be told as a story about the necessary moral calculus of scarce resources in a dehumanizing economic system: it could be a story about capitalism. Or it could be a story about a foolish new captain and the pressures of command. It could be a story about the slave who was so terrified by the screams of the drowning men and women that he asked the sailors to starve them to death rather than throw them overboard. It could be a story about some of the slaves who jumped in suicidal defiance rather than let themselves be thrown. It could be a story about one of the sailors. It could be a story about one of the survivors. It could be a tragedy. It could be a gospel.

The documents that preserve the record of the event are material texts, already formed according to certain narratives (such as the British legal system, narratives of property, et cetera), but they are archaic and abstract and hence, for most of our contemporaries, alien, foreign, hard to understand and relate to. Making sense of *Gregson v. Gilbert* demands close reading, knowledge of historical context, some fluency with legal jargon, some fluency with eighteenth-century British speech, and a sympathetic imagination. Still, any college-educated American could probably read the report and have a basic understanding of the case, and most Americans with a high school degree or GED could probably work through it with a little help. It's not a radically difficult document. But while the key narrative event—the throwing overboard of 150 slaves—stands out clearly and memorably, the train of events is vague, there are no distinct characters, the story does not flow, and the text does not sing. For some readers, that very vagueness provokes the imagination to fill in the gaps. Most, though, will be left wandering in a cloud of ignorance. The narrative doesn't "perform." The "through-line" is not clear.

Canadian lawyer and poet M. NourbeSe Philip took up *Gregson v. Gilbert* as the material for her book of conceptual poetry *Zong!*, which is, as Philip insists repeatedly in her explanatory essay at the end of her book, not a telling of the story, because the story cannot be told. Rather than tell the story, Philip takes the words of *Gregson v. Gilbert* apart and recombines them, sometimes whole, often broken, into gestures, phrases, Yoruba words, African names, page after page of scattered language. She compares her work to that of the Language poets, such as Charles Bernstein and Rae Armantrout, arguing that her poem questions "the assumed transparency of language and, therefore, employs similar strategies to reveal the hidden agendas of language." As she explains, "The not-telling of this particular story is in the fragmentation and mutilation of the text, forcing the eye to track across the page in an attempt to wrest meaning from words gone astray." Consider these lines, taken at random:

tunis for the bones   the ruins of my
            story their s & y ours
                    our story it hides
      the secret that   in the rift between
            cain & abel there
rome founds her   self on murder &
      on death come   strum the lute some
                    more for my late
soul *sum*   *sum sum sum* i am
            sum i am i   am *sum* sum
                              of all ned
                  s story no more
than eleven when   he ran a
            way to sea not   that far from the lisp
                    of ma
ma pa   pa he too had
      heard of a seam
                                          of gold so
                        broad & so
      wide in an age   of lust what
                  are we
to do but lust
                                          let
                  us wed then ruth
            when the ship sets   me d

own on land   again and
            be done i   am a new
        man sift the air   for enemies
            of my soul   they are many sh h
                        hush can you not
    hear the plea s   we were deaf to
            how to   mend this i am
god s agent here   on earth our rule   is
            just and   we
                    must but   to err so far
        from reason   it is a leaky tale i
                    recite it   holds no water with
map and wind   rose and lamp
            to see them   by we set
sail crates   of portginwinebeercider   & water there were[2]

    There are two basic conceits to this kind of writing, and three basic reading practices for approaching it. The two primary conceits of conceptual writing such as this are, first, that the ideas structuring the work as a whole are more important than the formal construction of particular phrases, sentences, sections, et cetera, and, second, that aesthetic effects are more usually found in moments of contrast, juxtaposition, disjunction, unexpected repetition, and isolated fragments than in any sense of symmetry, suspense, coherence, wholeness, order, or measure. As Vanessa Place and Robert Fitterman write in their theoretical manifesto, *Notes on Conceptualisms*, "Conceptual writing mediates between the written object (which may or may not be a text) and the meaning of the object by framing the writing as a figural object to be narrated."[3] According to Place and Fitterman, in conceptual writing "prosody shuttles between a micro attention to language and macro strategies of language, e.g., the use of source materials in reframing or mixing. The primary focus moves from production to post-production. This may involve a shift from the material of production to the mode of production, or the production of a mode."[4] What they mean is that while traditional "micro attention" strategies of close reading may be useful in particular instances, these should be balanced with a consistent attention to the work as a work in relation to its contexts—questions about who the language is for, what it is supposed to represent, who "owns" it, and how it circulates within culture.

With our sample from *Zong!*, for instance, we might track how the "u" phoneme/grapheme shifts from "ruin" to the close pairing "strum/lute" then to the ambivalent "*sum*," in English the word *sum* meaning the result of addition, an accounting term, in Latin *sum*, pronounced "soom," resounding back to "ruin" phonetically but looking like "strum" and meaning, of course, "I am," then shifting through "lust," "ruth," "hush," "just" and "must," all terms resonating within a narrative of racialized slavery, the historical framework of the British legal system, and post-structuralist literary theory critical of the concept of narrative itself. At the same time, much of the work's power, even in this moment of micro-reading, comes from attending to *Zong!*'s intervention as a work of language or conceptual poetry insisting on a moment of "reality" beyond language that language can never fully contain or inscribe (as Philip insists, the story cannot be told), yet constructed through the explicitly political transformation of nineteenth-century British legal language into affective representations of individual and collective suffering.

The best ways to read such a work are by skimming, free-associative close reading, and allegorical reading. Skimming provides a sense of linguistic atmosphere, a feeling of lexicon and grammar that offers a thin and mutable affective experience. Words never signify without affect, not only in their connotations but in their syntax, and skimming helps make that affective valence accessible across broad swaths of text. Free-associative close attention to specific phrases takes the text as a kind of machine for producing a reader's own creative response, opening the text into a form of dialogue. Reading allegorically, on the other hand, means thinking about what the text *means* in relation to the world, and specifically what the text represents or speaks of in its coded ways. Place and Fitterman begin their manifesto with the declaration that "Conceptual writing is allegorical writing," and define allegory as follows:

> The standard features of allegory include extended metaphor, personification, parallel meanings, and narrative. Simple allegories use simple parallelisms, complex ones more profound. Other meanings exist in the allegorical "pre-text," the cultural conditions within which the allegory is created. Allegorical writing is a writing of its time, saying slant what cannot be said directly, usually because of overtly repressive political regimes or the sacred nature of the message. In this sense, the allegory is dependent on its reader for completion (though it usually has a transparent or literal surface). Allegory typically depends heavily on figural or image-language; Angus Fletcher's book *Allegory: The Theory of a Symbolic Mode* argues that this heightened sense of the visual results in stasis.[5]

Straight narrative reading ("reading for the story") doesn't work that well with such poetry, nor does formalist appreciation. Consider our sample from *Zong!* While the story of the *Zong* is marked by an allusion to the biblical tale of Cain and Abel and briefly elaborated through an individuated narrative ("ned / s story no more / than eleven when / he ran a / way to sea"), these narrative gestures scatter into the dispersed language of the poem and cannot be clearly reconstructed. There are no "characters" as such who might personify values or with whom we might sympathize. As well, many of the typical reading strategies taught in English courses—historicism, psychoanalytic reading, Marxist criticism, reading for race or gender—are often not very productive or helpful with language and conceptual poetry, because these strategies rely on formal qualities, hermeneutic depths, and thematic interests which such poetry typically disavows.

Poetry in the traditions of concrete, language, and conceptual poetics, whether the dense abstractions of J. H. Prynne or the typographic experiments of Christine Wertheim, are made within a tradition of "avant-garde"–coded art practice that takes an explicitly ideological position against three concepts fundamental to capitalist art, which is to say art as commodity production. Those fundamental concepts are identity, transmission, and pleasure. An art object as a commodity must be branded, it must be able to circulate, and it must have use value. Conversely, art objects in the modernist experimental tradition resist identity, resist circulation, and resist being entertaining or instrumental (a poem should not sell you a Coke). It is in doing just these things, of course, that they assert their value *as* art objects, as objects definitionally beyond the sphere of capitalist production and thus available for exploitation, thus inspiring capitalism's future conquests by bodying forth the eternally promised desideratum of the always new. Art for art's sake has always been capitalism's spirit, even as its makers have always insisted that the role they are playing is capitalism's conscience. But conceptualism knows this, and turns its own ideologies inside out with strategies that many people find difficult or disagreeable. While offering work that attacks the idea of individual identity, conceptual poets brand themselves as consumer objects. While offering work that resists reading and retransmission, they often make their work freely available. While eschewing instrumentality, they make deliberately didactic works that offer pointed ideological, political, and moral criticisms of contemporary society and art production. Beginning from the choice between aestheticized politics and politicized art offered by Walter Benjamin in his essay "The Work of Art in the Age of Mechanical Reproduction," the very choice we face every day in a social world wholly given over to the suicidal self-consumption of its own grotesque nihilism, certain practitioners of conceptualism have decided to insist once again that art is, necessarily, political.

Zong! is an interesting example of conceptual poetry for several reasons, not least because it operates at the intersection between Benjamin's two choices. It is clearly politicized art, in that it manifests a critique of narrative power, institutional history, and the reproducibility of an event. At the same time, it is a work of aestheticized politics: by insisting on the traumatic unintel-ligibility of human sacrifice as an originary historical moment, Philip valorizes and calls into being a political community formed around that sacrifice. In *Zong!*, Philips works to keep alive a collec-tive identity—a political identity—through the memorialization and consecration of the death of representative members. Hence her focus on constructing *names* for the murdered slaves out of *Gregson v. Gilbert*, names that were never recorded but which she writes into her text, e.g., "Bomani Yahya Modupe Jibowu Fayola."[6] Hence her otherwise inexplicable fictional attribution of the work's origins to oral history: the cover of the book says the story was told to the author by Setaey Adamu Boateng, a name Philip has invented to invoke the authority of direct physical (genetic) transmission. As critic and scholar Evie Shockley wrote in the online poetry journal *Jacket2*, "*Zong!* enacts a critique, but also effects a catharsis or, more accurately, works through a problem that lies at the intersection of the emotions, the psyche, and the soul, if such a thing can be spoken of in the twenty-first century's secular spaces."[7] It is precisely at this intersection of mind and body, word and thing, nation and sacrifice, history and blood, that *Zong!* does its work as *tragōidia*.

Or as Philip herself writes elsewhere (in an essay titled "Wor(l)
ds Interrupted"):

> is zong! perhaps a ritual work masquerading as a
> conceptual work mirroring the act of stripping away
> the spirit of the african mask or carving leaving only the
> form the work masquerading as something else while
> doing another kind of work this is how african spiri-
> tual and cultural practices have survived the hostile
> societies of the afrospora it is how certain indigenous
> cultural practices survive the present day christianiza-
> tion and islamicization in africa
>
> there is very little space to speak of the ritual function
> of poetry particularly as it relates to a work like zong! it
> comes out of a particular historical moment that is the
> kya kya kya kari basin a moment that extends into the
> present is resonant am tempted to say redolent with
> aspects of ritual and spirit i think of zong! as doing a form
> of soul work for those who died unmourned i think of
> the impossibility of ever knowing what happened the
> impossibility of making whole that which has been rent
> asunder i think of writing in the face of the yawning
> chasm of oblivion that was the lot of africans . . .[8]

The key sentence here is: "I think of zong! as doing a form of soul
work for those who died unmourned." With this, the truth of
Zong! is revealed: its effort to insist on the incomprehensibility of
the event does not work *against* identity, but insists on the event's
ontological reality beyond language. *Zong!* does not critique the
story of the *Zong*, but reconstructs it, honors it, consecrates it. It
is not a "not-telling" at all, we realize. *Zong!* performs the truth of
collective identity, specifically racial identity, by ritually reenacting
a moment of violence as a sacred origin. It turns a murder into a
sacrifice. It is a gospel.

4. Desecration

I woke the morning after Victory Day to find Moscow silent and seemingly empty, haunted now by the absences of the teeming crowds, late drunken celebrants, and uniform-clad kids who had filled the streets the day before, as the day before had been haunted by great-grandfathers and great-grandmothers seventy years dead. On my morning run, I weaved through unmanned metal detectors guarding entrances to vacant plazas. Back at the university dormitory where I was staying, the campus was deadly silent. I had dinner plans to meet a friend of a colleague, a German historian working on the question of how Ukrainians in the 1950s remembered World War II, and took advantage of the quiet morning to work on my presentation for the conference. In the afternoon, I went out to a nearby Coffee House, a Moscow chain, for a cappuccino, one of the few things I could reliably depend on being able to order without confusion.

While I sat outside in the glorious May sun sipping my foamed milk, I checked in on Facebook and scrolled through my Twitter feed. I soon found a string of tweets posting a story from the *London Review of Books* by Seymour Hersh. It was a story about a CIA coverup, Obama administration lies, the construction of narratives, and the need to define collective identity against an excluded other. It was a story about Osama bin Laden. It was a story about a body.

Hersh's basic story was that the Obama administration constructed most of its narrative about the Osama bin Laden raid out of lies in order to obscure and efface the facts of the case. Hersh argues that what really happened in the Osama bin Laden raid was not at all like how it was portrayed. Whereas the government claimed to have found bin Laden through interrogation and spycraft, Hersh's informants say bin Laden was being held by the Pakistani secret police in Abbottabad and someone connected with the Pakistani secret police told the US about this fact. Whereas the US government

claimed to have sent a highly secretive special-operations team
into hostile territory without the knowledge or permission of the
Pakistani government, to capture bin Laden if possible or in the last
resort to kill him, Hersh's informants say that the US government
worked in collusion with Pakistan's, which made sure bin Laden was
left unguarded the night of the raid, and that there was never any
question of capture, that the American SEALs went in that night to
commit state murder. Finally, whereas the US government claimed
to have flown bin Laden's body out to sea, where it was properly
buried in accordance with Islamic ritual, Hersh's informants say that
in fact bin Laden was dumped unceremoniously out of a helicopter
over the Hindu Kush mountains. According to Hersh's story, the
Obama administration made up its cover story on the fly to protect
the Pakistani secret police and American-Pakistani relations and to
glorify American spycraft and military heroism.

I read Seymour Hersh's troubled and troubling account with
wonder but no surprise, with skepticism about Hersh's reliance on
so few sources but no faith in the official narratives as they were
told, and with a feeling of disappointment and dread that had
become familiar over the past decade as revelation after revelation
of US government torture, surveillance, assassination, bald-faced
lies, illegal aggression, and bad faith exploded into the public sphere
like so many canisters of toxic gas, spreading neither clarity nor
accountability but only nausea, moral poison, and obscurity. I knew
that like Wikileaks's Julian Assange, Edward Snowden, and Chelsea
Manning, Seymour Hersh would be pilloried in the mainstream
press and probably targeted by the Obama administration, his
report would be attacked ad hominem by media jackals questioning
Hersh's character, integrity, and sanity rather than dealing with the
substantive issues raised, and the report would be dismissed as a
scandalous mire of hearsay rather than taken seriously as a piece
of investigative reporting by the same journalist who broke My
Lai and Abu Ghraib. Hersh and his report would be derided, then

forgotten, much like the other numerous revelations of government incompetence, skullduggery, and evil we've been granted since 9/11 and forgotten with a vengeance, since Hersh wasn't only telling Americans a disagreeable truth (that our leaders and high officials are lying buffoons) but also taking away from us one of the few sacred symbols of national pride we had managed to salvage from more than a decade of frustrated military adventurism: the mutilated body of our superhuman enemy, Osama bin Laden.

I remember when the story broke that bin Laden had been killed. College students all over the country joined together to shoot off fireworks, sing patriotic songs, and wave American flags. Fans at sporting events burst into chants of "U-S-A! U-S-A!" Major broadcast networks interrupted their scheduled programs with live feeds of celebrants screaming and hooting in Times Square, near the ruins of the World Trade Center, and outside the White House. For a brief, blazing moment, a nation usually defined by bitter political feuding, racial strife, and brazen class inequality came together to celebrate its unity over the dead body of an Arab. Whether the moment was glorious or grotesque depends, I suppose, on your point of view. Ismail Haniyeh, for example, a senior leader of Hamas and at the time the elected prime minister of the Gaza Strip, told reporters: "We condemn the assassination and the killing of an Arab holy warrior. We regard this as a continuation of the American policy based on oppression and the shedding of Muslim and Arab blood."[9]

Whatever you thought about the war in Iraq, then coming to a close after eight years of mistakes, lies, profiteering, and blood, or the war in Afghanistan, a grim confusion then in the midst of an ambiguous drawdown, and whether or not you agreed that the appropriate response to the news was a crass display of idiotic jingoism, most Americans would agree that bin Laden's death was a good thing, and most Americans would feel that his killing was a kind of justice putting paid the crime of the 9/11 attacks. As the mythology around the bin Laden killing was spun, spun, and glammed up by talking heads, government officials, cryptofascists, and Hollywood, the highly trained, prodigiously equipped and supported assassins sent in by the US to murder a crippled, diabetic, middle-aged man came to be portrayed more and more as stoic knights in holy armor, cyborg cowboy warriors fighting evil in the demonic shadows of the desert night. From the Riefenstahlish film *Zero Dark Thirty* to Lea Carpenter's literary adoration of masculine power *Eleven Days*, American culture makers told and retold the moment's narrative of American glory, a story of white techno-righteousness overcoming the brown-faced devil and his heathen legions.

For Seymour Hersh to then come along and say that bin Laden was trapped, unguarded, unarmed, and handed over to the SEALs for slaughter, for him to tell a story wherein it wasn't American prowess that conquered the devil but rather the devil's own weakness, for him to remind us that Osama bin Laden wasn't a devil at all but a man, in a world of men and women, and that the men who killed him were only men as well, and for him to assert that we didn't give our enemy a proper burial but treated him with the savagery and disrespect for human life that we insisted were the very essence of his character, the very qualities that distinguished him from us, well—Hersh was desecrating a holy truth.

Of course, that's been Hersh's mode. He's a debaser, a desecrator, an enlightener, someone interested in piercing power's veils of hypocrisy, illusion, and obfuscation to bring hidden truth into the purifying light of rational thought. He's made a career out of exposing lies, unearthing conspiracies, and uncovering buried crimes. I've long admired Hersh's work and thought of him as a hero, though serious questions have been laid against the credibility of some of his recent work. Hersh is a journalist and freethinker in the best tradition of critical enlightenment thought, one in a long line of muckrakers, whistleblowers, cynics, and gadflies.

The idea in this line is to demystify the sacred, dispel illusion, and increase understanding. Somehow the former two lead to the latter, though it's not always clear how that happens. Nevertheless, it seems laudable to me, *sapere aude* and all that, and it forms the motivation for much of my own work, not least the paper I'd be delivering in Moscow on Tuesday, which was part of a longer project offering a critique of post-1945 American war culture. One of the main arguments of my project is that understanding war as trauma is a political act, in that trauma recuperates and glorifies nationalist military sacrifice under a language of psychopathology, elides structural and political realities by focusing on the experience of individuals rather than on social or systemic forces, and effaces enemy and civilian dead by substituting for their bleeding bodies the psychologically wounded soul of the trauma hero.

Understanding war as trauma is a relatively new way of thinking, available only since World War I and dominant in the United States only since the 1970s. The narrative of war as trauma took hold in the US because it helped solve ideological problems that had erupted in the 1960s between the ideal of American liberal democracy and the reality of American imperial power, and ease generational conflicts between those who'd won World War II and their children who'd inherited the postwar liberal order. Understanding war as trauma and focusing on the damaged souls of individual American soldiers allows us to ignore the reality of war as political policy and to ignore the effects our war policies have on those on whom they are imposed. It allows us to reconcile our idea of liberal American virtue, embodied by American soldiers who suffer psychological injury for the violence they are forced to commit, with the industrial violence by which America maintains its global political and economic hegemony. Our soldiers kill for us, and we demand that they suffer the blood guilt—in today's language, PTSD—so that we don't have to.

The talk I was to give on Tuesday focused on an earlier moment, before the idea of war as trauma had come to dominate American culture. In my paper for Tuesday, I compared Wallace Stevens's World War II poetry with James Jones's Proustian combat novel *The Thin Red Line*. What Stevens's poems and Jones's novel had in common was a serious concern with the problem of the individual nationalist hero in industrial warfare. In the traditional form of the sacrificial narrative, a hero dies for his community. A single name, a singular life, a unique body is sacrificed for an abstract ideal—in modern war, "the nation"—and the power of his sacrifice makes the ideal real. His blood has paid the price to consecrate national identity; the idea of the nation has become physically real in his body. One of the problems that arose with industrialized warfare in the nineteenth and twentieth centuries was that the single hero, the singular life, the unique sacrificial body wasn't unique at all, but horrifically multiple: industrialized war made a grotesque parody of the idea of sacrifice, sending millions of men to die in great putrescent piles of guts and limbs, over and over and over. Nevertheless, awards were still given, heroes still named, and nations still forged out of bloody bodies. How? And how could you reconcile that grotesque repetition with the idea of human dignity? And further yet, how could you accept that horrific process as the foundation of any kind of legitimate public order? James Jones and Wallace Stevens both made these questions a subject of their art, creating complex, difficult meditations on the problem, meditations that don't ever quite settle, though they both manage to achieve their own moments of tense equanimity.

I was nervous, preparing my paper, about how my Russian audience would take it. Were my desecrations of the formal structure of nationalist sacrifice coming too soon on the heels of Victory Day? Were my efforts to rend the veil of military honor under even traumatic narratives too pointed a critique to keep from offending sacred Russian memories of their own historical traumas? Millions had just marched in the streets carrying pictures of the dead. On

Saturday, the whole nation had turned out to honor the bodies of the fallen. On Tuesday, I was going to say that such honor was nothing more than political propaganda woven over the grotesque truth of the modern state. Would they boo? Would they hiss? Would they shout me down?

I needn't have worried. The soft abstractions I spun fell harmlessly down on my audience like so many flakes of ash. My talk was about America, anyway, American war, American heroes, American empire, and the arc that red, white, and blue flag danced across the seminar room kept them focused on the specifics of the case rather than inviting thoughts about how it might have applied to Putin, Moscow, and Saint George. What's more, these were scholars, academics, ideologues only when it served them, and what reason would they have had to rebuke me? No, the truth is that my desecrations fell on ears that were if not deaf at least disposed to be kindly, and I troubled no one, offended no one.

5. The Rising of the Dead

Four days after I came home from Russia, the Association of Writers and Writing Programs removed the poet Vanessa Place from their National Conference Los Angeles 2016 Subcommittee, in response to a petition circulated on the internet through Change.org ("Victories every day") arguing that Place's work was "at best, startlingly racially insensitive, and, at worst, racist," and a robust shaming campaign on Twitter by an anonymous internet collective that calls itself the Mongrel Coalition Against Gringpo. On May 13, the Mongrel Coalition launched its campaign by tweeting: "VANESSA PLACE IS RACIST. DEFEND HER AND YOU ARE COMPLICIT. VP WORE BLACKFACE. VP TWEETS GONE WITH THE WIND. GO AHEAD, DEFEND HER." The petition, which was not written by the Mongrel Coalition, followed a few days later.

The specific offensive work in question was a Twitter feed in which Vanessa Place was tweeting Margaret Mitchell's Civil War romance, *Gone with the Wind*, line by line, 140 characters at a time. The AWP, one of the most important institutions in the United States involved in the cultural production of what we call literary fiction and poetry, claimed that they "believed in the freedom of expression," and offered no judgment about whether they agreed that Place's work was racist or not, but had decided to remove Place from their subcommittee in order to avoid controversy. In their words: "The group's work must focus on the adjudication of the 1,800 submitted proposals, not upon the management of a controversy that has stirred strong objections and much ill-will toward AWP and the subcommittee. Perpetuating the controversy would not be fair to the many writers who have submitted the proposals."[10]

The petition against Place's work was written by a white poet named Timothy Volpert, who lives in Topeka, Kansas. The petition reproduces a screenshot of the Twitter feed in question, which features a production still of the actress Hattie McDaniel in her "Mammy" costume from the film *Gone With the Wind* and a backdrop banner with an archaic caricature of a black-faced woman. You can see from the screenshot that the feed had been running since 2009 and had produced 16,200 tweets. The complete petition reads:

> We find it inappropriate that Vanessa Place is among those who will decide which panels will take place at AWP Los Angeles. We acknowledge Place's right to exercise her creativity, but we find her work to be, at best, startlingly racially insensitive, and, at worst, racist. We do not believe it is right that she have a hand in deciding whether panels having to do with race and identity will be a part of next year's AWP. Her recent work with "Gone with the Wind" re-inscribes that text's racism—she does not abate it—in the flesh of every

descendant of slaves. Indeed, she herself claims to be constructing "a slave block" with the work. AWP's stated desire for inclusivity and diversity in the panel makeup requires an atmosphere of trust on the part of POC, LGBTQIA, and Disabled panel applicants, and Place's racially insensitive, if not downright racist, projects violate that sense of trust. She furthers her career on the backs of Black ancestors—the hands that filled the master's pockets now fill hers. We ask that you remove her from her position of authority over writers of color.

Thank you for the work you do. We trust you will make the right decision in this instance.[11]

It will be noticed at once that Volpert's claim that Vanessa Place's body of work is racist is based on one piece of evidence, "Gone with the Wind." Volpert argues that Place's whole oeuvre is "at best, startlingly racially insensitive," and that her judgment as a professional artist is compromised. Volpert strongly implies that Place is herself "racially insensitive," and also implies that if she were given the power to decide who should be on AWP panels, she would discriminate against writers of color and possibly even take advantage of them. These are heavy charges, and they have been made on the basis of one work of art, a work of art that Volpert interprets literally, ungenerously, mistakenly, hyperbolically, and out of context. Volpert describes Place's Twitter feed as a "recent work of art," but anyone can see from the image of the feed used in the petition itself that the work had been going on since 2009. Volpert says that the work "re-inscribes [*Gone With the Wind*'s] racism," when it would be more accurate to say that the work reframes or remediates it, since Place is tweeting Margaret Mitchell's novel, not "inscribing" it, but that's beside the point because Volpert goes further to say that the work "re-inscribes [*Gone With the Wind*'s] racism . . . in the flesh of every descendent of slaves." This is hyperbole, of course, a metaphoric expression. Vanessa Place has not written a single word "in the flesh" of anyone. What Volpert seems to want to say is that Vanessa Place's repetition of *Gone With the Wind* is harmful, and he presents that idea of harm as a metaphor of physical violence that explicitly invokes the lash. Volpert's broad stroke makes it impossible to judge whether Place's work is really harmful or not, since he's not making a serious claim about the world but a rhetorical gesture expressing a certain emotion. Volpert conflates Place's Twitter feed with a similar work of the same title published in the poetry journal *Drunken Boat* in 2010 by quoting out of context a phrase from Place's artist's statement explaining that piece saying that she is "constructing 'a slave block' with the work," which statement Volpert lets stand as a literalized metaphor that is expected, apparently, to speak for itself. He goes on to assert that Place "furthers her career on the backs of Black ancestors," an assertion made without explanation or evidence.

Volpert doesn't make a case building on a long trend in Vanessa Place's work over her career. He doesn't provide evidence of specific acts of racist discrimination that Place herself has committed. He doesn't bother to try to understand what Place's intent was with the Twitter feed he calls "racially insensitive." He offers no sustained engagement with conceptual poetry, the problems of representing and reframing race in terms of intellectual property rights, or even what it means to remediate a historical text in a new context.

To take Volpert's stance as he presents it, replicating *any* act of racism is itself racist (and moreover an act of physical violence). To take his tack, every text or image that represents slavery is as racist as slavery itself, and all representations of racism are equal, since all of it "re-inscribes . . . racism . . . in the flesh of every descendant of slaves." If Volpert had his way, there would be no representations of slavery at all, ever, not literary, not historical, not factual, nothing, because for Volpert mimesis is repetition, and repetition is reenactment. By this logic, Volpert himself is as guilty of being "racially insensitive" as Place is: if the Twitter feed is as racist as the novel being tweeted, then Volpert's "re-inscription" of Place's Twitter feed is as racist as the feed. "Remove Vanessa Place from the AWP Los Angeles conference committee" is as racist as "Gone With the Wind" is as racist as *Gone With the Wind* is as racist as actual plantation slavery. It's all the same.

Despite the patent absurdity of this position, the lack of real evidence for his claim, the manifest shoddiness of his argument, and its reliance on a strikingly ungenerous reading of a single work of art, Volpert's petition was signed by more than 2,100 people, including well-known and respected poets. Volpert's petition and the AWP's decision to remove Place from its committee set off a firestorm of controversy within the teacup of American poetry, including flame wars between poets, bitter arguments on Facebook, and yet more hyperbole in response to Volpert's, including Language poet Ron Silliman comparing the signers of Volpert's petition to Spanish fascists, Nazis, and Saïd and Chérif Kouachi. He went so far as to call them an "online lynch mob."

I was disturbed by the AWP's decision to remove Place based on Volpert's petition and angry with people I knew for supporting what looked to me like scapegoating. Vanessa Place's Twitter feed was offensive and dull, certainly, but her work in general has been thoughtful and intelligent, even if often discomfiting and difficult. I'd been following her work for years with admiration. I had invited her to be part of a symposium on conceptual poetry and poetic freedom I had organized at Princeton University in 2013, where she sat on a panel with Timothy Donnelly, Kent Johnson, Jena Osman, and Mónica de la Torre. Place's work is often emotionally difficult to read, because so much of it focuses on racial injustice and sexual violence; the challenge her work presents is substantial. Part of her gambit, as a conceptual poet who uses mainly found or appropriated texts, seems to be to turn the act of reframing into a painfully lucid steel mirror.

Her work had been, since before I had been following it, always presented within a clear theoretical and political approach. Place uses her work to attack the idea of the self, especially the lyric self, in part because, so she argues, behind the idea of the modern self lies the idea of property. She is a profoundly insightful critic of the role contemporary poetry plays in capitalism, and has made her work that of critiquing and, yes, desecrating what remains holy, sacrosanct, or metaphysically privileged around the idea of poetic production, poetic identity, and the voice.

As Place said in the address she delivered at Princeton:

> It has become apparent to me that poetry is funda-mental to capital, just as the humanities are desperately needed, though there is an obfuscation of the need through a stupid insistence on functionality. What is poetry/art for, et cetera, and while there is an easy answer about the utility of critique and interrogation, for plodding logic and pedantic insistency that science rewards less often than the humanities, there is a better, more transcendental, more obvious, response . . .
>
> Poetry is what poetry is, and what poetry is has everything to do with the packaging of the imaginary libratory subject. It has to do with other soft-eyed dreams—that clouds mean, that representations are, that language matters, that at any moment there can be a pivot-point at which a terrible beauty may be born. Beauty, it could be noted, being the beast that is abso-lutely indifferent to the corpse before it. And that these things are as true as anything else. Or, more precisely, as tragically true as everything else.
>
> The poetic subject is us, here, now, the point at which the false may be beautifully, horribly, real.
>
> Or, to misquote Eric Hoffer, "Every great cause

begins as a movement, becomes a business, and eventually degenerates into a racket."
    Put another way, "I" is not a subject.
    I is a racket.[12]

Place's work with *Gone With the Wind* is also about property,
as she explained after the AWP removed her from its committee:
part of the point of the Twitter feed was to draw legal action from
the notoriously litigious Margaret Mitchell estate, in the hopes of
provoking a legal battle about who "owns" the racist language in
Mitchell's novel. Her work with *Gone With the Wind* is also about
desecration. For, as a white author from Virginia, Place recognized
that Mitchell's novel was considered by many to be a sacred object.
As she wrote in the artist's statement that Volpert quoted from,
describing a work of text published in *Drunken Boat*:

> In May 2009, I was in Berlin, where the multifarious
> reminders of Nazism seemed more properly to be
> Germany's historical focus, rather than the Holocaust.
> For the Holocaust was an event, a singular horror,
> whereas Nazism was the formal manifestation of anti-
> Semitism as sociopolitical philosophy and ethical/
> aesthetic modus operandi. Similarly, slavery is not the
> issue for the United States today as much as racism is
> as ever was and ever will be, at least historically. This
> piece—the gleaning of all passages in *Gone With the
> Wind* in which "nigger" features prominently (omitted
> are other racial epithets or denigrating enactments),
> then set in a block of text, a slave block—aims to
> remind white folks of their goings-on and ongoings.
> Self included, for there is personal guilt there as well,
> given my family is not just Caucasian American, but
> Southern, Virginian, as they say, "by the grace of God."

And God's grace carries with it a certain responsibility
for the error of blind loyalty (see, Abraham & Isaac).
Too, GWTW is still a very much beloved bit of Ameri-
cana (Molly Haskell recently published a book on
Scarlett O'Hara as feminist icon, and last year's Best
Actress Oscar was announced to the soaring strains
of "Tara's Theme"), with very little attention paid to
its blackface, or that its blackface is blackface. Or that,
in such texts, characters are to people as people may
be to property. So I have stolen Margaret Mitchell's
"niggers" and claim them as my own. In a funny way,
I am replicating Huck Finn's dilemma/conversion: to
understand that keeping (not turning in runaway)
Nigger Jim is stealing, for which one may well go to
hell, and to do it anyway.[13]

The reference to Mark Twain—a great American desecrator
if ever there was one—is pointed. In emulation of Twain's novel
The Adventures of Huckleberry Finn, Place is positioning her work
in terms of a critique not just of slavery but of the connections
between private property and racism, with an awareness of its being
trapped in the very system it's trying to critique. In Twain's novel,
Huck Finn's moral options with regard to Jim are circumscribed
by the ridiculous horror of slave society, in which Jim is *property*.
Huck can return Jim or he can steal him, but he *cannot free him*.
Furthermore, stealing Jim means not only breaking the law for
Huck, but accepting social ostracism and his soul's damnation.
Place positions herself in a similar double bind as Huck by stealing
Margaret Mitchell's racist language. Place can choose to ignore
Mitchell's racist novel, or she can steal it, but *she cannot erase it*. In
effect, Place is dramatizing the intolerable position we're all trapped
in, the horrific idea of order we impose upon ourselves through the
concept of racial discrimination. We can try to ignore it or we can

claim our complicity, but we don't know how to get outside of it. We cannot simply erase our own history.

Pointing out painful double binds has long been part of Place's project. I suspect this is part of what makes her a figure of contention and fixation. For some time she took to appropriating Facebook posts by poets announcing publications or readings; recontextualized, the posts made a mockery of the writers' adroitly performed "humblebrags" and exposed the self-promotion so fundamental to social media. For this, Place was rebuked and criticized. I am convinced as well that Place's stark, intense, serious poetic persona grates on many poets today. Vanessa Place does not play nice, and the whole point of poetry today is that you play nice: you listen to other poets so they'll listen to you, and around and around it goes. The problem is that while everybody can read and write poems, not everybody gets a job doing it. Poetry pretends to operate like a gift economy, but in fact it's an industry, an industry whose product is poets—or, more precisely, paying MFA students.

Yet all this—the emotional, aesthetic, and moral complexity of Place's work, her theoretical rigor and conceptual brilliance, her explicit and laudable efforts to desecrate shambolic notions of poetic identity, poetic voice, and poetic community, the affective reaction her persona provokes, even her being lumped in with Kenneth Goldsmith—none of this explains the explosive emotions ignited by Volpert's petition, nor does it finally weigh in quite enough to make "Gone With the Wind" okay. I think only someone who deliberately ignored Vanessa Place's exhaustive theoretical work could charge her with being "racially insensitive," for she is nothing if not sensitive to the language used to construct race. Nevertheless, her work is also deliberately offensive. Even if the work shows a deep sensitivity to the language of race, "Gone With the Wind" is still racist.

So there's that. What's more, while I was disturbed by the AWP's fear of scandal and angry at fellow writers for supporting a half-baked petition rebuking a poet for doing challenging work, I was also confused, because a few weeks earlier I had found myself supporting the other side of a similar issue. When Deborah Eisenberg and other writers at PEN America publicly disavowed their support for the PEN Gala at which the French satirical magazine *Charlie Hebdo* would be awarded the Toni and James C. Goodale Freedom of Expression Courage Award, I thought their position was clear and unimpeachable. Never mind the disgust engendered by the opportunistic waving of JE SUIS CHARLIE placards, never mind the magazine's own complex relationship to satire and French Catholicism, and never mind the fact that *Charlie Hebdo* were desecrators, critics, cynics, debasers committed to puncturing facile credences and upsetting conventions. There were serious problems with the idea of PEN American giving an award for courage in freedom of expression to *Charlie Hebdo*.

First, allowing desecrators to do their cynical work, which work is not only a cornerstone of democratic and egalitarian thought but also essential to fostering intellectual maturity and social enlightenment, is not the same as rewarding them for it. One can support extreme examples of free speech, satire, and even hate speech, without rewarding and honoring their speakers simply because they persist in being offensive. Second, all this shit happens in a context. The context for Place's "Gone With the Wind" happens to be systemic oppression and racialized murder. The context for PEN America's award to *Charlie Hebdo* was fourteen years of aggressive American military action against Islamic countries and peoples. Keith Gessen wrote what seemed to me one of the best explanations of how this worked in his piece in *N+1* describing why he signed the letter protesting the PEN Gala:

> When twelve staff members and friends of the satirical cartoon newspaper *Charlie Hebdo* were killed at their offices by Saïd and Chérif Kouachi this past January,

several things happened. First, there was an outpouring of grief for the victims. There had been many other attacks on editors and writers in recent memory, but not at this scale and not with such brazenness. The brothers came in, announced that they were from al Qaeda, and started killing.

But in addition to the grief, in America at least there was something else: I would call it an attempt to assimilate the shootings to the ongoing American "war on terror." My friend George Packer, writing at the *New Yorker* website, immediately warned against ascribing the killings by two second-generation Algerian Muslims to the failure of France to integrate people like them, or to the ongoing Western participation in wars in the Middle East. The culprit, Packer wrote, was none of these things, but rather militant modern Islam: "an ideology that has sought to achieve power through terror for decades." It's the same ideology, Packer wrote, "that murdered three thousand people in the U.S. on September 11, 2001." And it was: the brothers had even pledged allegiance to al Qaeda. Packer's language took one back to the days after the September 11 attacks, when Western politicians and intellectuals began gearing up for a long protracted war with "Islamic terror." That war, obviously, continues.

When people in France, in their mourning, declared "Je suis Charlie," they were expressing grief, an identification with the victims of horrific violence. But what were people expressing when they said "Je suis Charlie" in the US? It was a tragedy. But what did it mean to identify with those particular victims, at this particular time? I could be wrong, but it seemed to me that "Je suis Charlie" was a way for people to re-pledge

their commitment to the War on Terror that had been
announced by the United States in 2001.[14]

The *Charlie Hebdo* award scandal was a story about bodies,
because the *Charlie Hebdo* shooting was a story about bodies. Whose
bodies? Arabic bodies or French bodies? Arabic bodies or American
bodies? *Gone With the Wind* is a story about bodies, because the
Civil War is a story about bodies. Whose bodies? Black bodies or
white bodies? Southern bodies or Yankee bodies? The story of the
Baltimore riots is a story about bodies, because the stories of Freddie
Gray, Eric Garner, Michael Brown, and Trayvon Martin are stories
about bodies. Whose bodies? Desecrated bodies or sacred bodies?
Bodies that matter or bodies that don't?

The angry, mournful cry echoing out from the protests last
winter was simple: Black lives matter. Black lives matter.

Black and white protestors came together over the dead bodies
of Michael Brown and Eric Garner, doing what communities do
over dead bodies, which is to make meaning. *These bodies are sacred*,
they said, every time they chanted "Hands up! Don't shoot!" or "I
can't breathe." *These bodies are sacred.*

Formally, the act is homologous to other acts of sacrificial
understanding and communion. The dead editors at *Charlie Hebdo*
became the sacred embodiment of French nationalism or, as Keith
Gessen suggested, the American war on terror: "Je suis Charlie."
The twenty-six million Russians killed in World War II became the
sacred embodiment of the Russian state, a Saint George's ribbon
tying a country together. The three thousand people killed in the
attacks on the World Trade Center became the sacred embodiment
of the American nation: Remember 9/11. The anonymous soldier
killed on the battlefield becomes the sacred embodiment of his
nation's spirit: the Tomb of the Unknown Soldier.

Structurally, the difference between a heroic sacrifice and a
scapegoating is merely a matter of identification. In both cases it's

a story about a body, a ritual, a sacrifice: a *tragōidia*. In both cases a group of people come together in bloody communion. In both cases the murdered body becomes sacred, either totem or taboo, lifted up or cast out. The community says, "We are the same as the dead," or the community says, "We are different from the dead." Either way, the community becomes *real* in its relationship to the dead: this is a story about a body. "We" cheer the death of Osama bin Laden. "We" stand over Eric Garner as our brothers in blue choke him to death. "We" say, "Je Suis Charlie." "We" lynch a nigger. "We" burn a witch. We decide who's in, who's out, who's right, who's wrong, who's good, who's evil, who lives, who dies. Typically, too, one follows hard upon the other, first the sacrifice, then the scapegoat, first the "Us," then the "Them."

I am constitutionally repelled by such acts of consecration. They make me want to be a debaser. I cannot believe in a nation or a peace that's founded in blood. I refuse to believe that violence brings us together. I cannot accept that death justifies death, war justifies war, and hatred justifies hatred. I refuse to pick sides. I don't want to eat the dead, wash myself in their blood, or claim their names. If I could, I would desecrate all these altars, tear down every veil, piss on every christ.

I admire the desecrators and cynics in history because they strike at idols of dogma and irrationality, because they strive to pierce through to reason and truth, because so often they stand alone and embattled against institutions, mobs, and blind adherence to tradition. But there's something else at work, too, because every act of desecration—like every act of consecration—happens in a context. We reason and criticize in social contexts, and I don't get to refuse mine. I don't get to refuse to pick sides. All too often, however alone they might think they are, it turns out that the desecrators, debasers, and cynics stand not against but alongside the mighty. And it turns out that sometimes when they thought they were spitting on a false idol, they were desecrating the faith and hope of those who have been told again and again that their lives and dreams don't matter.

When we think about *Charlie Hebdo* and Vanessa Place, we need to think about Saïd and Chérif Kouachi, Hattie McDaniel, and Michael Brown. When we think about 9/11, we need to think about Osama bin Laden and a hundred years of Western military and political intervention in the Middle East. When we think about the avant-garde's critique of the Self, we need to think about the dead bodies dumped over the side of the *Zong*. And as we think, we might begin to realize that the sides we get to choose between are not enlightened desecrators and unenlightened mobs, but those with the power to name the sacred and those whose lives are spent fighting for that dignity.

Some lives matter more than others: that's why protestors have to form a group called Black Lives Matter. Some lives matter more than others: that's why French satirists desecrating Christianity is different from French satirists desecrating Islam. Some lives matter more than others: that's why Russian propaganda valorizes the Russian dead and American propaganda, the American dead. Some lives matter more than others: that's why US audiences flocked to watch *American Sniper* but have forgotten Abu Ghraib.

Some lives matter more than others because that's how humans do politics, but can you, cynical reader, *mon semblable, ma sœur*, begrudge a people their right to insist on their dignity? Can you deny your own need for the sacred, your own deep thirst for an existence that's more than mere matter? Can you truly tell me that you have not, in haunted moments, called upon the names of the dead?

Everything happens in a context. The context we live in now is one in which carbon waste from the richest countries is rapidly warming the planet, threatening infrastructure and agriculture around the world, destabilizing weather patterns, and raising sea levels to inundate coastal cities. As a species, we face our greatest collective threat. For decades, the only hope for humanity has been for all the peoples of the world to unite in common cause and limit our carbon emissions. The wealthiest need to give up their cheap energy, the poorest needs to give up their dreams of wealth, and our collective fate needs to be grounded in economic and environmental justice. That has not happened, and most likely never will. We remain as divided today as ever, and as environmental disaster endangers food and water resources, economic precarity narrows opportunities, and war spreads, each group insists on its exceptional difference: Sunni, Shiia, French, Algerian, Western, Islamic, American, Russian, the 99 percent, the 1 percent, White, Black . . .

Some lives matter more than others. That's how we make collectives—identities—peoples—nations—wars. The bloody ritual of sacrifice and communion through which we manifest what "we" means won't end until we learn to sacrifice ourselves first, in every case, for every brother and sister, every other Other. Those with wealth and power must scatter it. Those with privilege must dismantle it. Those caught in the complicity of repression must lay down their own bodies to end it. Those who suffer violence must turn the other cheek. The impossible demand for infinite compassion is our only hope, the only way we might be saved.

And when that bright day comes it will be the last day, and all the dead of every race, creed, gender, and nation will rise from their graves together as one, finally equal. [2015]

War of Choice

By the time the English Civil War had ended, after nine years of brutal fighting, well over half a million people had been killed throughout the three kingdoms of England, Scotland, and Ireland. England alone suffered approximately 190,000 war-related deaths out of a population of five million, a death rate of nearly 4 percent— making the English Civil War almost twice as deadly, per capita, as the American one two centuries later.

Across the Channel in Paris, Thomas Hobbes watched the war end with grim relief. He had fled England in 1640, and reports of the war's devastations spurred him to deepen his reflections on sovereignty and power. In 1651, he published *Leviathan*, almost instantly recognized as a major work of political philosophy. One of the most influential ideas in the book was Hobbes's new story of the "State of Nature": whereas the Bible described humanity's exile from an innocent Eden, Hobbes told a tale of humanity's escape from an constant, anarchic war for resources, where "the life of man [was] solitary, poor, nasty, brutish, and short."

In joining "Nature," "War," and primitive man, Hobbes's story of the "state of Nature" as a war of all against all implicitly justifies any amount of violence committed by a sovereign power, since the sovereign is by definition working against violence and toward civilization and peace. War, for Hobbes, is not a specific kind of social action that groups of people undertake against each other but is defined by its very distinction from social life.

This was a powerful idea, especially if you happened to be a white

European during the age of colonial expansion. It still often determines how we think and talk about war today. It shapes the stories we tell about going to war and coming home, it undergirds what we mean when we talk about "trauma," and it provides the conceptual basis for universalist claims to be waging a "war on terror." Looked at through the Hobbesian frame, wars waged by one group of people against another are transformed, as if by magic, into metaphysical struggles against our own primitive nature.

Hobbes doesn't come up much in Georgetown University philosopher Nancy Sherman's book *Afterwar: Healing the Moral Wounds of Our Soldiers*, but his definition of War as Nature implicitly informs everything she says. Like Hobbes, Sherman would have her readers forget that war is a thing humans do to each other. Like Hobbes, Sherman would like to believe that war is somehow separate from civilization.

Sherman is primarily a moral philosopher, with a background in Kant and Aristotle, and her research focuses on military ethics, the "battlefield mind of the soldier," and "the moral weight of war." According to Sherman, *Afterwar* is "a manifesto for how to engage in moral repair, one on one, with individual service members and veterans so that we can begin to build a new kind of integrated community." This call raises as many questions as it answers, one of the most important of which is about the relationship between this unidentified "we" and American soldiers.

Sherman's best chapter, "Don't Just Tell Me 'Thank You,'" explores precisely this question. It begins with a familiar scene: A civilian tells a veteran "Thank you for your service." The veteran says, "No problem" or "You're welcome." After an awkward pause, the conversation resumes, nobody feeling satisfied with the exchange, the civilian vaguely guilty, the veteran resentful. Sherman carefully unpacks the many complexities at work within this interaction, elucidating how the actors involved are performing ritualistic observances of social norms and committing themselves to shared values, but from different perspectives and with radically different senses of investment and sacrifice. For civilians to say "Thank you for your service" is for them to say "Thank you for doing what I did not, or would not, do for our community."

So much for civilian guilt. But why are soldiers so resentful? Sherman explains that soldiers might feel resentful if they feel that civilian "gratitude is merely instrumental, for the sake of getting them to renew their service," or if they feel more alienated than recognized—if they feel, that is, that civilians don't really understand what they're being thankful for. Veterans might feel resentful as well because they feel guilty, angry, or confused about their deeds. They might feel resentful because they suspect the ritual is just that and no more, an insincere formality. The issue, as Sherman frames it, is one of veterans holding citizens accountable.

Sherman's analysis here is nuanced and illuminating, but it fails to adequately address two significant problems. The first is the issue of Sherman's "we." Her book relies throughout on an implicit identification between American citizens and government policy, as if what soldiers did in Iraq or Afghanistan was an expression of national political will. This easy correlation between the values and thoughts of American citizens and the decisions made by the United States government simply cannot be made, especially when it comes to military action, and it is disingenuous to imply that soldiers are acting on behalf of the "American people." No doubt there are many who would like to believe they are, but Sherman needs a better account of how beliefs about national unity match reality, and what disjunction between the two might mean. In this light, veterans might well be resentful of what they see as citizens' false claim to agency or their naïveté in confusing polyglot America with the United States government.

The second major problem Sherman downplays is that veterans might feel "used," not just because the gratitude offered might be instrumental, but because they did some evil shit. Veterans might feel they don't deserve to be thanked for what they did; they might see what they did not as a service, but as a crime. Sherman touches on this lightly, but only very briefly and only in the most specious way. She brings in the example of Jean Améry, a Holocaust survivor who argued that his refusal to forgive his Nazi torturers had moral power. As Sherman quotes him, "Only I possessed, and still possess the moral truth of the blows that even today roar in my skull, and for that reason I am entitled to judge, not only more than the culprit but also more than society—which thinks only about its continued existence." Sherman quotes Améry to "remind us of limiting cases for relieving moral resentment, where there can be no possibility of moral healing," but she doesn't address the fact that if you map Améry's situation onto the last fourteen years of war, her example of irrecuperable moral injury lines up not with American soldiers but with orange-suited, force-fed detainees at Guantanamo Bay and naked, tortured Iraqis in Abu Ghraib. Simply put, the victims tortured by the wars in Iraq and Afghanistan weren't American soldiers, but Iraqis and Afghans.

Sherman relies here and elsewhere on a conflation between Holocaust victims and American veterans of the wars in Iraq and Afghanistan, as if there were any moral equivalence between the targets of the Final Solution and the agents of the global "War on Terror." This thoroughly irresponsible equivalence illuminates the great moral vacuum at the heart of Sherman's book, which is in the way she persistently turns the question of moral responsibility into a narrative of moral injury. Much of *Afterwar* comprises stories from soldiers who served in Iraq and Afghanistan, yet all but one of those stories are about what those soldiers suffered, not what they did. This is an enormous failing.

Key to this failing is Sherman's uncritical reliance on the idea of "moral injury." She writes that it "refers to experiences of serious inner conflict arising from what one takes to be grievous moral transgressions that can overwhelm one's sense of goodness and humanity," but she never unpacks this definition. She never explains how inner ethical conflict leads to injury or what, precisely, is being "injured." She never makes a case for why this language of victimization and injury ought to replace a language of responsibility, nor why "moral injury" might be more useful than the more conventional language of "guilt," "shame," and "betrayal" she uses elsewhere. Nor does Sherman ever make a clear distinction between "moral injury" and PTSD, or discuss why one way of talking about war might be better than the other. Rather, Sherman conflates moral injury with several other diagnostic terms, from survivor guilt to traumatic brain injury, in ways that only obscure what she means. Most disturbingly, Sherman's phenomenon of "moral injury" produces a victim without a perpetrator: no agent is ever named who does the injuring, nobody is responsible, no one is at fault.

Sherman's lack of philosophical rigor here might be an oversight, or it might be bad faith. "Moral injury" turns out to be an empty sophism, more useful for David Brooks–style cant than for serious thought about war or morality. With it, you can imply some airy recognition that something went wrong with America's most recent military adventure but still advertise your support for "the troops," all while dodging the indelicate question of who exactly might be responsible for injuring whom.

Whatever one might say about the corrupt boondoggle of Afghanistan, the war in Iraq was an aggressive power grab executed with astonishing idiocy, enriching companies such as Halliburton, DynCorp, Bechtel, and ExxonMobil at the cost of hundreds of thousands of Iraqi lives and ongoing human suffering almost incomprehensible in its meaninglessness. Anyone doing moral philosophy of war needs to make sense of what it means to know you have committed evil, not as a victim but as a perpetrator, and anyone talking about morality and the Iraq War needs to account for the gross irresponsibility, outright lies, and pointless waste of human life that characterized that conflict. What kind of "moral healing" is appropriate for Specialist Lynndie England, who tortured prisoners in Abu Ghraib? Sergeant Frank Wuterich, whose Marines killed twenty-four civilians in Haditha? Colonel Michael D. Steele, whose soldiers testified that he ordered them to "kill all military-age males" in their area? General George Casey, senior commander in Iraq from 2004 to 2007, who incompetently oversaw Iraq's descent into civil war? What kind of community expresses gratitude for such behavior? While Sherman claims academic expertise on the "battlefield mind of the soldier" and "the moral weight of war," she doesn't seem much interested in such questions. Nor does she spend much time on how the "battlefield mind of the soldier" reckons with killing and torturing innocents, or how "we" might carry the moral weight of an unjust, illegal, and aggressive war.

A work of moral philosophy about war that doesn't discuss agency and what it means to do evil, or how the discrepancy between claims to moral goodness and knowledge of moral evil might be made sense of, isn't doing philosophy. To be fair, Sherman never claims that's what *Afterwar*'s about. She is quite explicit that she has written a manifesto, a call to "build a new kind of integrated community." The problem is that the community she seeks to build is one for whom war isn't a moral or political choice, but a moral accident, an abstract force—something like an act of Nature.

Another important thing Sherman leaves out is the fact of war's tremendous appeal. "Even war has something sublime about it," wrote Kant, arguing that it is "all the more sublime in proportion to the number of dangers" faced. The sublimity of war is captured in the epic scenes written by Tolstoy in *War and Peace*, in Ernst Jünger's memoir *Storm of Steel*, and in the helicopter assault in Francis Ford Coppola's *Apocalypse Now!* Throughout history, people have found war not only sublime but exhilarating, purifying, sexually charged, liberating, and ennobling. For many veterans, war was and will remain the most profound experience of their lives. As

Supreme Court Justice Oliver Wendell Holmes Jr. wrote, looking back on his service in the Civil War: "The generation that carried on the war has been set apart by its experience. Through our great good fortune, in our youth our hearts were touched with fire."

Some of the men and women who go to war find not only sub-limity but vocation. For professional soldiers especially, war is the summit of their life's work. Peace for such warriors is a dull prison. Some of the assorted disorders that plague veterans after war are doubtlessly attributable to feelings of frustration and diminishment. The contrast between the thrilling power one wielded in war and the petty constraints imposed by civilian life is a familiar theme in veterans' writing.

Michael Putzel's hybrid work of journalism, history, and biog-raphy, *The Price They Paid: Enduring the Wounds of War*, illustrates this theme, focusing on the story of Major James Newman, a career soldier whose sublime moment as an air cavalry commander came during the darkest years of the Vietnam War. According to the accounts and recollections Putzel weaves together, Newman was a bold, charismatic, fiercely competent leader, once nominated for the Congressional Medal of Honor for a daring helicopter rescue. Yet as soon as Newman came home, his career imploded and his life took a sudden swerve. Newman assaulted his wife, illegally mar-ried the wife of a fellow officer, then tried to hire a cab driver to kill his new wife's husband (she was still married) and burn down his own home.

Newman had earned stellar evaluations in Vietnam, had been promoted on his return, had been awarded a Distinguished Service Cross, and was being groomed and recommended for a career path that gave him a "good shot at eventually earning a general officer's star, perhaps even two." After the grand jury indictment charging him with two counts of conspiracy and one of bigamy, though, his military career was over. Less than eighteen months after coming home from Vietnam, where he had commanded dozens of men flying millions of dollars' worth of military equipment, directing them through complex, coordinated aerial and ground combat with the highest imaginable stakes, James Newman left the military, got divorced, and a few years later went to work as a Buick dealer. He sold cars for the rest of his life.

Putzel makes a great mystery out of Newman's self-destruction, but it's not so hard to understand. Newman identifies the problem himself: "'I couldn't go kill somebody every day,' he lamented years later. 'I didn't have a mission of no kind.'" When Newman boarded the plane in Vietnam to come back to the US, he was leaving behind his status, his command, his community, the work that made his life meaningful, and the intensity that made his life sublime. He came home to guilt, boredom, and constraint. Is it any wonder he started lighting fires?

The Price They Paid offers insight into what it means for a professional soldier to go to war. What it helps us see best is that war isn't a state of nature or a moral accident but can be a way of life and, what's more, a meaningful one. As with Sherman's book, though, and as in Hobbes's naturalization of war, Putzel leaves aside the wider questions of war as a political or social activity, especially the war in Vietnam. Yet as long as we refuse to look at the wider political questions of war, we will be able to see it only as disconnected stories of isolated individuals suffering in a state of nature. As long as we refuse to see war as an action for which people and institutions are responsible, we will continue to mistake imperial soldiers like Major James Newman for unfortunate victims.

———

Over the past two years, police killings of unarmed black men have become prominent in national discussion. The problem is not a few bad apples, but a system of institutionalized racist violence and the people who serve it. As Ta-Nehisi Coates wrote, "There is nothing uniquely evil in these destroyers or even in this moment.

The destroyers are merely men enforcing the whims of our country, correctly interpreting its heritage and legacy."

Coates was writing about Ferguson, Baltimore, Cincinnati, and Staten Island, but he could have been writing about Iraq and Afghanistan. Indeed, it is puzzling to me that we have talked so little about the connection between a decade of reckless American military aggression abroad and the police brutality we see today at home. While commentators have expressed alarm at the militarization of police equipment across the US, fewer have been willing to discuss the militarization of American culture. It was not ever thus. During the 1960s, the Vietnam War was often connected to police violence at home, and the struggle for civil rights was allied to the struggle to end the war. We seem reluctant today to connect the War on Terror with the war on black lives, but how many videos do we need of police snipers, police tanks, police drones, and police violence before we recognize chickens that have come home to roost?

Imagine if instead of having a conversation—insufficient as it has been—about systematic racism, we were having a conversation about the moral and psychological stress American police suffer in the course of patrolling their communities. Imagine that instead of talking about Black Lives Matter, we were talking about police health care, police pensions, and police suicide rates. Imagine that instead of hearing about how Rekia Boyd, Michael Brown, John Crawford, Samuel DuBose, Eric Garner, Freddie Gray, Dante Parker, Tamir Rice, Tony Robinson, and Walter Scott were killed, we never learned their names but instead were treated to stories about Ray Tensing's posttraumatic stress, Darren Wilson's marital problems, and Daniel Pantaleo's moral injury. Imagine that instead of trying, however inadequately, to address America's long history of racial violence, we were spending our time trying to educate civilians in their obligation to "bridge the police-civilian divide."

Of course you don't have to imagine: that's the very conversation we've been having these last fourteen years about war. And as long as we continue having the same conversation, talking as if war were a fact of nature and not a political choice, we're going to stay locked in the same wartime mentality. As long as our government keeps showing the world that Iraqi lives don't matter, Afghan lives don't matter, Muslim lives don't matter, Arab lives don't matter, then our police will keep drawing the same conclusion about black lives. Until we reckon with the things we've done, we will find no peace, because we will not have owned up to the fact that war is not "nature," but a choice, a choice we keep making again and again. [2016]

My Flesh and Blood

My body keeps channeling so many contradictory feelings around the figure of the soldier *intensity of shame* as his body becomes the object of my lust and my violence. I want to kill him for blocking my dream of a demilitarized future, and I want to be fucked by him because the repressive sublimation of his body has become unbearable.

—Rob Halpern, *Music for Porn* (2012)

1.

Men in tights and spandex clutch each other, hold each other, sweat and bleed together under the white lights, slamming each other to the mat, to the ropes, to the climax, the final turnabout and inspired last-minute rise from soul-obliterating suffering to throw off the hurt and confusion and fear, lay evil low with a perfectly executed suplex, and restore the scales of justice.

The 1980s were a golden age for American professional wrestling, and like a lot of kids, I watched it on TV. My friend Jeff, though, was serious. Maybe it had to do with his being raised in a Catholic church that still observed the Tridentine Mass, or maybe it was the magic of the moment, the conflation of Cold War fears and charismatic freaks—Macho Man Randy Savage, Rowdy Roddy Piper, André the Giant—but he approached each week's match with religious devotion.

"It's not real," I objected. Jeff insisted it was. We argued for weeks, then hashed out a reading that satisfied us both, locating the real in the wrestlers' bodies: The stories were managed and constructed, we agreed, but Junkyard Dog really did clamber up the ropes in the corner and leap down at Ricky "The Dragon" Steamboat, clothes-lining him with his forearm. Yes, the feuds between Hulk Hogan and the Iron Sheik were cooked up, but the bodies slamming to the mat each week were raw. It wasn't until years later, after I'd been to war and had long ago left off watching wrestling, that I realized we were still missing the point.

Meat is not truth. The truth of wrestling cannot be the wrestler's body, since an infinite number of actual bodies could be destroyed on the mat and wrestling would still go on. No, I began to see, the truth of the event was actually much closer to Jeff's Tridentine Mass: The bodies lent their substance to the semiotic exchanges of narrative, face and heel, peripeteia and revenge, all of which shaped and channeled viewers' desires. The truth was the whole: The ritual synthesis of blood and word, flesh and mask, was what gave those falling bodies weight.

2.

I remember first seeing Omer Fast's video installation *The Casting* at the 2008 Whitney Biennial. I'd been out of the army two years, and back from Iraq for four. The installation consisted of two screens with projections on both sides. I found myself transfixed by the flicker in the images, the way the performers blinked and wobbled, mimicking still photos, and was moved by the seamless interweaving of an American soldier's story about killing an Iraqi with the same soldier's story about dating an unhappy, self-harming German girl. I didn't know whether the stories were real, but that didn't seem to matter: The actors were, and they lent their substance to the semiotic exchanges of the narrative, Germany and Iraq, killing and burning, all of which shaped and channeled viewers' desires to consume the soldier's trauma.

The situation Fast's film dramatizes is suggested in its title: a collective casting an individual in the role of scapegoat. On one side of the screens, there are the lights, the screens, the cameras, the actors playing the interviewer, producers, and staff, the whole spectacular apparatus of consumer capitalism attending to its altar, the screen, and the body upon it.

On the other side of the screens, Fast interviews a man who seems to have been a soldier. "So how do you feel about improvising?" he asks, to which the man responds ambivalently: "It depends on how you feel at the time." Fast presses: "Can you improvise now?"

The man submits and tells his two stories, twisted together in Fast's deft editing, offering up a perfect proportion of innocence and blood guilt. We drink down his pain, confusion, and desire to be seen, all mediated through gorgeous shots (on the screens' other sides) of a burning Humvee, a bloody scarf, an autobahn, American soldiers.

The Casting ends abruptly, ambiguously, with the artist suggesting that the story might not work because it's too long, then delivering a few spliced-together sentences that have since been interpreted as Fast's artistic statement: "I'm definitely not so much looking for a political angle. I'm more interested in the way that experience is turned into memory and then the way that memories become stories, the way that memories become mediated."

With these sentences, Fast offers the exact ideological formulation justifying the consumption of wartime sacrifice as art. Our aesthetic engagement with war, it insists, is not about power but about narrative. We cast the traumatized soldier as our scapegoat, the one bearing the sins of war, and ignore numberless dead Iraqis in favor of attending to one American's psychological suffering. Politics—the objective fact of the soldier's existence as an agent of state violence—is displaced by an insistence on "memory" and "experience." We're not interested in blood, we tell ourselves. We're interested in stories.

Fast later called his statement "a complete lie."

3.

Omer Fast's 2016 film *Continuity* is a feature-length revision of his videos *Continuity* (2012) and *Spring* (2016). It's also an expansion and elaboration of *The Casting*. The film crew has been replaced by a middle-class German couple. The singular actor has been replaced by a series. The soldiers now serve in the Bundeswehr rather than the American army, and the war is in Afghanistan rather than Iraq, but the relationships are homologous. The ritual sacrifice is the same.

Watching *Continuity* carelessly, it's easy to piece together a troubling but comprehensible narrative: An aimless, hash-smoking German kid named Daniel joins the Bundeswehr, looking for something that will feel as real as flame burning flesh. While in Afghanistan, he makes a pass at a fellow soldier and is gang-raped by several men in his unit. Later, on patrol, Daniel leaps out of his vehicle and runs into the desert. Several soldiers follow him. They are ambushed and killed.

Back home in Germany, Torsten and Katja Fiedler are crippled by grief, and hire a succession of young men, possibly prostitutes, to act out Daniel's homecoming. They pick the men up at the Bahnhof, one after another, bring them home, and serve them dinner. The Daniels hallucinate maggots and fingers in the food, an eyeball in the wine, whether from self-medication or being drugged we don't know. After each dinner, Katja tries to sleep with them. Three Daniels later, the Fiedlers change the game and hire an even younger boy, Felix, to role-play the events leading to their son's enlistment. On his way to the Fiedlers' one afternoon, Felix is hit and killed by a stolen sports car driven by a male prostitute, the protagonist of a second narrative strand.

The last Daniel's disappearance renews Katja's grief. Driving through the woods with Torsten, presumably to pick up yet another Daniel, she sees a camel walking down the highway and stops. She gets out of the car and follows the camel into the forest, Torsten close behind, to a clearing overlooking a sandy trench full of dead and dying soldiers, some of them Daniels. She watches an Afghan man collect the soldiers' weapons. Is Katja hallucinating? Did Torsten drug her too? Has the fantasy somehow become real? Does it matter?

The film offers its most delicious pleasures in the domestic theater of the Fiedlers' dining room, where each new Daniel negotiates a fresh performance of Oedipal fantasy. The second fake Daniel is particularly fun to watch, as he spools out a story in which a chance meeting between Bundeswehr soldiers and an Afghan family erupts into violence, which is then patched over with the gift of an Audi. It's virtuosic storytelling, and the details are so perfect we're left to wonder whether the young man is a gifted liar or himself a veteran.

"It's true," Daniel number two assures us.

"No it's not," says Katja.

"It is," he says.

"I don't believe you," she says.

"Doesn't matter," Daniel number two admits. "What would you rather hear?"

4.

On closer viewing, there are several knots in *Continuity*'s seemingly linear trajectory. The Fiedlers' drama unspools one scene after another, but Daniel's Afghanistan comes to us in flashbacks which, on closer examination, don't quite cohere: the soldier we thought was Daniel wears a nametag reading Vogel and is played by the same actor who hits Felix with a sports car. What had seemed to be one narrative arc dissolves into fragments, while what had been two stories merge, a narrative double exposure filling out a unified symbolic economy.

Working with and against the ideology of trauma, *Continuity* explores how war functions in the Western bourgeois imagination, how those of us back home projecting our shame, grief, and lust onto the screens of soldiers' bodies are less interested in the fate of any specific individual than we are invested in a ritual economy of sacrifice. We are more than willing to overlook discrepancies between Soldat Fiedler and Hauptgefreiter Vogel, Daniel number one and Daniel number two, imagination and fact, so long as these young men can fill out the formal roles in our ritual *fort-da* of trauma and recovery. Like Katja and Torsten and the interviewer in *The Casting*, we are ambivalent about particular soldiers' stories— this one is too long, that one strains belief, this other doesn't match our expectations—but we need their bodies to make our stories about who we are feel real.

Whereas *The Casting* offers one single soldier performing his trauma, *Continuity* gives us the performance again and again, as body after body cycles through the role of symbolic sacrifice. The continuity is explicit. A tattoo on Daniel number two's forearm reads *in saeculo saeculorum*, "for a lifetime of lifetimes," a phrase from the Vulgate that recurs twelve times alone in the Book of Revelation and is sung in the Tridentine Mass. Torsten tells young Felix, playing Daniel, played by Bruno Alexander: "You are my flesh and blood."

But meat isn't truth. The truth of war cannot reside in the soldier's body, because any number of young men could be ground to pulp and the war would still go on, just as any number of wrestlers can fall to the mat, and any number of wafers can become the flesh of Christ. Rather, the truth of war is something like a mass. The soldier's body lends its substance to the semiotic exchanges of the narratives—freedom and terror, trauma and recovery—shaping and channeling our desires for identity and transcendence. *Continuity* helps us see how the truth of war is the Eucharistic whole: Through the ritual synthesis of word and blood, fantasy and flesh, we assert our communion in the face of death. [2017]

IV.

LAST
THOUGHTS

What Is Thinking Good For?

Spend a couple of hours online skimming think pieces and hot takes, bouncing from *Slate* to the *New York Times* to Twitter to *The Chronicle of Higher Education* to Reddit, and you'll soon find yourself either nauseated by the vertigo that comes from drifting awash in endless waves of repetitive, clickbaity, amnesiac drek, or so benumbed and bedazzled by the sheer volume of ersatz cognition on display that you wind up giving in to the flow and welcoming your own stupefaction as a kind of relief.

Nevertheless, one can, out there among the hired trolls, scum-slingers, professional identitarians, pundits, and charlatans, still reliably find good work: courageous investigative journalism; thoughtful, witty, and erudite reflections on complex cultural phenomena; heartfelt, perceptive essays exploring intricate ethical and social dilemmas, each piece the assiduously hewn product of countless hours of labor. And all of it eminently disposable, fated to be consumed and retweeted and referred to for a few hours then forgotten, like everything else passing through the self-devouring gullet of the ouroborosian media Leviathan we live within, picked up and dropped as we keep searching for newer confirmations of our half-articulated hopes and fears, more recent pictures to prove to us our world makes sense, fresher flags to wave telling other people who we are and that we exist. The internet's total instrumentaliza-tion of thought, in which every shared #mustread is repurposed to accessorize an online persona, has created a constant demand for new content, a great vortex sucking every half-formed attitude and clever tweak into its gaping maw, which is also its anus, spewing and eating and spewing again in an interminable grotesque mockery of public intellectual life, Hegel's world spirit as human centipede.

Flee from the trashfire of the agora to the fluorescent-lit labyrinths of the ivory tower and you find yourself in another world, yet a recognizable one, in which the same faddishness and basic disposability holds sway as in the broader culture, but wrought in strange tongues and played out for much smaller audiences. Despite the vestigial guild system regulating entry into the academy, Sturgeon's law—which proposes that 90% of everything is crap—still holds, and thought is as instrumentalized in the university as it is out in the marketplace: articles and books are mainly valued not for their wisdom, aesthetic qualities, rigor, or information they hold about the world, but rather as entries on a CV, points toward promotion, testimony to the university's glory, and provocations for further "knowledge production."

On the humanities side, at least, since that is what I am familiar with, specifically literature and English, all too often what one finds are conversations driven by relentless self-absorption in debates about the field and relentless demands for "ground-breaking" research agendas, neologisms, and epistemic revolutions, since these are the easiest ways for new scholars to distinguish themselves and for older scholars to stay excited about their profession. Each new crop of PhD students confronts a brutally competitive job market in which the individual odds for making a good career out of their long and arduous training are slim: thus the intellectual freedom and sense of discovery which may have drawn them to graduate school in the first place are displaced by powerful compulsions to produce consumer objects *à la mode*, conventional enough to be recognizable, different enough to be interesting, shaped to the needs of the market, forgettable and ultimately forgotten. And yet, despite the neoliberalization of the university, the casualization of academic labor, the ridiculous workload most teachers carry, the catastrophe of the academic job market, the herd-thinking that characterizes academic fads, and the all too real assault on public education, higher education, and the humanities coming from anti-intellectual Republicans and Koch-funded libertarian cadres, good scholarship still somehow gets done. But who has the time to read it?

Across the spectrum of cultural production, the same phenomenon holds: our attention to any particular object of human thought or passion is fleeting, for we know as soon as we start reading one article that six more wait to replace it, and more behind those, more books, more TV shows, more movies, more reviews, more lists. Our relationship with the objects of human intellectual and artistic production is no longer characterized by sustained attention and reflection, but rather swift and relentless consumption: absorb as much as you can in a skim, post or repost it on social media, move on. You're wondering right now how long this piece is, thinking about skipping ahead, anxious if and when I'm going to get to a 280-character takeaway you can tweet to your followers. The important thing is not the object or its effect on us, but rather what stance or opinion the object makes possible. In this way, what was once recognized as thought, facilitated in literate culture by the circulation of texts, has become something else: on one side a shifting array of shallow reactions and poses, on the other a virtual hive mind. The individual thinker, like the individual artist, has been subsumed into the relentless and sterile abundance of consumer capitalism, having become in the process either a pop idol whose output is nothing but variations on a brand, or just another worker bee.

The point here is not to lament the loss of the individual, nor to speak ill of pop idols, though the anthropological implications of the way that the internet and mass society are transforming our conception of the individual and evacuating that interiority which is the *sine qua non* of the literate self are profound and still not yet fully articulated, but rather to ask what it all means for thought. What does it mean today *to think*? What is thinking *good for*?

It sometimes seems as if the only socially valued forms of intellectual labor are the production of ideology ("think tanks"), the production of attention ("think pieces"), and the production of reproducible consumer objects (i.e., books, not necessarily for reading but for discussing, ideally big books with simple arguments that can be repeated ad nauseam across multiple platforms—think Steven Pinker or Malcolm Gladwell). Producing knowledge about the world is still compensated, if not as well as producing opinions, but when it comes to serious thought the situation seems bleak. Yes, "critical thinking" is still spoken of as a value in the humanities wing of the educational industry, even though it's under profound attack across the culture and even if critique has by and large devolved into a set of rote gestures, but the arduous liberation of consciousness from dogma and self-imposed ignorance is as unwelcome today as it was in Socrates's Athens. And even if you do find solid journalism, beautiful writing, profound analysis, or edifying thought, what do you *do* with it? Read it, tweet it, then move on to the next, and the next, and the next? A stream of language passes into you through a screen then back out through another screen, and can you even say it touched you? Were you even there? Or was it just a momentary shudder of the hive?

Now that we're here, though, I see that I've begun *in media res*, or rather, *in media media*, begging the question before I even asked it. We cannot ask what thought means today, that is, until we have some sense of what we mean by "thought." *Is* it the same as critique, in a sense Kantian or Marxian or otherwise? Is it the love of wisdom? Learning to die? The sedulous apprehension of universal abstract forms of truth? The elaboration of mental architecture justifying otherwise meaningless lives? A game?

The answer's not immediately clear, though we might make some intuitive claims. We can be certain that thought has something to do with consciousness, and something to do with language, though what exactly the relation is in each case is not entirely transparent.

Thought has its pre-conscious insight, its structures and images, its relations and systems; half the difficulty in thinking is putting thought into words. Yet thought is not reducible to language, much less to text. The argument Socrates makes against writing in Plato's *Phaedrus*—that writing isn't properly philosophical because a text always says the same thing to whoever questions it—suggests a way of approaching the question that sees thought not in terms of its product, the philosophical argument, but as a process, a dialectic, and considered from this angle, perhaps my initial concern over our relentless inattention to textual objects is misplaced. Thought, after all, does not inhere in ink and paper, much less in pixels on screens, but in the human social world. Yet the *Phaedrus* offers a paradox, because it is itself a text, and as Derrida demonstrated in his famous essay on Plato's *pharmakon*, it is a rather ambiguous and dialectical text—as might be, Derrida argues, every text, since any given piece of writing is not a dead letter transmitting self-evident truth but a medium, and a medium not only connecting the present reader and absent writer, but connecting the thinking writer and language, *logos*, both in the writer's time and in the reader's: thought as social media.

Thinking is indubitably a social activity, though the archetypal image of the thinker as hermit would suggest otherwise. In the apartness of the eremite image, whether it takes the form of Socrates standing ruminating in his sandals, Siddhartha sitting under his lotus tree, Rodin's bent thinker perched pondering the gates of hell, or Hannah Arendt smoking over her desk, we find something essential represented, which is that while thought is undeniably a social activity, it is not continuous with social life. Thought is something that happens in a strange relation to society, at some distance from day-to-day human rhythms, in a different kind of time, attentive to other cares. The thinker is a public figure, no doubt, since to keep one's thoughts private, unarticulated, unwritten, and unshared is to abjure the dialectical process of thought itself, the difficult translation of ideas and phenomena into the very fabric of sociality, language.

But there remains about the thinker something isolate, some quality that sets her apart. This quality is not accidental but essential, for it is that which separates the thinker from the ideologue, the preacher, the "thought-leader," and the sophist: it is the quality of dedication to thought itself, a refusal to accept thought's subordination to other social values, even to society as such. It is a willing and deliberate self-estrangement from "what is known," the unexamined and taken-for-granted premises upon which the collective imaginary structures we live within are founded. It is an effort to ask hard and perhaps unanswerable questions about our most sacred beliefs and our most obvious truths. Which is why the thinker remains alienated from society even as she walks within it, and why so many people find her threatening and annoying.

What is thought, then? Thought is the willed suspension of thought. It is what the ancients called "pondering," what Zen Buddhists call *shikantaza*, or "just sitting," what Adorno called "negative dialectics," and what German philosopher Peter Sloterdijk calls the suspension of "stress-semantic chains." Thought is the opposite of a hot take, which channels an emotional reaction through a preexisting pattern of rhetoric back into the ebb and flow of social meaning. Thought is a practice which the philosophical text assists through its demand for rigorous attention to language, but which is, as Socrates argued in Plato's *Phaedrus*, never reducible to the text. It cannot be replicated, reproduced, remediated, or retweeted because it's an event in a moment of social relation, nothing more, nothing less: a pause, a suspension, a temporary liberation from the psychosomatic chains that bind us to the collective dream we call reality, an opening in which new possibilities might emerge.

So what's thinking good for, then? What's it good for today, or, frankly, ever? Why should we take the time to ponder complex and difficult arguments about abstract concerns, suspend our emotional and moral reactions to confusing and provocative claims, and cultivate our alienation from the 24/7 cycle of mediated outrage and despair that shapes so much contemporary social life?

Or let's put the question another way. Over the past thirty years, hundreds of books and thousands of articles have been written about the urgent, catastrophic threat that climate change poses to the world, exploring the problem in its technical, historical, ethical, and philosophical aspects. These books and articles have been talked about in the mainstream media, even on TV, and nearly everyone who has access to the internet today knows about sea level rise, the greenhouse effect, and the melting Arctic. Yet in spite of all this intellectual work, all this research and rhetoric and effort and thought, we seem unable to act coherently and collectively to address this grave existential threat. Part of the problem is the "we" here, because that "we" includes almost two hundred sovereign nations, each with its own political and economic agendas, various corporate entities whose very existence depends on perpetuating the extractive fossil-fueled capitalist economy that's killing us, and an elite group of rich and powerful decision makers who believe that they will be protected from the danger by their wealth, regard flagrant waste and conspicuous consumption as status symbols, and are deeply invested in business as usual even if it means global apocalypse.

And climate change is only the most egregious example. Think about our inadequate gun laws, the appalling regularity of school shootings, and the innumerable think pieces, personal essays, and legislative proposals that have been impotently put forth addressing the problem. Think about the outrageous persistence of systemic and ideological racism, founded in a notion of human difference thoroughly discredited by science more than a century ago, fought against by brave people who risked their lives for basic dignity and justice, and argued against by some of America's most brilliant thinkers. Think about the ongoing stupidity of our war in

Afghanistan, the stubborn persistence of aggressive sexism, our soul-sucking addiction to our phones, the rise of Trumpism, the opioid epidemic, et cetera. If you take all the seemingly intractable ills of modern life and compare them against the vigorous, dedicated, earnest efforts made by countless talented and educated thinkers, writers, journalists, policy wonks, scholars, activists, students, and artists to address them, you might be forgiven if the conclusion you come to is one of puzzled despair: we seem incapable of listening to reason.

In the late eighteenth century, German philosopher Immanuel Kant articulated an ideal of collective, self-conscious rational self-determination that remains one of the noblest achievements of human thought. In his famous essay "What Is Enlightenment?", written in the years between the signing of the American Declaration of Independence and the ratification of the US Constitution, Kant argues that free thought leads to better government, writing: "Free thought gradually acts upon the mind of the people and they gradually become more capable of acting in freedom. Eventually, the government is also influenced by this free thought and there it treats man, who is now more than a machine, according to his dignity." It's a beautiful concept: the idea that we can all come together as equals and, through the free use of our reason and open discussion, not only decide what is best for us as a group and how to live together, but also achieve the highest fulfillment of our personal and collective existence. This concept undergirds our idea of the public sphere, what some call the marketplace of ideas, the value we ostensibly place on public education and higher education, our notions of citizenship, American civic religion, and the root of what we understand thinking—reason—writing—to be *good* for. Thinking is good, we tend to assume, because it helps us make life better. Thinking is good, we tend to believe, because it makes us free.

Yet everywhere we look today, from Twitter to the White House to Raqqa to the melting Arctic, human reason stands defeated. Our seemingly rational decisions turn out to have fatal consequences we never anticipated, free and informed public discourse has given way to propaganda, lies, harassment, and censorship, and many free citizens of open democracies no longer see the value in making judgments based on evidence, but rather seek evidence only to confirm their pre-existing judgments, heedless of whether they are accurate or erroneous. Pizzagate? Pee tape? Russian hackers? Vaccines? Who knows? The only thing you can be sure of is that the other side is lying.

Kant's motto for the Enlightenment was *Sapere Aude!*: "Dare to Know!" The motto for twenty-first-century America seems to be taken from Weird Al Yankovic's song, "Dare to Be Stupid." And from a certain point of view, it's not wholly irrational to choose to be irrational. After all, the Enlightenment agenda of rational control over the human and non-human world is exactly what has led to most of our modern ills, from the hectic, Taylorized grind of our spiritually empty lives, relieved only by binge-watching Netflix, to our dependence on pills to stave off depression, from climate change, mass extinction, and an increasingly toxic and degraded environment to nuclear war. What's more, as Friedrich Nietzsche realized in the late nineteenth century, radical free thought leads ultimately not to an increase in human dignity, as Kant argued, but to nihilism and apocalyptic violence. Philosophy has struggled from the beginning to make sense of the Enlightenment's internal contradictions, and those contradictions have only grown. In the words of Theodor Adorno and Max Horkheimer, written during World War II but holding just as true today as they did then, "The wholly enlightened earth is radiant with triumphant calamity."

Alas, the Enlightenment's humanistic ideal was a delusion from the beginning, premised on a deliberate misapprehension of empiricism that built a giant loophole into what otherwise seems to be a wholly deterministic universe. The great problem empiricism poses, articulated variously by Hume, Spinoza, and La Mettrie, is that once you accept the underlying premise that the universe in which we live operates by predictable mechanisms (or "laws") which can be quantified and modeled, you lose any basis for free will. A truly deterministic universe is mechanistic turtles all the way down, and there's no justified exception for human consciousness. The best one can do with any kind of intellectual integrity is maintain a faith in generative chaos, or bracket the question of whether free will actually exists at all and assert that we should believe in it regardless, neither of which—generative chaos or a pragmatist will to believe—comes close, you'll notice, to anything like our actual experience of freedom, which when you pay attention to it looks less like reason and more like rationalization. We act, and only after come up with the reasons why. Kant, following Descartes, dispensed with the problem by a clever bit of sophistry and an abiding faith in a Christian God. Reason offered Kant an escape from determinism because he held that reason comes from God, connects to God, in some way *is* God. The Enlightenment wasn't so much the triumph of reason as the subordination of scientific empiricism to Christian metaphysics.

Freedom, it turns out, is the whole problem: on the one hand, the conceit necessary to make sense of a moral order structured by a choice between eternal reward and eternal punishment, and on the other the idea that conscious control over nature, from the outward conquest of the farthest reaches of Earth to the zealous inward self-denying asceticism of the Protestant believer, can free us from nature's limits and dictates. Freedom to choose sin or virtue, on the one hand, and freedom from nature on the other. It is a conception of freedom founded not only in Christian metaphysics, but in the material history of modern Europe, namely a staggering influx of wealth plundered from the Americas, Africa, and Asia, human slavery, and an industrial revolution that opened up vast reserves of solar energy stored in the form of fossilized carbon—first coal, then oil. From the beginning, our modern sense of being free meant *not* being a slave, whether to a plantation master or to natural powers like wind and water. Indeed, as Andreas Malm painstakingly shows in his book *Fossil Capital*, coal won out over wind and water as a power source for early industrialization not because it was cheaper, but because it gave factory owners more control over their workers—which is to say, more "freedom."

If we are honest with ourselves and take a broad enough historical view, we must humbly submit that thought has never really been all that good for all that much. It's never been especially *useful*. Oh, there's invention and law and utopian ideals and so on, which have provided designs and justifications for innumerable human artifacts, institutions, and projects. But thought isn't engineering, despite Marx's famous eleventh thesis on Feuerbach, which contends that "philosophers have only interpreted the world" while "the point is to change it." On the contrary, thought resists instrumentalization because it resists subordination to all social value. Thought is good for thought; it is its own end. Socrates didn't save Athens, the Buddha didn't save India, Walter Benjamin didn't save the Jews, and philosophy has never cured a disease or conquered a country or rescued a village or raised a child. It might help you become more compassionate, though that didn't seem to work for Arthur Schopenhauer, who's perhaps better known for shoving his landlady down the stairs than he is for his magnum opus, *The World as Will and Representation*. It might help you be more prudent, though, again, the biographies of well-known philosophers from Mary Wollstonecraft to Ludwig Wittgenstein suggest this is not necessarily the case.

Since thought has never been able to save us in the past, it might be a little unreasonable to expect it to do so now. Thought simply cannot solve the root problems of human existence—desire and mortality—and thought cannot tell us what is good, what we ought to do, or how to live, because these questions have no final answers. Thought cannot make us free, from nature or from each other, since

human consciousness is determined by countless factors from gut
bacteria, neurochemistry, and genetics to acculturation and the
weather, and human politics is the product not of logical proposi-
tions but of situational negotiation within social power relations.
And finally, thought cannot make us gods. It cannot free us from
our animal, material existences, the demands of embodied life, and
the fact of our finitude. As long as human spirit inheres in matter—
even if that spirit is a cloud stored on a server farm in Iowa—we
remain mortal, dependent on the Earth, and subject to physical
forces which exceed our control. This is what thought truly struggles
with: not the possibility of escape, but the inevitability of death.

Only by coming to terms with this conundrum do we realize,
at last, that the worm gets one more turn. Thought is, in the end,
the only thing that *can* save us. Here we stand, each one of us one
primate among billions in a species that has overrun and ruined
its habitat, heading for a population correction the likes of which
the human world has never seen, on a wobbly spinning rock with
a rapidly warming atmosphere in a distant corner of the galaxy, a
temporary accumulation of star dust, once was nothing, will again
be nothing, is nothing now but electrochemical pulse and biological
striving, a flicker in the web of being. Only thought can help us see
who we are, *know* who we are, and help us reconcile our imaginary
collective models of the world, so rich and so vital and so often
false, with the truth of our worldly being. Only humble and diligent
thought, uncomfortably estranged from daily life, can bring to light
our total dependence on other humans and the non-human world
we live within while opening the way to the joyful communion our
dependence makes possible.

True freedom emerges not from domination or even from
escaping domination, but from recognizing and accepting those
forces which shape our lives, cultivating detachment, and interrupting the cycle of reaction and desire. Thought slows being,
suspends our participation in social life, opens a gap between cause

and effect that is in the end our only true sovereignty. The thinker, that is to say, is an interrupter: not merely a node or an amplifier within social circuits, but a place of stillness. An active pause. A total ecstatic absorption in the now.

What is thinking good for today, among the millions of voices shouting to be heard, as we stumble and trip toward our doom? Not much, maybe nothing, maybe less. Certainly memory can help preserve the wisdom of the past and set the record straight, understanding can help us see our situation more clearly, and the two together can help us make sense of how we got to where we are. Questioning our accepted beliefs can reveal to us our hidden selves. Cultivating an awareness of our dependence on others, human and non-human alike, opens the way to compassion, humility, and joyful communion with all being. Practicing detachment vitiates desire and accommodates our souls to death. And finally, ultimately, deliberation slows and limits action. Pondering your situation keeps you from reacting to it, which is, in the end, the highest good thought can offer: doing less, doing nothing, being nothing more or less than we are—a gathering of dust and light, a universe—awake.

Raising a Daughter
in a Doomed World

I.

My partner Sara woke holding her belly. "What time is it?" she said. "Write down the time." It was late, well before sunrise, and within a few hours contractions were coming on strong, a full sixty seconds every four minutes, so we called the hospital and texted our doula and grabbed our go bag and drove. The next morning, after twenty-seven hours of labor and five hours of pushing, after nine months of worrying and hoping and looking at ultrasound scans, after years of deliberating and wondering and negotiating between the demands of being on the academic job market and our deeper biological cycles, a new human emerged into the world yowling like something feral: our daughter. Tears spilled from my eyes as I hugged her and Sara together, my chest opening like I'd found the source of all joy in the universe and plugged in, streaming total utopian *agape*.

First I cried for joy; the second time I cried for sorrow, a few minutes later, holding my daughter, Rosalind, and looking out the window over the hospital parking lot, the rows of cars, the strip mall across the street, the flat, ugly, rust-belt sprawl of northern Indiana, box stores and drive-thrus, drainage ditches and concrete and waste fields that might have once been oak groves, a world in which the landscape had been ravaged and brutalized as a matter of course, and in which any possibility for living in harmony with nature had been evacuated. Birds and bees and frogs were all dying, the seasons were out of joint, and instead of grieving, people were on their phones. My partner and I had, in our selfishness, doomed our child to life on a dystopian planet, and I could see no way to shield her from the future. "I'm sorry," I told her, weeping, as her tiny fingers gripped mine. "I'm sorry you have to live in this broken world."

Anyone who pays much attention to climate scientists or to reporting by journalists on climate change knows that the outlook is grim. It's a tired story by this point, since scientists such as James Hansen have been warning us for thirty years, but it goes like this: Waste carbon dioxide from burned fossil fuels is accumulating in the atmosphere and trapping solar energy, which is warming the planet at an astonishing rate. This global warming is radically transforming environmental conditions all over the planet, leading to a range of second-order effects including rising seas, destabilized crop yields, mass extinction, unpredictable and dangerously intense storms, drought, floods, and heat waves. The stress these effects are putting on human political, economic, social, and agricultural infrastructure, already intense, will eventually be greater than anything we've seen since the twentieth century's two world wars, and will probably outstrip those. It's not unreasonable to say that the challenge we live with today is the greatest the human species has ever faced.

Anyone who pays much attention to politics can assume that we're almost certainly going to botch this challenge. In order to stop emitting waste carbon dioxide completely within the next five or ten years, we would need to radically reorient all human economic and social production, a task that is scarcely imaginable, much less feasible. It would demand centralized control of key economic sectors, massive state investment in carbon capture and sequestration, and global coordination on a scale never before seen, at the very moment when the political and economic structures that held the capitalist world order together under American leadership after World War II are splintering, and extremist libertarians are dismantling the

United States government from the inside. The very idea of unified national political action toward a single goal seems farcical, and unified action on a global scale mere whimsy. What's more, significant and dangerous levels of warming are already baked in to the system from all the carbon dioxide we've already dumped. There's a time lag between CO_2 increase and subsequent effects, between the wind we sow and the whirlwind we reap. Our lives are lived in that gap. My daughter was born there.

Barring a miracle, the next twenty years are going to see increasingly chaotic systemic transformation in global climate patterns, unpredictable biological adaptation, and a wild range of human political and economic responses. These likely trends pose unanswerable dilemmas: Should I start a college fund for my daughter, or would she be better served by learning to shoot, hunt, and live off the land? Should we raise her where we live now, in a state on the cutting edge of privatization, where public services like school buses and 911 call centers and highways are failing but our middle-class income allows us to own a home, far from the rising ocean? Or should we try to move back to one of the blue-bubble cities on the coast, where we'd struggle just to pay the rent, and where floods, wildfires, and drought threaten even the wealthiest? There are no clear answers. Every choice is a gamble.

The next twenty years will be tough. After that, it gets worse. The middle and later decades of the twenty-first century—my daughter's adult life—promise a global catastrophe whose full implications any reasonable person must turn away from in horror. Recall that World War II, including the Holocaust and other atrocities, saw about 3 percent of the entire global population annihilated. It staggers the soul to imagine what going through a population bottleneck that entailed losing 70 percent of the human species would look like, but that's what it would take to get us back to population levels circa 1940.

In the almost eighty years since then, the human species has burst the boundary conditions for sustainable life on Earth through what some scientists call the "Great Acceleration," an unprecedented spike in socioeconomic and earth systems trends—everything from carbon dioxide emissions, surface temperature, and tropical forest loss to fertilizer consumption, water use, and population (from approximately 2.3 billion in 1940 to 7.6 billion today)—a spike which represents "the most anomalous and unrepresentative period in the 200,000-year-long history of relations between our species and the biosphere," in the words of J.R. McNeill and Peter Engleke. And while we might hope that world leaders will correct course and somehow bring this Great Acceleration under control, human history suggests that this bubble will burst like every other, in crisis and chaos. One thing is certain, as McNeill and Engleke testify: "The Great Acceleration in its present form cannot last for long." On the other side of the inevitable correction, a hundred years from now, whatever *Homo sapiens* are left on Earth are going to be struggling to adapt to a hot, unstable, and hostile planet.

Why would anyone choose to bring new life into this world? How can I explain my decision to my daughter? And isn't there anything we can do about it?

It's true that numerous engineering solutions are available that might help decrease and mitigate carbon emissions, but the social and economic costs of these solutions are so unclear and contentious that widespread agreement on implementation seems practically impossible. Meanwhile, in the US, our political system has been hijacked by thieves seemingly interested only in looting the republic and undermining democratic rule. Faced with such systemic failures, many adopt an individualist approach, arguing that it's up to each of us to make the personal sacrifices necessary to stop global warming.

According to a widely cited 2017 research letter by geographer Seth Wynes and environmental scientist Kimberly Nicholas, the most effective things any of us can do to decrease carbon emissions are to eat a plant-based diet, avoid flying, live car free, and have one fewer child, with the latter choice having the most significant impact by far. Wynes and Nicholas argue for teaching these values in high school, thus transforming society through education. The real problem with this proposal isn't with the idea of teaching abstention and thrift, which is all well and good, but rather with the social model their recommendations rely on. Contra Adam Smith and Margaret Thatcher, society is not simply an aggregate of millions or billions of individual choices, but a complex recursive dynamic in which choices are made within institutions and ideologies which then subtly change over time as these choices feed back into the structures that frame what we consider possible, all the while being disrupted and nudged and warped by countless internal and external drivers, including environmental factors such as global warming, material and social innovation, and the occasional widespread panic. Which is just to say that we are not free to decide how we live any more than we are free to break the laws of physics. We choose from possible options, not *ex nihilo*.

It's clear that we should all go vegan for the sake of the planet. It's a sacrifice I'm reluctant to make, despite the moral and eco-logical costs of factory farming, because I know, through my years as a vegetarian, that totally forgoing meat leaves me depressed and lethargic. Wynes and Nicholas don't define what "plant-based" means, though, so if it just means *less* meat, and especially less beef and pork, then it's certainly something we could all do without too much hassle. No more steak, no more cheeseburgers, no more pork belly ramen—okay, fine.

And I would love to avoid flying and to live car free. (Truly. I can't even properly express my loathing for flying.) I lived without a car for several years in my twenties and early thirties, so I know it's possible, but my world then was largely limited to the range I could walk or bike or get to on public transit, and my work was usually casual and close by. Now, like most Americans, I live and work in a city that was built for cars and has totally inadequate public transit, and which also happens to be thousands of miles away from my extended family and my oldest friends. No car? No job. No flying? No Thanksgiving with the family.

As for not having a child, of course nobody *needs* to have children. It just happens to be the strongest drive humans have, the fundamental organizing principle of every human culture, and the *sine qua non* of a meaningful human world, since it alone makes possible the persistence of human meaning through time. My partner and I didn't *need* to have a child, but without one, our lives felt like they lacked something important.

To take Wynes and Nicholas's recommendations to heart would mean cutting oneself off from modern life. It would mean choosing a hermetic, isolated existence and giving up any deep connection to the future. I know because I've lived like that, and I sometimes even daydream about returning to it: everything seemed so pure then, so simple. But like most of us, I can't or won't; I'm committed to *this* world, the world I live in, in all its stupidity and doom, because this world is the one everyone else lives in too: my colleagues and students, my friends and family, my partner and daughter. This world is the only one in which my choices have meaning. And this world, fucked up as it is, is the only one that offers joy. As George Orwell wrote in 1946, in another time of global crisis, in an essay on the mating habits of the common toad, "If we kill all pleasure in the actual processes of life, what sort of future are we preparing for ourselves?"

Furthermore, taking Wynes and Nicholas's argument seriously would mean acknowledging that the only truly moral response to global climate change is to commit suicide. There is simply no more effective way to shrink your carbon footprint. Once you're dead, you won't use any more electricity, you won't eat any more meat, you won't burn any more gasoline, and you certainly won't have any more children. If you really want to save the planet, you should die.

And I, for one, would salute you. Such self-sacrifice would be admirable, even heroic, but it still won't save us. Even if millions suddenly went vegan, swore off airplanes, sold their cars, and had themselves sterilized, it wouldn't significantly slow down global warming. Billions of human beings already live a subsistence existence right now, and most carbon waste is due to a small percentage of people who don't seem to care much about the consequences. Recalling Thorstein Veblen's theory of conspicuous consumption, we might even speculate that the freedom to pollute is a kind of status symbol (a point Michel Serres makes in his book *Malfeasance*). If that's right, then we can assume that the wealthy parasites killing the planet are never going to give up their privileged and destructive habits, because those very habits are how they maintain their sense of self-worth.

The real choice we all face is not what to buy, whether to fly, or whether to have children, but whether we are willing to commit to living ethically in a broken world, a world in which human beings are dependent for collective survival on a kind of ecological grace. There is no utopia, no Planet B, no salvation, no escape. We're all stuck here in the same shithole together. And living in that world, the only world there is, means giving up any claims to innocence or moral purity, since to live at all means to cause suffering. While you could, if you had the will for it, go off the grid, your subsistence farm would still be a tiny holocaust for the pests who would seek to live off your bounty, your land deed would still need to be recognized by the state, and you would almost certainly need to enslave animals, if not for food and material such as milk, leather, and bone, then at least for labor. Living ethically means understanding that our actions have consequences, taking responsibility for how those consequences ripple out across the web of life in which each of us is irrevocably enmeshed, and working every day to ease what suffering we can. Living ethically means limiting our desires, respecting the deep interdependence of all things in nature, and honoring the fact that our existence on this planet is a gift that comes from nowhere and may be taken back at any time.

I chose to have a child with my partner because I believe in life, because I want the wheel of life to keep turning. I believe in old people dying and new people being born. I believe in the winter's first snow, and the first pink cherry blossoms bursting and falling in the spring. I believe in squirrels chasing each other through maple branches, toads mating by the river, herons nesting in the bogs, and knobby-kneed fawns bounding through open meadows. Sometimes I think focusing on the horror of our coming civilizational collapse is just a way for me to avoid the grief I feel at losing the natural rhythms that climate change is already beginning to warp. The seasons are confused, the animals are confused, and nothing feels right, not the land, not the weather. But for all my grief and horror, I can't seem to let go of the dumb hope that we might somehow find the wisdom to live within our planet's ecological limits.

It's not really rational. Politically, realistically, making human life sustainable at this point would demand a world socialist revolution, since only a unified world government committed to radical economic redistribution and ecological justice would be able to initiate and manage transitioning the global economy off fossil fuels. Socially, spiritually, we'd need a world religion that worshipped Mother Earth and put harmony with nature over all other values. We'd need to throw away our bedazzling hi-tech toys and turn our gaze back to the land, the air, the water, the rhythms of the natural world, and the other beings who live there. While we're at it, we should also probably put women in charge, get rid of nuclear weapons, and outlaw racial and ethnic discrimination.

I could spin out the fantasy further, and maybe that's a fine way to pass the time until we die. But I doubt we'll see anything like it come to fruition. I'm pretty sure we're going to keep fumbling along toward our doom, just like we've fumbled our way into breaking the planet. Human beings are dependable like that. Nevertheless, the dire and seemingly unsolvable fact of climate change—just like the unsolvable fact of our own mortality—doesn't signify the end of ethical thought but its beginning, for it's only in recognizing the fact that our lives are limited, complicit, imperfect, and interdependent that we begin to understand what it means to live together in this world.

When my daughter was born I felt a love and connection I'd never felt before: a surge of tenderness and care harrowing in its intensity. I knew in a moment that I would kill for her, die for her, sacrifice anything for her, and while those feelings have become more bearable since the first delirious days after her birth, they have not abated. And when I think of the future she's doomed to live out, the future we've created, I'm filled with rage and sorrow.

Every day brings new pangs of grief. I'm excited to see the world afresh through my child's eyes, as any parent would be, but I have also found her every new discovery haunted by death. Reading to her from *Polar Bear, Polar Bear, What Do You Hear?*, I can't help but marvel at the disconnect between the animal life represented in that book and the planet-wide mass extinction happening right now. When I sing along with Elizabeth Mitchell's version of "Froggie Went a-Courtin,'" I can't help but feel like I'm betraying Rosalind by filling her brain with fantastic images of a magical non-human world, when the actual non-human world has been exploited and despoiled. How can I read her *Winnie the Pooh* or *The Wind in the Willows*, when I know the pastoral harmony they evoke is lost to us forever, and has been for decades? How soon do I explain to her what's happening? In all the most important ways, it's already too late.

There's no way to win this game, no way to hack life in a doomed world. I can't protect my daughter from the future and I can't even promise her a better life. All I can do is teach her: teach her how to care, how to be kind, and how to live within nature's grace. I can teach her to be tough but resilient, adaptable and prudent, because she's going to have to struggle for what she needs, but I also need to teach her to fight for what's right, because none of us are in this alone. I need to teach her that all things die, even her and me and her mother and the world we know, but that coming to terms with this difficult truth is the beginning of wisdom.

It's not enough, though, just to teach the next generation how to cope with our failures. Off-loading responsibility for the world onto the future is ethically inexcusable, precisely the kind of short-term selfish behavior that led us to this precipice, and illogical to boot. Our children learn early to distinguish what we do from what we say, and they model their own behaviors on the former, not the latter. So no matter how much we talk about children being the future, if we keep acting like their future is disposable, they'll take that action for truth, regardless of how convincing we find our own hypocrisy.

But there are even bigger issues with seeing climate change as the future's problem instead of our own. One is time. A major reason coming to terms with climate change is so difficult is because it takes time, it unfolds in time, and we're not great at foreseeing trend lines that go against our narratives of how things should be. We tend to rely on two kinds of temporality, which the Ancient Greeks called *chronos* and *kairos*, which we might call "day-to-day time" and "event time." In day-to-day time, we tend to assume everything is going to be much the same as it was yesterday, within the predictable cycles of change to which we have become accustomed. The sun will rise and fall, we'll wake up and go to work, we'll get a bunch of emails and take too long to answer them, while football gives way to basketball and we celebrate the various shopping holidays that mark our calendar, and children get older and go to college and have their own children and eventually disappear into retirement homes. The regular unfolding of life as we conceive it is the basis for our sense of normality, the frame that shapes our decisions, and the implicit backdrop against which we judge new information. In event time, on the other hand, day-to-day rhythms are suspended. A carnivalesque mood takes over, our social structures reveal themselves as the willed collective illusions they are, and we see ourselves emerge for a moment into an open clearing of nearly infinite possibility. Event time is precisely the moment of action in crisis, the "now" when everything can change.

These two kinds of temporality constitute a dynamic back-and-forth in which everything is normal until it isn't, and then there's a new normal. Unfortunately for us, and somewhat ironically, climate change doesn't fit this dynamic, because climate change is a gradual process happening year by year, punctuated not by one global event but by an unpredictable series of increasingly damaging local disasters. Hurricane Katrina, Superstorm Sandy, the monsoon floods in India and Bangladesh that killed more than a thousand people in 2017, the California drought—any one of these catastrophes might have been the event which changed everything, except that each one was in the end no more than a regional phenomenon, swiftly superseded.

There is as yet no "we" who might respond to climate change, no universal political subject, only an abstract "we" comprising billions of individuals who are all going to die in our own individual ways. For most of us, the day-to-day time of global capitalist civilization remains the beating pulse of our lives, even as the world around us changes into something strange and awful. By the time the event we seem to be waiting for happens, we will have already lost too much to be able to do much about it. By the time the moment of decision arrives, our fate will have already been sealed.

Thus, even though we live in the gap between the wind and the whirlwind, taking that gap for a momentary reprieve is a mistake. The catastrophe is *now*, even if it's almost impossible for most of us to see that fact through the blinders of day-to-day time. That very dissonance is perhaps the defining truth of our era, the key to its anxious, bipolar character, the red thread that connects #MeToo, the Middle East, Arctic sea ice collapse, Russian hacking, #BlackLivesMatter, Trumpism, the rise of the libertarian political right and the socialist left, the banality of our workaday lives, and the dramatic fever dreams we live out online. I could raise my daughter to be a member of the Post-Apocalyptic Vuvalini Resistance, but we still have to live through the next twenty, fifty, seventy years, and how do we do that?

The other major issue with framing climate change as our children's problem is that while some degree of warming now appears inevitable, the range of possible outcomes over the next century is wide enough and the worst outcomes extreme enough that there is some narrow hope that revolutionary socio-economic transformation today might save billions of human lives and preserve global civilization as we know it in more or less recognizable form, or at least stave off human extinction. The range of outcomes decreases every day, though, shifting month by month toward the more apocalyptic end of the spectrum, and waiting twenty years—fifteen years—even five years may well see the window for saving humanity slam shut. Our children will not face the choices we face. They won't have the opportunities we now have for action. They'll confront a range of outcomes whose limits were determined by the choices we made.

So we're back to the problem of what to do. It seems clear that if we want to transform the global economy by shifting to renewable and nuclear energy (supplemented with carbon capture and sequestration), then we need to impose some kind of centralized global economic control. We could start by nationalizing energy production and other major industries, expropriating and redistributing the wealth of the 1 percent so that it can be put to work for the rest of us, then joining together with the other nations of the world in a single government that sees the needs of all humans as equal, regardless of race, creed, color, sexual orientation, homeland, or gender. This world government would necessarily have to have the legal power to enforce its decrees however they were legislated, so it would also need a monopoly on force. First dismantle the plutocracy, then dismantle the nation state. If you think this sounds like socialism, you're not wrong.

Many people are afraid of socialism, and it's true that there are a range of worthy arguments against it, from the historical atrocities of Stalinist Russia and Maoist China to liberal Western concerns about the sacred integrity of the individual. Such arguments raise legitimate issues, but unfortunately we lack the luxury of having time for such debates. We face a global collective emergency which can only be addressed by a global collective response. Individual choice and market-based solutions are wholly inadequate to the urgency and scale of the problem, which demands dedication and sacrifice from all quarters under a unified central leadership, meaning global leadership.

In a way, Trumpism has done us a great service by driving apart the contradictory poles of individual greed and collective good, which had been uneasily joined under capitalism, and forcing a new articulation of collective political life free from the dead hand of the market. But the challenge of figuring out how we might form a world socialist government is almost as difficult a question as figuring out how to address climate change. Wars are fought over such questions. I just don't see any other option that offers a real chance for navigating and coping with global warming and its ramifications without risking apocalyptic devastation. Non-binding treaties like the Paris Agreement aren't going to do it. Carbon markets aren't going to do it. Broken democracies like are own aren't going to do it.

To be honest, though, having a child hasn't really inspired me to acts of self-sacrifice in the service of abstract and doubtful goals. Rather the opposite. I've had to start thinking about schools, health care, housing, and investment in whole new ways. I feel a deep obligation to "provide for my child's future" within the constraints of contemporary American society, which demands making some kind of uneasy peace with America's brutally hierarchical, racist, and individualist culture. This is how young radicals become middle-aged liberal hypocrites. My love for my daughter is overwhelming and irrational, and consumer capitalism exploits that every day by whispering—screaming—in my ear that if I don't do everything I can to make sure my child has more than yours, more whatever, the best whatever, then she's going to fall behind; that if I don't push her to learn her alphabet before the other kids she'll never pass the tests to get into the prestige kindergarten which means she'll never get into college and she'll wind up wasting her life as a checker in a grocery store; that if I don't buy her the expensive wooden skill-building puzzle or the organic kale-avocado puree then I'm condemning her to a slippery slope of disappointment, failure, and drug addiction. The immense engines of capital, I have learned, possess a formidable array of forces that only activate once you've had children, when they fall on you with the force of a thousand suns.

It takes real effort to remember that my daughter's fate is not hers alone but shared, inexorably, inevitably, despite the fact that the rich will be able to cope with climate change better than the poor, for a while. Money means you can flee, so you don't get stuck in the Superdome. Money means access to institutional and governmental resources hidden from the poor behind complex, unwelcoming bureaucracies. Money means you can prep for disasters with insurance, kitted-out go bags, and second homes. Money means you can rebuild. But money won't stop the seas from rising or the wind from blowing. Money won't save the Arctic and it won't save Miami. And once the system falls apart, all those ones and zeros in your bank account will evaporate, and all the gold you've carefully hidden for the end times will be revealed for what it is, a not especially useful yellow rock.

The choice we have to make isn't whether or how to save

ourselves, but, as I said before, whether we're willing to commit to living ethically in a broken world, in which human beings are dependent for collective survival on respecting the ecological limits of our planet. Signing up for a world socialist revolution might be a start. But then what? And what else? How do we live with—in— *within* this crisis? How do we change the world on a human scale? How do we teach our children by example, and not just with words and stories?

I'm too much an individualist to want to tell anyone how to live, too much a child of pioneers, committed *a priori* to the idea that each of us has to work out our own salvation, and skeptical of the claims of gurus who give you twelve easy rules to follow. But in the spirit of American can-do pragmatism, I will offer a few broad suggestions. First, we should organize locally and aggressively. This will not only connect us to our neighbors, but it's also the most likely path to world socialist revolution. It's extremely unlikely that we'll bring about a revolution from outside the system—as long as it's "us and them," they have the guns, the laws, and the money, and will beat us every time. But as Trump has shown, the system itself is far more vulnerable to takeover than anyone had suspected. A socialist revolution from within now seems possible, though it's going to take dedicated cadres and bold individuals committed to a long-term strategy of dominating state and local governments while building a national and international movement.

Second, and perhaps counter-intuitively, we need to do less. Our daily lives are caught in manic cycles of pointless production and frenzied consumption, desperate bids for connection and whiplash reactions, from your morning coffee to Twitter outrage to the stiff drink or dank bud you need to chill at night, all of it powering a vast cultural machine that feeds on our anger and fear as much as it feeds on coal, oil, and natural gas. One must labor in order to eat, it's true, and we must work to repair the broken world, but so much of what we do is unnecessary, unconsidered, and reactive that we live out our days distracted and drained and unfocused. Slow down. Do less. Do the one thing that matters, rather than the fifteen that don't.

Finally, we need to learn to die. It's not only our thoughts and feelings that are entangled in frenzied cycles of fear and desire, but our very selves, our egos. Yet this self we cling to so fiercely is nothing but an ephemeral moment, a transient emergence of self-conscious matter, a passing cloud of being. We each have our allotted span of years on the planet, some more, some less, and then return to the nothing from which we came. Learning to accept this simple fact is a difficult, lifelong task, but it's the first step in understanding that the self isn't a unique, isolated thing at all but a product of generations enmeshed in a world, a transmaterialization of stellar dust, the expression of a vibrant, buzzing universe, a future and a past.

Everything dies, but what we do while we live lives on, in our sons and daughters, in the worlds we make or destroy. We're all doomed. That's simply the condition of being born. But it's also the condition that makes a new future possible. Now what?

Endnotes

We're Doomed, Now What?

1. No doubt this is Nietzsche's revision of his predecessor Spinoza's ideal of *amor dei intellectualis*, the intellectual love of god (or nature), which for Spinoza took form in the practice of rational inquiry.

2. According to Climate Central scientists working from NASA and NOAA data, February 2016 was 1.63° Celsius above preindustrial temperatures, and March 2016 was 1.54° Celsius above. See "Earth Flirts with a 1.5-Degree Celsius Global Warming Threshold," *Scientific American*, Apr. 20, 2016, www.climatecentral.org/news/world-flirts-with-1.5C-threshold-20260. Tobias Friedrich and others have predicted temperature increases of up to 7.36° Celsius by 2100. See Friedrich, Tobias, et al. "Nonlinear Climate Sensitivity and Its Implications for Future Greenhouse Warming," *Science Advances* 2:11, Nov. 9, 2016, http://advances.sciencemag.org/content/2/11/e1501923.

Arctic Ghosts

1. Hadn't found them, that is to say, until recently: the wreck of the *Erebus* was discovered in 2014, and the wreck of the *Terror* in 2016.

The Precipice

1. Philip Shabecoff, "Global Warming Has Begun, Expert Tells Senate," *New York Times*, June 24, 1988, www.nytimes.com/1988/06/24/us/global-warming-has-begun-expert-tells-senate.html.

2. Thomas A. Boden, Gregg Marland, and Robert J. Andres, "Global, Regional, and National Fossil-Fuel CO_2 Emissions," Carbon Dioxide Information Analysis Center, Oak Ridge National Laboratory, U.S. Department of Energy, Oak Ridge, TN, 2017, http://cdiac.ornl.gov/trends/emis/tre_glob_2014.html.

3. Scott Waldman, "Rise in Global Carbon Emissions Slows," *Scientific American*, Nov. 14, 2016, www.scientificamerican.com/article/rise-in-global-carbon-emissions-slows.

336 ROY SCRANTON

Hannah Arendt, introduction to Walter Benjamin, *Illuminations: Essays and Reflections*, ed. Hannah Arendt, trans. Harry Zohn (New York: Schocken, 1969), 3–4.

Walter Benjamin, "Theses on the Philosophy of History," *Illuminations*, 257–58.

Memories of My Green Machine

1. J. Glenn Gray, *The Warriors: Reflections on Men in Battle* (Lincoln: University of Nebraska Press, 1958), 21.

2. Michel Foucault, *The History of Sexuality*, vol. 1, *An Introduction* (New York: Vintage, 1990), 143. For an interesting and provocative exploration of the "biopolitical" question in terms of nuclear war, see Jacques Derrida, "No Apocalypse, Not Now (Full Speed Ahead, Seven Missiles, Seven Missives)," *Diacritics* 14:2, Nuclear Criticism (Summer 1984): 20–31.

3. Giorgio Agamben, *Homo Sacer* (Palo Alto, CA: Stanford University Press, 1998), 8.

4. Jacques Derrida, *The Animal That Therefore I Am* (New York: Fordham University Press, 2008), 31.

5. Neil Badmington, "Theorizing Posthumanism," *Cultural Critique* 53 (Winter 2003): 10.

6. Daniel T. O'Hara, "Neither Gods nor Monsters: An Untimely Critique of the 'Post/Human' Imagination," *boundary 2*, vol. 30, no. 3 (2003): 121–22.

7. Jacques Derrida, "'Eating Well,' or the Calculation of the Subject: An Interview with Jacques Derrida," in Eduardo Cadava, Peter Connor, and Jean-Luc Nancy, eds. *Who Comes After the Subject?* (New York: Routledge, 1991), 109. See also Jacques Derrida, *Specters of Marx* (New York: Routledge, 1994), 17.

8. Bernd Hüppauf, "Experiences of Modern Warfare and the Crisis of Representation," *New German Critique* 59 (Spring–Summer 1993): 62.

9. "Identity, seen as a complex and continuous process of indentifying

with or rejecting other individuals, values, social and natural sur-roundings, was subjected to crisis very soon after soldiers experienced conditions of the front. There was very little to identity with or to relate to. Soldiers felt cut off from real life." Ibid., 58.

10. Martin Heidegger, "The Question Concerning Technology," *The Question Concerning Technology and Other Essays* (New York: Harper & Row, 1977), 12.

11. Karl Marx, *Capital*, vol. 1 (New York: Penguin, 1976), 286, 493ff.

12. Heidegger, "Question Concerning Technology," 27.

13. Ernst Jünger, *On Pain* (New York: Telos Press, 2008), 31–32 (author's italics).

14. Donna Haraway, "A Cyborg Manifesto: Science, Technology, and Socialist-Feminism in the Late Twentieth Century," *Simians, Cyborgs, and Women: The Reinvention of Nature* (New York: Routledge, 1991), 150; and Alphonso Lingis, "The Effects of the Pictures," *Journal of Visual Culture* 5, no. 1 (2006): 84.

15. Russell A. Berman, preface to Jünger, *On Pain*, xxv.

16. Wolf Kittler, "From Getalt to Ge-Stell: Martin Heidegger Reads Ernst Jünger," *Cultural Critique* 69 (Spring 2008): 84.

17. Jünger, *On Pain*, 30.

18. Paul Richards, "New War: An Ethnographic Approach," in Paul Richards, ed., *No Peace No War: An Anthropology of Contemporary Armed Conflicts* (Athens: Ohio University Press, 2005), 3. See also Jonathan Shay, *Achilles in Vietnam: Combat Trauma and the Undoing of Character* (New York: Scribner, 1994), 6. Additionally, interesting discussion of some contemporary issues in the anthropology of war can be found in Keith Brown and Catherine Lutz, "Grunt Lit: The Participant-Observers of Empire," *American Ethnologist* 34, no. 2 (May 2007): 326–27; Steve Featherstone, "Human Quicksand: For the US Army, a Crash Course in Cultural Studies," *Harper's*, Sept. 2008,

pp. 60–68; Danny Hoffmann, "Frontline Anthropology: Research in a Time of War," *Anthropology Today* 19, no. 3 (June 2003): 9–12; and David Rohde, "Army Enlists Anthropology in War Zones," *New York Times*, Oct. 5, 2007.

19. Susan Sontag, *Regarding the Pain of Others* (New York: Picador, 2003), 74.

20. Phillip L. Walker, "A Bioarchaeological Perspective on the History of Violence," *Annual Review of Anthropology* 30 (2001): 590.

21. Ibid., 586.

22. Allen Feldman, "Memory Theaters, Virtual Witnessing, and the Trauma-Aesthetic," *Biography* 27, no. 1 (Winter 2004): 186.

23. Yuval Noah Harari, "Martial Illusions: War and Disillusionment in Twentieth-Century and Renaissance Military Memoirs," *Journal of Military History* 69 (Jan. 2005): 72.

24. Gray, *Warriors*, 116.

25. Sontag, *Regarding the Pain of Others*, 126.

26. Ivana Maček, "Sarajevan Soldier Story: Perceptions of War & Morality in Bosnia," in Richards, ed., *No Peace No War*, 64.

27. Ibid., 73.

28. "In his study of the technological changes in warfare over the course of civilization, for example, William McNeill finds the creation of the modern army in the seventeenth century 'as remarkable in its way as the birth of science or any other breakthrough of that age,' and lists as a major effect of drill—the rhythmic movement of marching in step with many men or of firing a gun by following a precise series of forty-two successive acts performed identically by all participants— the disappearance from the soldier's body of the signs of a particular region or country: 'the psychic force of drill and new routines was such as to make a recruit's origins and previous experience largely irrelevant to his behavior as a soldier.'" Elaine Scarry, *The Body in Pain* (New York: Oxford, 1985), 118.

29. Gray, *Warriors*, 27.

30. Shay, *Achilles in Vietnam*, 82–99.

31. Ernst Jünger, *Storm of Steel* (New York: Penguin, 2003), 239.

32. Simone Weil, *The Iliad; or, The Poem of Force* (Wallingford, PA: Pendle Hill, 2001), 26.

33. Sigmund Freud, "Why War?" *The Standard Edition of the Complete Psychological Works of Sigmund Freud*, vol. 22 (1932–36): *New Introductory Lectures on Psycho-Analysis and Other Works*, www.pep-web. org/document.php?id=SE.022.0195A, p. 204.

34. Nietzsche's insistence on the bodily animal being of man is well known, and his influence on Jünger, Heidegger, Derrida, twentieth-century thought, notions of the "end of man," and even this paper—while they cannot be addressed here—should not be left unnoticed: "But the awakened, the enlightened man says: I am body entirely, and nothing beside; and soul is only a word for something in the body. The body is a great intelligence, a multiplicity with one sense, a war and a peace, a herd and a herdsman." Friedrich Nietzsche, "Of the Despisers of the Body" *Thus Spoke Zarathustra*, part 1 (New York: Penguin, 1969).

35. Richard W. Wrangham, "Evolution of Coalitionary Killing" *Yearbook of Physical Anthropology* 42 (1999): 1–30.

36. Ibid., 2.

37. Ibid., 26.

38. Although there may be problems with his hypothesis and its political implications certainly make it very controversial, it nevertheless remains convincing. For one (rather flat) criticism of Wrangham, see Paul Roscoe, "Intelligence, Coalitional Killing, and the Antecedents of War," *American Anthropologist* 109, no. 3 (Sept. 2007), 485–95.

39. Hüppauf, "Experiences of Modern Warfare," 60.

40. Jünger, *Storm of Steel*, 92.

41. Jünger, *On Pain*, 22.

42. Shay, *Achilles in Vietnam*, 15.

43. Gray, *Warriors*, 179.

44. Ibid., 53.

45. Ibid., 28–29.

46. Jünger, *On Pain*, 1.

47. Allen Feldman, "Political Terror and the Technologies of Memory: Excuse, Sacrifice, Commodification, and Actuarial Moralities," *Radical History Review* 85 (Winter 2003):, 62.

48. Scarry, *Body in Pain*, 81.

49. Jünger, *On Pain*, 16–17.

50. Scarry, *Body in Pain*, 65.

51. Weil, *Iliad*, 3.

52. Hanna Arendt, *On Violence* (New York: Harcourt, Brace & World, 1970), 46.

53. "Although in all forms of work the worker mixes himself with and eventually becomes inseparable from the materials of his labor . . . the body in war is, to an extent found in almost no other form of work, inextricably bound up with the men and materials of his labor: he will learn to perceive himself as he will be perceived by others, as indistinguishable from the men of his unit, regiment, division, and above all national group . . . as he is also inextricably bound up with the qualities and conditions—berry laden or snow laden—of the ground over which he walks or runs or crawls and with which he craves and courts identification . . ." Scarry, *Body in Pain*, 83, cf. 88.

54. Richards, "New War," 17.

55. See, for example, Gray, *Warriors*, 148–58; Scarry, *Body in Pain*, 88; Shay, *Achilles in Vietnam*, 103–20; and Slavoj Žižek, *Violence: Six Sideways Reflections* (New York: Picador, 2008), 42–73.

56. See Robert Graves, *Goodbye to All That* (New York: Anchor, 1998), 137, 188–90; Gray, 142–48; and Jünger, *Storm of Steel*, 216 for accounts of warriors who face their enemies with respect.

57. Shay, *Achilles in Vietnam*, 103.

58. Gray, *Warriors*, 163.

59. Ibid., 81.

60. Michael Taussig asserts that fetishes "come across more like people than things, spiritual entities that are neither, and this is what gives them their strange beauty . . . Unwinding the fetish is not yet given on the horizon of human possibility." Michael Taussig, *My Cocaine Museum* (Chicago: University of Chicago Press, 2004), xviii. Consider this passage from *The Things They Carried*: "The things they carried were determined to some extent by superstition. Lieutenant Cross carried his good luck pebble. Dave Jensen carried a rabbit's foot. Norman Bowker, otherwise a very gentle person, carried a thumb that had been presented to him as a gift by Mitchell Sanders. The thumb was dark brown, rubbery to the touch, and weighed 4 ounces at most. It had been cut from a VC corpse, a boy of fifteen or sixteen." Tim O'Brien, *The Things They Carried* (New York: Broadway Books, 1990), 13. On the superstitiousness of soldiers and the myth-making elements at work in the combat zone, see particularly Paul Fussell, *The Great War and Modern Memory* (New York: Oxford University Press, 2000 [1975]), especially pp. 114–54; and Shay, *Achilles in Vietnam*, 30–32, 137–48.

61. "There are . . . three arenas of damage in war, three arenas of alteration: first, embodied persons; second, the material culture or self-extension of persons; third, immaterial culture, aspects of national consciousness, political beliefs, and self-definition." Scarry, *Body in Pain*, 114. Discussion of the Heideggerian sense follows.

62. Martin Heidegger, "Question Concerning Technology," 8, 16–17.

63. Martin Heidegger, *Being and Time* (New York: Harper & Row, 1962), 97.

64. Ibid., 101.

65. Ibid., 104. I would add, as a point of interest, the possibility that aesthetic withdrawal opens another path to the gestalt of Things, an epiphanic meditation that allows the Being of things to disclose itself without the imposition of instrumental utility.

66. Ibid., 105.

67. Scarry, *Body in Pain*, 61–63, on the "civilization-destroying" or "culture-destroying" aspect of injury.

68. Ibid., 135.

69. Gray, *Warriors*, 179.

70. Jünger, *Storm of Steel*, 255–56.

71. Hüppauf, "Experiences of Modern Warfare," 61. The preceding text reads: "In contrast to [a] 'humanist' vision of modern warfare, a vision of the faceless gray warrior emerged. Linked to the disintegration of the bourgeois ego and its meaningful psychological construction was the reconstitution of man as a fighting machine. The hardened man with his steel helmet, emotionless, experienced, with no morality apart from the value of comradeship and no obligation or attachment other than to his immediate group of warriors, fitted the imagery of futurism and soon degenerated into the fascist myth of the new man. However, this ideological straightjacket, with its looming deformation into fascist attitudes and the Nazi killer mentality, was only the most openly menacing but short-lived political materialization of this experience. Jünger's idea of the *Arbeiter*, for all its now-dated characteristics, is a typified construction with considerable significance for western man in the second half of this century."

72. Kittler, "From Gestalt to Ge-Stell," 92. For more on the relation between Heidegger and Jünger, see Eduardo Mendieta, "Imperial Geographies and Topographies of Nihilism: Theatres of War and Dead Cities," *City* 8, no. 1 (2004): 20; and, of course, Richard Wolin, ed., *The Heidegger Controversy* (Boston: MIT Press, 1992).

73. Gray, *Warriors*, 103.

74. Weil, *Iliad*, 22.

The Terror of the New

1. Translation by Christian Hänggi, "Stockhausen at Ground Zero," *Fillip*, Fall 2011, http://fillip.ca/content/stockhausen-at-ground-zero.

2. Anthony Tommasini, "The Devil Made Him Do It," *New York Times*, Sept. 30, 2001, www.nytimes.com/2001/09/30/arts/music-the-devil-made-him-do-it.html.

3. Theodor W. Adorno, *Aesthetic Theory*, ed. Robert Hullot-Kentor (Minneapolis: University of Minnesota Press, 1997 [1970]), 6, 8, 29, ibid., respectively.

4. Don DeLillo, *Mao II* (New York: Viking, 1991), 41.

The Idea of Order I Can't Breathe

1. It turns out that I was conflating various quotations. One is from *The Autobiography of Alice B. Tokias* where she writes: "Americans . . . are like spaniards, they are abstract and cruel. They are not brutal they are cruel. They have no close contact with the earth such as most europeans have. Their materialism is not the materialism of existence, of possession, it is the materialism of action and abstraction." In other places Stein compares Spanish and Russians and finds them similarly "oriental" and "callous." She writes in *Everybody's Autobiography*: "And then it came to me it is perfectly simple, the Russian and the Spaniard are oriental, and there is the same mixing. Scratch a Russian and you find a Tartar. Scratch a Spaniard and you find a Saracen."

2. M. NourbeSe Philip, *Zong!* (Middletown, CT: Wesleyan University Press, 2008), 117.

3. Vanessa Place and Robert Fitterman. *Notes on Conceptualisms* (Brooklyn, NY: Ugly Duckling Presse, 2009), 17.

4. Place and Fitterman, *Notes*, 18.

5. Ibid., 15.

6. Philip, *Zong!*, 43.

7. Evie Shockley, "Is 'Zong!' Conceptual Poetry? Yes, It Isn't," *Jacket 2*, Sept. 17, 2013, http://jacket2.org/article/zong-conceptual-poetry-yes-it-isn%E2%80%99t.

8. M. NourbeSe Philip, "Wor(l)ds Interrupted: The Unhistory of the Kari Basin," *Jacket 2*, Sept. 17, 2013, http://jacket2.org/article/worlds-interrupted.

9. Ned Parker, "Hamas Denounces Killing of Bin Laden," *Los Angeles Times*, May 2, 2011, http://articles.latimes.com/2011/may/02/world/la-fgw-bin-laden-hamas-20110501.

10. Association of Writers and Writing Programs, "Update Regarding the AWP Los Angeles 2016 Subcommittee," May 18, 2015, www.awpwriter.org/magazine_media/writers_news_view/3716/update_regarding_the_awp_los_angeles_2016_subcommittee.

11. Timothy Volpert, "Remove Vanessa Place from the AWP Los Angeles Conference Committee," Change.org, May 2015, https://www.change.org/p/association-of-writers-and-writing-conferences-remove-vanessa-place-from-the-awp-los-angeles-conference-committee.

12. Vanessa Place, "I Is Not a Subject: Part 5 of 5," *Harriet: A Poetry Blog*, May 1, 2013, www.poetryfoundation.org/harriet/2013/05/i-is-not-a-subject-part-5-of-5.

13. Vanessa Place, "Artist's Statement," *Drunken Boat* 10 (Summer 2009), www.drunkenboat.com/db10/06fic/place/statement.html.

14. Keith Gessen, "On PEN and *Charlie Hebdo*: Why I Signed the Letter Protesting the PEN Annual Gala," *N+1*, May 5, 2015, https://nplusonemag.com/online-only/online-only/on-pen-and-charlie-hebdo.

Acknowledgments

These pieces were written over the course of the past eight years, and several were published elsewhere before being collected here. I'm deeply grateful to the editors who helped me think through what I was trying to say, challenged me on unresolved obscurities and half-baked assumptions, and sometimes even gave me the opportunity to do the work in the first place: thanks to Jo Anne Colson, Nikki Columbus, Will Dana, Jodi Dean, Kali Handelman, Paavo Järvensivu, Michael Kazin, Lee Konstantinou, Sarah Leonard, Davide Panagia, and the anonymous reviewers, unsung copy editors, and stalwart fact checkers who back them up. My greatest thanks go to Peter Catapano, at the *New York Times*, who published my first major piece, in his Home Fires series, and who has since been not only an exemplary editor but an advocate, an advisor, and a friend.

Thanks go as well to other readers, interlocutors, guides, and friends along the way, including Aziz Alwan (RIP), Jane Arraf, Charles Bernstein, Patrick Blanchfield, Dominic Boyer, D. Graham Burnett, Meehan Crist, Andrew Cole, Tagak Curley, Borzou Daragahi, Timothy Donnelly, Jeff Dolven, Maria DiBattista, Nadia Faydh, Matt Gallagher, Rachel Galvin, Christopher Hitchens (RIP), John Houston, Cymene Howe, Dale Jamieson, Josh Kotin, Quil Lawrence, Meredith Martin, Eduardo Mendieta, Ian Miller, James Miller, Peter Molin, Melissa Monroe, Tim Morton, Maggie Mustard, Deak Nabers, Perry O'Brien, The Order of the Third Bird, Ned Parker, Vanessa Place, Hilary Plum, Ross Poole, Ahmed Qusay, Lisa Robertson, Joydeep Roy-Bhattacharya, Zach Savich, Jacob Siegel, Susan Stewart, Cedar Swan, Ian Tamblyn, Diana Thater, Dorothea von Moltke, Bruce Weigl, Martin Woessner, and everyone aboard the MS *Ocean Endeavour*. Much gratitude as well goes to Mark, Bronwen, Abby, Rachel, Juliet, Janine, Amara, Steven, Paul, Rudy,

Kevin, Monica, Gary, and everyone else at Soho Press, a superb team putting out brilliant, exciting work. I'm exceedingly proud to be working with them. In addition, I am gratefully indebted to the American Councils for International Education, the Center for Energy and Environmental Research in the Human Sciences at Rice University, the Finnish Cultural Institute in New York, the Los Angeles County Museum of Art, the Mahindra Humanities Center at Harvard University, Princeton University's Program in American Studies, the Russian State University for the Humanities, and the Whiting Foundation for research and travel support that made this work possible.

Finally, Sara: what can I say? None of this would be imaginable without you. Even as the world rushes to its doom, your love and courage fill each new day with light.

The previously published essays in this collection are reprinted more or less as they first appeared, as of the date noted at the end of each piece in brackets. Aside from three exceptions, only minor edits have been made, mainly to clean up nagging infelicities. Those exceptions are "We're Doomed. Now What?," "Arctic Ghosts," and "Back to Baghdad." The former two were updated to include information that emerged after publication, in the one case the winner of the 2016 US presidential election and in the other the Arctic's continued death spiral. The last of the exceptions, "Back to Baghdad," is notably different from the version that was published in *Rolling Stone* in 2014, and nearly three times as long: it is the version I wish the magazine could have published. I'm grateful to Will Dana and to *Rolling Stone* for helping me craft the version that saw print that summer, and I'm very pleased to be able to offer readers the rest of the story today.

One piece in this collection is exceptional in another way: "Rock Scissors Paper" plays with fact and fiction in ways that betray the standard, which holds in every other case, of fidelity to evidence and sources, a fidelity born out of both scholarly concern for citation and journalistic respect for verifiable facts. This Borgesian bastard is included not because I mean to fuck with the reader but because it is relevant to the topic of climate change and, despite its factitiousness, still an *essay*, faithful in its wayward way to the need to see things clearly.

"Anthropocene City" was originally published in significantly different form as "Another Storm Is Coming," in the *New York Times* (October 2, 2016), and published in its current form in *Mustarinda* (2017).

"Arctic Ghosts" was originally published in slightly different form as "Tourists at the End of the World," in *The Nation* (November 9, 2015).

"Back to Baghdad" was originally published in significantly different form as "Back to Baghdad: Life in the City of Doom," in *Rolling Stone* (July 31, 2014).

"Climate Change and the Dharma of Failure" was originally published in *The Revealer* (October, 19, 2015).

"The Fantasy of American Violence" was originally published in the *New York Times* (July 3, 2016).

"Memories of My Green Machine" was originally published in *Theory & Event* 13, no. 1 (March 2010).

"My Flesh and Blood" was originally published in *Parkett* 99 (2017).

"The Precipice" was first presented as a talk at the Mahindra Humanities Center at Harvard University, on February 23, 2017.

"Rock Scissors Paper" was first presented as a talk at the Los Angeles County Museum of Art, on February 16, 2016.

"The Terror of the New" was originally published in *Sierra Nevada* 25 (2014). It was recognized as a notable essay in *The Best American Essays* 2015.

"The Trauma Hero" was originally published in the *Los Angeles Review of Books* (January 25, 2015).

"War and the City" was originally published as a five-part essay in the *New York Times* (September 3, 6, 8, 10, and 12, 2010).

"War of Choice" was originally published in *Dissent* (Winter 2016).

"We're Doomed. Now What?" was originally published in the *New York Times* (December 21, 2015).

These pieces are reprinted here with permission.